comforting
foods

compiled and edited by

Norman Kolpas

Macmillan • USA

MACMILLAN
A Simon & Schuster Macmillan Company
1633 Broadway
New York, NY 10019

Library of Congress Cataloging-in-Publication Data

Comforting foods / compiled and edited by Norman Kolpas; Project Open Hand.
p. cm.
Includes index.
ISBN 0-02-566401-8
1. Cookery. I. Kolpas, Norman. II. Project Open Hand (Organization)
TX714.C627 1995
641.5—dc20
95-11422
CIP

Manufactured in the United States of America
10 9 8 7 6 5 4 3 2 1

Dedication

Every morning at 8:30, a very special group of people arrives at the Project Open Hand kitchen. Rain or shine, bone-chilling cold, or pea-soup–thick fog, these men, women, and children begin cutting carrots, peeling potatoes, and slicing tomatoes with one goal in mind: to give life-sustaining nourishment to people who are sick; people who struggle daily for health and life; people fighting AIDS.

Throughout the day at Project Open Hand, in the kitchen, the offices, the food banks, and throughout San Francisco and Alameda counties, our volunteers give their time, hands, and hearts. They assemble "meals with love," pack grocery bags, stuff envelopes, or greet our clients at their doors with a smile, chitchat, and a hot meal. They help people with AIDS stay strong for another day, help keep them at home and out of the hospital, and show them that they are not alone, no matter what their circumstances, and that they are important enough for other people to go out of their way. All this for people they do not even know.

Different reasons have brought these volunteers to AIDS services and to us: Some have lost loved ones from the disease; others have someone close to them who is fighting for life now. Still others, though not personally affected, see the suffering in the community and want to do something about it. They come to us and say, "I care and I want to help."

Whatever their motivations, they have joined the Project Open Hand family. In fact, these 2,400 volunteers are Project Open Hand. Should our corps of volunteers walk away tomorrow, our doors would close on that day—forever. At Project Open Hand, we get to witness every day the amazing things that a group of people with vision, compassion, and commitment can do. We watch people give of themselves so that others may have a better life. They show us the humanity present in us all.

This book is dedicated to these inspiring people, our volunteers. They make it all possible.

Project Open Hand,
San Francisco, 1995

Acknowledgments

Norman Kolpas would, most of all, like to thank the chefs and restaurateurs from across the nation who contributed their recipes for this book with their open hands and hearts. Thanks, also, to Pam Hoenig of Macmillan for involving me in this project; to Jane Sigal for making the editing process a great pleasure; to Lynn Luckow for his kind guidance; and to my wife and son, Katie and Jacob, for their love and support.

Project Open Hand extends its heartfelt thanks as well to those who donated without remuneration their culinary secrets to make *Comforting Foods* possible. In addition, the generosity of Macmillan USA in supporting this book is gratefully acknowledged. The Publisher's decision to devote 100 percent of the royalties from the sale of this book to Project Open Hand is an extraordinary philanthropic act. These funds will directly effect the 2,800 men, women, and children living with AIDS who are comforted by Project Open Hand's daily hot meals and food staples.

Contents

Chapter 4   Desserts and Beverages

Foreword

Brillat Savarin, in his book *The Physiology of Taste*, wrote that *you are what you eat.* Your choice of food reflects your upbringing and environment, your social status, your aspirations and values, and possibly the influence of your travels. But this statement is only part of the equation. The way you eat also reflects the way you *feel.* When you are happily busy, perhaps in love, you often forget to eat; food is not in the forefront of your consciousness. When you are depressed or anxious, you may eat and eat but not feel satisfied; food cannot fill a void or ease an emotional pain. When you are feeling sick, you don't want very much to eat, but you do want loving care and comfort. The foods that fill that need are simple, easy to eat, and cooked with love.

In the wee hours of the morning, when you wake up feeling the start of a bad cold or the latest flu, perhaps you may have a fleeting remembrance of a similar time when you were a child. You awoke feeling achy and sick, and your mother touched your forehead and pronounced you "too sick for school." For what seemed like an eternity, you lay in bed, tossing, slightly feverish, alternately groaning and napping. After one of your fevered dreams, you opened your eyes, and there by your bed was chicken soup with rice or cinnamon toast and tea. And while you didn't feel ravenously hungry, you knew that if you ate this food, you would feel better. Your mom loved you, and you would get better. Although you were feeling miserable, your memories of those days are happy and precious. The creation of precious memories and happy times is the power of comforting food.

This book is dedicated to people who are sick and in need of comfort and love because in many instances they may not get well. By preparing food cooked with love, by taking the time to make chicken soup or cinnamon toast, rice pudding or applesauce, we tell them we love them and we care. That message of love lasts and enriches all our lives with greater meaning. We set an example for others to follow.

ix

That is the story of Project Open Hand. This organization, under the initial leadership of Ruth Brinker, set an example that is being followed in communities all over the country. Many years ago, too long ago, way too long ago, Ruth and her staff at Project Open Hand started delivering home-cooked meals to people with AIDS, people often too weak to cook, much less shop for food. Open Hand was the proverbial "mother" who touched their brows and pronounced them not well enough to go out so that dinner would be coming to them. From a small crew cooking out of a church kitchen, Project Open Hand is now in its own building with a professional kitchen and a large staff preparing 1,600 nutritious meals a day. These meals are delivered by an army of volunteers who understand the power of comforting food and compassion.

Over the years, I have cooked at innumerable fund-raisers so that Project Open Hand could continue its much-needed work. I am proud to serve on the board of directors of Project Open Hand. As a chef, my life revolves around feeding the general public, a very demanding clientele. For many diners, food serves as background to a business meeting, a family reunion, a romantic adventure. But Project Open Hand's dining public is a different audience, with an urgent agenda. I am happy that we are able to offer nourishment, both culinary and emotional. That is what real cooking is all about.

Many times I have brought food home to members of my staff who were sick, and I loved them and needed to tell them that in a personal way. The food I prepared was food I knew they loved because we had eaten together many times and shared our feelings and our food memories. I always chose to make the familiar food of their childhood or often-requested favorite dishes from Square One's repertoire. This book is a collection of recipes from chefs like myself who can recall what it is they want to eat when they need food and comfort, food that offers nurturing as well as nourishment. We feel better just thinking about our favorites and hope that this joy of cooking with love will be one you will want to share. —*Joyce Goldstein,*
Chef/Owner, Square One

Introduction

As our world hurtles toward the twenty-first century, we all seek more comfort in our daily lives. Food, like a loving touch or a glimpse of divine power, has that ability to comfort.

Now, more than ever before, we seek out foods that provide a feeling of warmth, good cheer, and well-being in our daily lives: steaming soups, stews, and casseroles; meatloaves and roasted chickens and heaping bowls of mashed potatoes; sandwiches piled high and pastas oozing with cheese; home-churned ice creams, fresh-baked cookies, and bread puddings hot from the oven.

We look for recipes that are fairly easy to prepare, yet fill the kitchen with their homey, tempting aromas. We return to favorite foods that recall, with every bite, happy meals of childhood—or we seek out dishes that provide us with heartwarming new memories.

A call for just such recipes went out to chefs in the San Francisco Bay Area, including many who had participated in *The Open Hand Cookbook* and *The Open Hand Celebration Cookbook*. The call went out as well to leading chefs and restaurateurs across the nation who appreciated the good work being done by Project Open Hand.

The request was a simple one: Please send your favorite recipes for comforting foods, whether they come from your restaurant's menu, from your home kitchen, or from your childhood. Aside from a few suggestions of possible categories into which those recipes might fall— soups and salads, pastas and risottos, quick breads and muffins, and so on—and a reminder that the recipes must be accessible to the average-skilled home cook, no further advice was given.

The response from these chefs was overwhelmingly positive and generous. It was also fascinating, reflecting an incredible diversity of backgrounds, experiences, and personal tastes.

As you browse through the pages of this book, you'll find, in effect, up to 173 different ways in which food can comfort. Some you'll instantly recognize as the kinds of dishes that give you warmth or solace. Others might surprise or intrigue you, and the personal comments that their creators provide could offer new insights into the myriad ways that food brings pleasure to all of us.

Apart from selecting recipes with the aim of achieving balance, variety, and interest, as well as making sure that the recipes would work for home cooks and were all similarly presented and phrased, I myself tried to meddle very little in the contents.

This book, to my way of thinking, has 64 separate and distinct authors (whose biographies you'll find in the contributors section beginning on page 227), all with his or her own unique way of cooking. No two necessarily purée a soup or mash potatoes or thicken the custard base of an ice-cream mixture in quite the same way. Certainly, no two think of food in precisely the same way, though all take obvious delight in preparing it as a form of self-expression and love.

I hope you'll find their approaches to comforting foods as enlightening, delightful, and warm-hearted as I did.

Norman Kolpas

chapter

1

First Courses

The first course sets the tone of a menu, and a meal that begins with a soothing, satisfying dish makes dining a comforting pleasure from the first bite or sip. On the following pages, you'll find myriad options for starting a lunch or dinner, ranging from hot and cold appetizers to soups to a wide variety of salads.

Like many of the best first courses, most of these recipes can be served in other ways as well. Most of the appetizers can be prepared in larger quantities, to be offered on a buffet or passed as cocktail-party hors-d'oeuvres; some also make satisfying main courses. Many of the soups and salads, too, require little more than some crusty bread to turn them into the featured course for an informal lunch or dinner. There's comfort to be found in such delicious versatility.

Goat Cheese and Roasted Tomatoes Wrapped in Phyllo

Sarah Stegner, The Dining Room, The Ritz-Carlton, Chicago, Illinois

Serves 4

Sarah Stegner took her inspiration for this savory combination from classic Greek appetizers like spinach-and-feta-filled spanokopita. Her filling, though, uses the classic Italian or southern French flavors of creamy goat cheese, fresh herbs, and intense roasted tomatoes. (The tomatoes, by the way, roast for 3 hours; they are nonetheless easily prepared and can be made the day before and refrigerated.)

You can serve these pastries as finger food (the recipe easily multiplies for a cocktail crowd). Sarah also suggests presenting them as a knife-and-fork appetizer, accompanied by a small salad of baby greens. Unlike the triangular phyllo packages favored in Greece, Sarah wraps hers much more simply, as you would a birthday present.

4 medium-size plum tomatoes, peeled, cut crosswise into halves, and seeded (see Box, page 3)

1/4 cup olive oil

Salt

Black pepper

1 package phyllo dough, thawed (see Note)

1/2 pound soft goat cheese

2 tablespoons finely chopped mixed fresh basil, Italian parsley, and thyme

1. Preheat the oven to 180°F.

2. Put the tomato halves cut sides up in a small, shallow baking dish. Drizzle lightly with some of the olive oil and season with salt and pepper. Roast until they look slightly dried, about 3 hours. Remove them from oven.

3. Increase the oven temperature to 375°F.

4. To assemble the hors-d'oeuvres, first unfold the packaged phyllo. Gently peel off one sheet (which should measure about 11 by 18 inches) and place it on a work surface. Brush the top lightly but evenly with some olive oil. Place a second sheet on top and brush with more oil. Repeat with a third sheet and then a fourth. With a long, sharp knife, cut the stacked sheets into 4 equal rectangular stacks.

5. In the center of each stack of phyllo, place 2 tablespoons of the goat cheese. Top with a roasted tomato half and sprinkle with 3/4 teaspoon of the herbs. Then, in the same way, add one more layer each of cheese, tomato, and herbs.

6. Fold the edge of each phyllo stack closest to you over the filling. Fold both sides over, then the edge farthest from you, to enclose the filling completely, pressing down gently to seal the oil-brushed phyllo sheets together. Brush tops lightly with oil.

7. Place the packages on a baking sheet or in a shallow baking dish large enough to hold them without touching. Bake until the phyllo is golden brown and the filling is hot and bubbly, 7 to 10 minutes. Serve immediately.

NOTE • *You'll find packaged phyllo dough in well-stocked food stores and Middle Eastern markets.*

Peeling and Seeding Tomatoes

Bring a medium-size saucepan of water to a boil. Fill a medium-size mixing bowl with ice and water. With a small, sharp knife, core the tomatoes and score a shallow X in the skin at their opposite ends. Immerse the tomatoes in the boiling water until the skins begin to peel, about 10 seconds; then, with a skimmer or a slotted spoon, remove and put in the bowl of ice water. With your fingertips or the knife, peel the tomatoes, starting at the Xs. Cut them in halves crosswise and squeeze gently to force out the seed sacs.

The Devil's Own Deviled Eggs

Chris Schlesinger, East Coast Grill, Cambridge, Massachusetts

"Whenever my folks would have people over in the summer, my mom would serve deviled eggs," recalls Chris Schlesinger. "For that reason, no summer function seems really complete to me without them. I always insist on serving this, my own peculiar version, at all such affairs."

By peculiar, Chris refers to his deviled eggs' incendiary spiciness—"a novelty that dates from a stage in my cooking career when people would dare me to make everything hot." You can, of course, tone it down to suit your own tolerance level, using milder fresh chilies or less of the Thai curry paste.

12 large eggs

1/4 cup mayonnaise

1 tablespoon Dijon mustard

1 tablespoon Thai curry paste (see Note)

2 tablespoons seeded and chopped fresh red or green jalapeño chilies

2 tablespoons trimmed and chopped green onion

2 tablespoons chopped cilantro (fresh coriander)

Salt

Black pepper

Bottled fruit chutney (optional)

Japanese pickled ginger (optional; see Note)

1. Fill a large mixing bowl half full of cold water and add a tray of ice cubes. Set aside.

2. Put the eggs in a large saucepan with enough cold water to cover them. Bring to a boil over medium-high heat and continue boiling for 10 minutes. Drain and immediately plunge into the bowl of ice water.

3. Shell the eggs, cut them lengthwise in halves, and scoop out the yolks.

4. In a medium-size mixing bowl, mash the yolks with the mayonnaise, mustard, and curry paste. Add the jalapeños, green onion, and cilantro. Mix well. Season to taste with salt and pepper.

5. Scoop the yolk mixture back into the whites and garnish, if you like, with the chutney or pickled ginger.

NOTE • *You'll find Thai curry paste, along with Japanese pickled ginger, in the Asian food section of well-stocked supermarkets, in Asian markets, or in specialty food stores.*

Artichokes with Onions, Lemon, Olives, and Mint

Serves 4 to 8

Judy Rodgers, Zuni Cafe & Grill, San Francisco, California

"I love this dish for the earthy, satisfying textures and flavors, which meld so well," says Judy Rodgers. "I find it especially delicious and comforting the next day, served at room temperature or just warmed."

3 pounds firm, sweet onions such as Vidalia, Maui, or red, thinly sliced

4 cloves garlic, trimmed of blemishes and thinly slivered

2 cups extra-virgin olive oil

4 teaspoons sea salt

1/2 cup Niçoise olives, rinsed

2 tablespoons packed fresh mint leaves, coarsely chopped

1 lemon, thinly sliced

4 large artichokes

1/2 cup dry white wine if necessary

1. In a mixing bowl, toss the onions and garlic with 1 cup of the olive oil and 2 teaspoons sea salt. Add the olives, mint leaves, and lemon and toss again. Set aside.

2. With a small, sharp, stainless-steel knife, cut away the bottoms of the artichokes' stems; then, carefully peel the remainders of the stalks. With kitchen scissors, trim off the sharp points of the leaves. Cut each artichoke lengthwise in half. Use a stainless-steel spoon to scrape out the fibrous choke from each half. Put the prepared artichoke halves in another bowl and, with your hands, toss with the remaining oil and sea salt, taking care to coat thoroughly and to rub the oil and salt between the leaves.

3. Preheat the oven to 350°F.

4. In a shallow baking dish large enough to hold the artichokes in a single layer, spread the onion mixture. Nestle the artichokes cut sides down in the onions. Cover the dish with its lid or heavy-duty aluminum foil and bake about 30 minutes. Uncover and check the onions: They should have sweated some of their liquid, but if the dish seems dry, pour in the wine. Cover again and bake until the artichokes are tender enough to be easily pierced at their base with the tip of a small, sharp knife, about 30 minutes more.

5. Uncover the baking dish, raise the oven temperature to 400°F and bake until the edges of the vegetables begin to brown, about 15 minutes more. Serve hot, warm, or cold.

Galettes de Crabe Le Bec-Fin
(Crab Cakes Le Bec-Fin)

Georges Perrier, Le Bec-Fin, Philadelphia, Pennsylvania

Generously serves 10

As their French name might imply, these crab cakes exceed expectations, foregoing the usual bread crumbs for a rich puree of shrimp, cream, and eggs that binds the crab mixture. The recipe may be halved easily.

1 teaspoon unsalted butter

1 bunch green onions, green parts only, cut crosswise into 1/8-inch pieces

1 pound jumbo lump crabmeat, picked over to remove any bits of shell or cartilage

14 ounces large raw shrimp, peeled and deveined

2 large eggs

1 pint heavy cream

Salt

Black pepper

2 tablespoons Dijon mustard

1 tablespoon Worcestershire sauce

1 tablespoon hot pepper sauce

Mild vegetable oil

Lemon wedges

1. Put the bowl and metal blade of a food processor in the freezer to chill thoroughly.

2. In a small saucepan, melt the butter over medium heat. Add the green onions and cook, stirring, just until they soften.

3. In a large mixing bowl, toss the green onions together with the crabmeat. Set aside.

4. Put the shrimp in the food processor with the cold metal blade. Process, stopping a few times to scrape down the bowl, until finely pureed, about 1 minute. Add the eggs and process until the mixture is smooth and shiny, about 2 minutes more. Scrape down the bowl again.

5. With the machine running, slowly pour in the cream. When it has all been added, stop and scrape down the bowl again. Add salt and pepper to taste and process briefly again to make sure the cream is fully incorporated. Scrape down the bowl, add the mustard, Worcestershire sauce, and pepper sauce; process briefly again.

6. Add the shrimp puree to the bowl of crabmeat and green onions and, with a rubber spatula, fold them together.

7. In a large nonstick skillet, pour enough oil to coat the bottom and heat over medium-high heat. Form cakes from 1/2-cup portions of the mixture. Taking care not to crowd the skillet, cook the cakes until golden brown, about 2 minutes per side. Serve as soon as possible with lemon wedges.

Moroccan Spiced Crab Cakes

Serves 8 to 10 *Matthew Kenney, Matthew's, New York, New York*

"Crab cakes remind me of my childhood home in Maine, where my father and I used to go crabbing at least once a week," says Matthew Kenney. "These crab cakes are light and flavorful, and the taste and smell—even with the addition of exotic North African spices—always send me back home."

2 tablespoons olive oil

2 small red bell peppers, halved, stemmed, seeded, and cut into 1/4-inch dice

2 ribs celery, cut into 1/4-inch dice

2 cloves garlic, finely chopped

1 bunch green onions, trimmed and thinly sliced

One 2-inch piece fresh ginger, peeled and finely chopped

1 tablespoon ground cumin

1 tablespoon ground turmeric

1 teaspoon ground cardamom

Pinch of cayenne pepper

Salt

1 pint heavy cream

1 1/2 cups Japanese bread crumbs (see Note)

1 1/2 cups ground almonds

1 pound jumbo lump crabmeat, picked over to remove any pieces of shell or cartilage

1/2 cup finely chopped Italian parsley

1 bunch chives, finely chopped

2 tablespoons grated lemon zest

Mild vegetable oil such as canola

1. In a large sauté pan or skillet, heat the olive oil over medium heat. Add the bell peppers and celery and cook, stirring, for 2 to 3 minutes. Add the garlic, green onions, and ginger and cook, stirring, for 2 minutes more. Add the cumin, turmeric, cardamom, cayenne, and salt to taste and cook, stirring, 1 minute more.

2. Stir in the cream. Bring to a boil and cook, stirring occasionally, until the liquid reduces by about a half, 7 to 10 minutes.

3. Meanwhile, in a small mixing bowl, toss together the Japanese bread crumbs and the almond flour.

4. Stir the crabmeat, 1 3/4 cups of the bread-crumb mixture, the Italian parsley, chives, and lemon zest into the pan. Taste and adjust the seasonings.

5. Remove the mixture from the heat and let cool to room temperature.

Recipe continues • • •

6. Spread the remaining bread-crumb mixture on a plate. With your hands, form the crab mixture into 8 to 10 round cakes about 1 inch thick. Lightly dip both sides of each cake in the bread-crumb mixture and transfer to a waxed paper–lined baking sheet or tray. Chill in the refrigerator for at least 1 hour or until ready to cook.

7. Put a shallow baking dish large enough to hold the crab cakes into the oven and preheat the oven to 400°F.

8. In a large nonstick skillet, pour enough vegetable oil to coat the bottom and heat over medium heat. Taking care not to crowd the skillet, add the crab cakes and pan-fry until golden brown, 2 to 3 minutes per side. Transfer the crab cakes to the heated baking dish and bake in the oven for 2 to 3 minutes more. Serve as soon as possible.

NOTE • *Japanese bread crumbs are available in Asian markets and in the Asian food sections of well-stocked supermarkets.*

Bay Scallops and Rock Shrimp with Herb-Vegetable Jus

Hans Wiegand, The Pavilion Restaurant, The Claremont Resort, Oakland, California

Serves 6

The secret behind this soothing yet elegant appetizer lies in the intense vegetable stock Hans Wiegand makes from scratch—a concoction easily prepared, yet so flavorful you could serve it on its own as a comforting broth.

While you could offer the seafood mixture by itself in small soup bowls, he suggests serving it over small pasta, rice, or polenta. Cut the number of servings to 4 and the dish becomes a light main course.

Vegetable Stock:

6 medium-size ribs celery, cut into 1/4-inch-thick slices

5 medium-size carrots, peeled and cut into 1/4-inch-thick slices

2 medium-size white onions, cut into 1/4-inch-thick slices

2 medium-size leeks, white and pale green parts only, halved lengthwise, thoroughly washed and cut cross-wise into 1/4-inch-thick slices

10 Italian parsley stems

10 black peppercorns

4 cloves garlic, cut into halves

2 small shallots, cut into halves

2 whole cloves

1 bay leaf

1 teaspoon dried tarragon

1 teaspoon dried thyme

1 teaspoon whole coriander seeds

Bay Scallops and Rock Shrimp:

1 tablespoon unsalted butter

1/2 pound bay scallops, trimmed, rinsed, and patted dry

1/2 pound peeled rock shrimp, deveined

2 ears corn, kernels cut from cobs

1 small leek, white and pale green parts only, halved lengthwise, thoroughly washed and thinly sliced crosswise

1/4 pound fresh shiitake, oyster, chanterelle, or button mushrooms, trimmed and cut into 1/4-inch-thick slices

1 tablespoon finely chopped shallots

3 medium-size tomatoes, peeled, seeded (see Box, page 4) and cut into 1/4-inch-wide strips

1 tablespoon finely chopped Italian parsley

1 tablespoon finely chopped fresh basil

Salt

Black pepper

For the vegetable stock:

Put all the stock ingredients in a large saucepan and add cold water to cover. Bring to a boil over high heat; then reduce the heat to low and simmer gently for 30 minutes. Remove from the heat, cover, and let the vegetables infuse in the liquid until cold. Pour the stock through a strainer set over a large bowl. Discard the solids. Store the stock in the refrigerator, covered, until ready to use.

For the bay scallops and rock shrimp:

1. In a large skillet, melt the butter over medium-high heat and as soon as it begins to foam add the scallops and rock shrimp. Cook, stirring, until the shrimp turn pink and the scallops look opaque and firm, about 3 minutes. Remove with a slotted spoon and set aside.

2. Add the corn, leek, mushrooms, and shallots to the pan and cook, stirring, until tender, 4 to 5 minutes. Pour in the reserved stock and deglaze by stirring and scraping with a wooden spoon to dissolve the pan deposits. When the liquid comes to a boil, stir in the tomatoes, parsley, and basil. Season to taste with salt and pepper. Put the seafood in shallow bowls. Ladle broth and vegetables over them.

Fresh Miyagi Oysters in Ponzu Sauce with Daikon Radish

Hiro Sone and Lissa Doumani, Terra, St. Helena, California

"Miyagi, about 200 miles north of Tokyo, is where I come from," says Hiro Sone. "I grew up with the oysters harvested there, topped with my mother's own ponzu sauce." Hiro serves them as an appetizer, 6 per person; but you could also offer the oysters as a cocktail hors-d'oeuvre.

Buy your oysters from only the most reputable seafood shop, and avoid any that gape open or smell like anything other than the fresh scent of the sea. If you aren't experienced shucking oysters, ask the fishmonger to shuck them for you, packing them on their half shells nestled in ice.

Ponzu Sauce:

2/3 cup rice wine vinegar

1/2 cup soy sauce

1/3 cup lemon juice

2 1/2 tablespoons mirin

Oysters and Daikon Radish:

1 pound daikon

1 teaspoon cayenne pepper

1 teaspoon hot paprika

36 fresh oysters, cleaned and shucked

One 1- to 2-ounce package daikon sprouts, washed and patted dry

Zest of 2 lemons, cut into thin strips

For the ponzu sauce:

Put all the ingredients in a small nonreactive saucepan and bring to a boil over medium-high heat. Transfer to a bowl and refrigerate, covered, until cold.

For the oysters and daikon radish:

1. While the ponzu sauce is chilling, peel the daikon and grate on the fine holes of a handheld grater. Drain liquid and put the grated daikon in a mixing bowl. Sprinkle with the cayenne and paprika, toss well, cover, and refrigerate.

2. Put the oysters in their half shells on a serving platter or individual dishes. Fill each shell with the cold ponzu sauce. Garnish with daikon sprouts, grated daikon, and lemon zest strips and serve immediately.

NOTE • *You can find the ingredients for this sharp, slightly sweet sauce as well as the fresh Japanese white radish known as daikon in any well-stocked supermarket or Asian food store.*

Spicy Angel Wings

Serves 4 to 6 *Chaiwatt Siriyarn, Marnee Thai, San Francisco, California*

Glazed with a sweet-hot garlic sauce that you'll want to lick off your fingers, these deep-fried chicken wings are an irresistible favorite at Marnee Thai, run by owner-chef Chaiwatt Siriyarn and his wife, May.

Mild vegetable oil

1 1/2 pounds chicken wings, rinsed, thoroughly patted dry, and cut into halves at the joints

1/2 cup packed whole fresh basil leaves, rinsed and thoroughly patted dry

1/2 cup chicken stock

1/2 cup sugar

2 1/2 tablespoons Thai fish sauce (see Note)

1/2 tablespoon paprika

1/2 tablespoon cornstarch

2 tablespoons finely chopped garlic

1/2 tablespoon seeded and finely chopped fresh hot chili pepper

1. In a large wok or deep fryer, heat 3 to 4 inches of vegetable oil to 375°F on a deep-frying thermometer. Add the chicken wings, in batches if necessary to prevent overcrowding, and fry until golden brown, 5 to 7 minutes. Remove from the oil with a wire skimmer and drain on paper towels. Set aside.

2. In the same hot oil, add a few basil leaves and fry just until they turn bright green and look slightly transparent, no more than 10 to 15 seconds; remove immediately and drain on paper towels. Repeat with the remaining leaves until all the basil is cooked. Set aside.

3. In a small mixing bowl, stir together the stock, sugar, fish sauce, paprika, and cornstarch until thoroughly blended.

4. In another wok or a medium-size saucepan, heat 2 tablespoons of vegetable oil over medium heat. Add the garlic and chili pepper and cook, stirring, until fragrant, about 1 minute. Add the stock mixture, raise the heat to medium-high, and bring to a boil, stirring; continue boiling, stirring constantly, until the sauce thickens and reduces to just over 1/2 cup, 5 to 7 minutes.

5. Add the fried chicken-wing pieces to the sauce and stir to coat them well. Transfer to a serving platter and garnish with the fried basil leaves. Serve immediately.

NOTE • *You'll find Thai fish sauce (nam pla), a salty, briny paste used as a seasoning, in Asian food stores and well-stocked supermarkets.*

Parma Prosciutto and Parmesan Croutons with Tomato-Basil Relish

Sarah Stegner, The Dining Room, The Ritz-Carlton, Chicago, Illinois

For this rustic version of the popular Italian appetizer known as crostini, Sarah Stegner recommends buying good-quality prosciutto imported from Parma. For added color, she suggests substituting, if available, a yellow tomato for one of the red tomatoes and purple-colored opal basil for one of the two bunches of basil.

The croutons may be served on plates for a first course, as here; or you could pass them as a cocktail hors-d'oeuvre, multiplying the recipe as needed.

1/4 cup olive oil

1 tablespoon balsamic vinegar

1 tablespoon lemon juice

Salt

Black pepper

3 medium-size ripe red tomatoes, peeled, seeded (see Box, page 4), and cut into 1/4-inch dice

2 bunches fresh basil, large leaves cut crosswise into very thin strips, small leaves reserved for garnish

1 loaf Italian ciabata bread or crusty French bread

2 large cloves garlic, cut into halves

1/4 cup grated Parmesan cheese

16 paper-thin slices prosciutto (about 1/4 pound total)

1. In a mixing bowl, stir together the olive oil, vinegar, lemon juice, and salt and pepper to taste. Add the tomatoes and the basil julienne and mix well. Set aside at room temperature.

2. Preheat the oven to 325°F.

3. Cut 16 long, thin slices of ciabata or French bread. Rub both sides of each piece with the cut edge of half a garlic clove. Put the bread slices in a single layer on a baking sheet and sprinkle their tops with the Parmesan. Bake until the cheese is golden brown, 10 to 15 minutes.

4. While the bread is still warm, wrap a slice of prosciutto around each piece. Place them on serving plates and top with the tomato-basil relish, garnishing with the small basil leaves. Serve immediately.

Prosciutto and Mission Fig Handrolls

Bruce Hill, Oritalia, San Francisco, California

8 pieces

Bruce Hill takes the form of the handroll—one of the most pleasurable sushi shapes—and transforms it into a sensuous composition in which succulent fresh figs and grilled mushrooms are enwrapped in peppery, bitter arugula leaves and slices of rich, salty prosciutto.

Serve two of the handrolls per person as an appetizer; or double or triple the recipe as needed and pass them as hors-d'oeuvres.

1 teaspoon balsamic vinegar

Salt

Black pepper

2 tablespoons olive oil

1 large portobello mushroom or 2 large fresh shiitake or 4 crimini mushrooms, stems removed

8 paper-thin slices prosciutto, each about 3 by 9 inches

16 medium-size arugula leaves, washed and dried

One 1- to 2-ounce package daikon sprouts, washed and dried

4 ripe black mission figs, stemmed and halved lengthwise

1. Preheat a grill or broiler.

2. In a small mixing bowl, stir the balsamic vinegar with a little salt and pepper to taste, until the salt dissolves. Stirring continuously, drizzle in 1 tablespoon of the olive oil. Set the dressing aside.

3. Brush the mushroom cap or caps on both sides with the remaining oil and sprinkle with salt and pepper. Grill or broil until golden brown, 1 to 2 minutes per side. Cut the portobello cap into 8 slices; if using shiitake or crimini mushrooms, cut each into 8 slices.

4. Lay the prosciutto slices on a flat work surface. Place 2 arugula leaves and 1/8 of the daikon sprouts at one narrow end of each slice. On top of the greens, distribute the mushroom slices and fig halves. Sprinkle with the dressing.

5. Starting at the end topped with the filling, tightly roll up each prosciutto slice, rolling at a slight angle to form a cone shape that encloses the filling. Serve promptly.

Stuffed Green Onion Pancakes

Law Ming, Harbor Village, San Francisco, California

Dim sum, the term for Chinese morning and lunchtime dumplings, is generally translated as "delight the heart," a perfectly poetic definition for any comfort food. Master dim sum chef Law Ming provides his recipe for one of the most popular such items, which may also be served in the evening as an appetizer or cocktail hors-d'oeuvre.

Pancake Wrappers:

3 cups cake flour or all-purpose flour

1 cup boiling water

1/2 cup cold water

3 to 4 tablespoons vegetable shortening

Salt

Filling:

3 ounces skinless, boneless chicken breast, well-chilled and cut into 1/4-inch dice

1/2 teaspoon cornstarch

1/4 teaspoon cooking sherry

Salt

Vegetable oil

1/2 Chinese air-dried sausage, cut into 1/4-inch dice (see Note)

1 tablespoon Chinese dried shrimp, finely chopped (see Note)

3 ounces Chinese barbecued pork (char-siu), cut into 1/4-inch dice (see Note)

1 bunch green onions, trimmed and cut crosswise into thin slices

1 teaspoon oyster sauce (see Note)

1 teaspoon soy sauce

1/4 teaspoon sugar

For the pancake wrappers:

Put the flour in a large mixing bowl. Stirring quickly with chopsticks or a fork, pour in the boiling water, then the cold water, mixing well. On a lightly floured work surface, knead the dough until smooth and supple, then form into a ball and return to the bowl. Cover the ball of dough well with plastic wrap or a damp kitchen towel and let rest at room temperature for 30 minutes.

For the filling:

1. In a small bowl, stir the chicken together with the cornstarch, sherry, and a pinch of salt. Set aside.

2. Heat 1 teaspoon of oil in a small skillet or wok over high heat. Add the Chinese sausage and dried shrimp and stir-fry for 1 minute. Add the chicken mixture and stir-fry for 2 minutes more. Quickly stir in the barbecued pork and 3/4 cup of the green onions, reserving the rest for the pancake wrappers. Immediately stir in the oyster sauce, soy sauce, sugar, and 1/4 teaspoon of salt, mixing well. On a large plate or platter, divide the filling into 16 equal portions and set aside.

To make the pancakes:

1. Unwrap the dough and, on a lightly floured surface, knead it gently again for a few minutes, until smooth and supple. Divide the dough into 16 equal portions, cover with plastic wrap, and set aside.

2. Take 1 piece of dough, rub it all over with about 1/4 teaspoon of the shortening, and use a small rolling pin to roll it into a circle 6 inches in diameter. Rub about 1/2 teaspoon of shortening onto the top of the circle of dough and sprinkle evenly with about 1/2 teaspoon of the remaining green onions and a pinch of salt.

3. With your fingers, tightly roll up the circle of dough into a narrow cylinder, enclosing the onions. Then, starting at one end of the cylinder, coil tightly, like a snail. Turn the coil on its side and roll into a circle again, about 4 inches in diameter. Place 1 portion of the filling in the center and bring up the edges of the circle around it, pinching them securely together at the top to seal in the filling. With the rolling pin, flatten it once more to form a plump pancake about 2 1/2 inches in diameter. Set aside and repeat the procedure with the remaining dough and fillings.

4. In a large skillet, pour a thin layer of vegetable oil and heat over medium-high heat. Add the pancakes, in batches if necessary to prevent crowding, and fry them until golden brown, about 2 minutes per side. Pat dry on paper towels to remove excess oil before serving.

NOTE • *You can find the special filling ingredients for this recipe in Chinese and other Asian food stores.*

Grilled Szechwan-Style Baby Back Ribs

Roy Yamaguchi, Roy's, Honolulu, Hawaii

Serves 4

"When I was growing up in Tokyo, my parents made ribs for us all the time," recalls Roy Yamaguchi. "Those foods you remember from childhood, prepared with love, are what I most enjoy to eat." He gives the ribs—which would also be good as hors-d'oeuvres—extra flavor by simmering them in a chicken stock perfumed with ginger, garlic, and cilantro (fresh coriander) before grilling them with a hoisin-based sauce.

1 small bunch cilantro (fresh coriander), stemmed

1/2 bunch Italian parsley, stemmed

2 cloves garlic, peeled

One 1-inch piece fresh ginger, peeled

12 cups chicken stock

2 racks (about 3 1/4 pounds) baby back ribs

2/3 cup hoisin sauce

2 tablespoons red or yellow miso (soybean paste)

4 teaspoons peeled and finely chopped fresh ginger

4 teaspoons finely chopped garlic

4 teaspoons sake or dry sherry

4 teaspoons soy sauce

2 teaspoons sugar

2 teaspoons Asian chili paste with garlic

1. In a food processor, finely chop the cilantro (fresh coriander), Italian parsley, cloves of garlic, and piece of ginger.

2. Transfer the mixture to a large Dutch oven and add the stock and the ribs. Bring to a boil over high heat, then reduce the heat to medium, cover, and simmer briskly until the ribs are tender, about 30 minutes.

3. In a medium-size mixing bowl, stir together the hoisin, miso, chopped ginger and garlic, sake, soy sauce, sugar, and chili paste. Set aside.

4. Drain the ribs well and transfer them to a baking sheet. Brush the ribs on both sides with some of the sauce and let cool at room temperature for about 1 hour. (If you like, the sauce and ribs can then be covered separately and refrigerated overnight.)

5. Preheat a charcoal grill or broiler.

6. Brush the ribs with more of the hoisin sauce and grill or broil until deep brown, about 4 minutes per side. Cut the racks into individual ribs and serve hot with the remaining sauce.

NOTE • *You'll find the few special ingredients called for here in a well-stocked supermarket or Asian foods store.*

Four-Onion Soup

Grant Showley, Showley's at Miramonte, St. Helena, California

Serves 4

"Great hot when the wind is blustery and the weather unfriendly, this soup is equally delicious chilled on a hot summer day," says Grant Showley of this fragrant soup, in which the fourth member of the onion family is actually a cousin, garlic. He suggests the option of swirling into each serving 1 teaspoon of pesto or pureed pimiento, for extra color and flavor.

3 pounds white potatoes, peeled and coarsely chopped

2 large onions, coarsely chopped

1 bunch green onions, trimmed and coarsely chopped

4 shallots, coarsely chopped

4 cloves garlic, coarsely chopped

2 cups dry white wine

2 cups heavy cream

2 cups milk

Salt

White pepper

1. Put all the ingredients except the salt and pepper in a large pot over high heat. When it approaches a boil, reduce the heat to low and simmer until all the vegetables are soft, about 1 hour.

2. Pour the soup through a strainer set over a large bowl; reserve the liquid. In a food processor, puree the vegetables, in batches if necessary. Stir the puree back into the liquid and season to taste with salt and pepper.

3. Serve immediately. Or let cool to room temperature and then refrigerate, covered, until chilled.

Sopa de Albóndigas (Meatball Soup)

Serves 6 to 8 · *Nestor Arrañaga, Project Open Hand, San Francisco, California*

"With all its various ingredients," says Nestor Arrañaga, "this traditional Mexican soup is very nutritious." Albóndigas, he adds, translates simply as "meatballs." He also points out that the soup will not be authentic without the inclusion of mint.

Albóndigas:

1 pound lean ground beef

2 tablespoons finely chopped fresh mint or 1 tablespoon dried mint, crushed

2 tablespoons fine fresh breadcrumbs

2 tablespoons uncooked white rice

1 tablespoon granulated garlic

1 tablespoon black pepper

1 tablespoon ground cumin

1/2 teaspoon salt

2 large eggs, slightly beaten

Broth:

1 tablespoon olive oil

2 cloves garlic, finely chopped

1/2 medium-size onion, finely chopped

6 cups cold water

1 pound tomatoes, coarsely chopped

2 medium-size carrots, peeled and cut into 1/2-inch-thick slices

2 medium-size zucchini, cut into 1/2-inch-thick slices

2 medium-size ribs celery, cut into 1/2-inch dice

1 medium-size potato, peeled and cut into 1/2-inch cubes

One 8-ounce can garbanzo beans, drained

Salt

Garnishes:

1 ripe avocado

1/4 cup coarsely chopped fresh cilantro leaves

1 cup sour cream

For the albóndigas:

In a medium-size mixing bowl, thoroughly mix together all the ingredients with your hands. Set aside.

For the broth:

1. In a large soup pot, heat the olive oil over medium heat. Add the garlic and onion and cook, stirring until tender, 3 to 4 minutes. Add the water, raise the heat to high, and bring to a boil.

2. Moistening your hands frequently with cold water to prevent sticking, form the meat mixture into small meatballs about 1 inch in diameter, dropping them carefully into the boiling water. Bring the water back to a boil, skimming the surface if

necessary. Reduce the heat to medium, add the tomatoes, cover, and simmer for 20 minutes.

For the garnishes:

1. Add the carrots, zucchini, celery, potato, and garbanzo beans. Season to taste with salt, cover, and continue cooking until the vegetables are tender, about 20 minutes more.

2. Before serving, peel and pit the avocado and cut into 1/2-inch chunks; toss the chunks with the cilantro. Pass the avocado-cilantro mixture and the sour cream for guests to add to the soup to taste.

Butternut Squash Soup with Sage

Maria Helm, The Sherman House, San Francisco, California

Serves 4 to 6

"On a cold day, this hearty bowl of soup is especially comforting," says Maria Helm. The recipe works fine with low-sodium canned chicken stock. Serve the soup with Maria's Buttermilk Biscuits (page 154).

1 tablespoon unsalted butter or olive oil

1 small onion (about 2 inches in diameter), coarsely chopped

4 fresh sage leaves, finely chopped

1 tablespoon honey

1 large butternut squash, halved, peeled, seeded, and cut into 1-inch chunks

6 to 8 cups water or chicken stock

1/4 cup heavy cream (optional)

Salt

Pepper

1. In a large saucepan, melt the butter or heat the oil over medium heat. Add the onion and cook, stirring, until golden. Add the sage and honey and continue cooking until the honey bubbles.

2. Add the squash and 6 cups of the water or stock. Raise the heat to high and bring to a boil. Reduce the heat to low and simmer, uncovered, until the squash is tender, about 45 minutes, adding more liquid if necessary to keep the squash submerged.

3. Remove the pan from the heat and let the soup cool for about 15 minutes. A few cups at a time, puree in a blender, taking care to avoid splattering. If you like, for extra smoothness, press the soup through a strainer or pass it through a food mill.

4. Return the soup to the pan and if you like, stir in the cream. Over medium heat, bring back to a boil and season to taste with salt and pepper. Serve immediately.

Red Bell Pepper Soup

*Christopher Gross, Christopher's and Christopher's Bistro,
Phoenix, Arizona*

Serves 6 to 8

"This rich and hearty soup is the perfect antidote to a winter chill, even in Phoenix,"
says Christopher Gross. Made in the style of a classic French cream soup, its smooth
consistency and vibrant color make it equally suitable for a family-style meal or for
elegant entertaining.

1/4 cup olive oil

7 medium-size red bell peppers,
halved, stemmed, seeded, and
coarsely chopped

3 medium-size leeks, white parts only,
halved lengthwise, thoroughly
washed and coarsely chopped

2 medium-size carrots, peeled and
coarsely chopped

2 medium-size onions, coarsely
chopped

7 cups chicken stock

2 medium-size potatoes, peeled and
coarsely chopped

2 sprigs fresh thyme

1 bay leaf

1 1/2 quarts heavy cream

1/2 cup (1 stick) unsalted butter,
cut into pieces

Salt

White pepper

1. In a heavy large saucepan, heat 1 tablespoon of the oil over medium-low heat. Add
   the peppers, leeks, carrots, and onions and cook, stirring, until they are softened,
   about 10 minutes.

2. Add the stock, potatoes, thyme, and bay leaf. Raise the heat to medium and simmer
   until the potatoes are very tender and the liquid has reduced by about a third, about
   30 minutes. Remove the thyme and bay leaf.

3. In batches, puree the soup in a blender or in a food processor. Pour the puree
   through a strainer and return to the saucepan. Stir in the cream and simmer about
   15 minutes more.

4. Remove the pan from the heat and stir in the remaining olive oil. Then stir in the
   butter until it melts. Season to taste with salt and pepper. Serve immediately.

Roast Butternut Squash and Pear Soup with Blue Cheese Cream and Toasted Hazelnuts

Philippe Jeanty, Domaine Chandon, Yountville, California

Serves 4

Blue Cheese Cream and Toasted Hazelnuts:

1 ounce good-quality blue cheese, at room temperature

3/4 cup mascarpone

1/2 cup shelled hazelnuts

Roast Butternut Squash and Pear Soup:

2 medium-size butternut squashes, halved, peeled, seeded, and cut into 1-inch pieces

Salt

Black pepper

1/2 cup (1 stick) unsalted butter

1 medium-size onion, coarsely chopped

2 sprigs fresh sage

4 medium-size pears, halved, peeled, cored, and coarsely chopped

4 cups chicken stock

For the blue cheese cream and toasted hazelnuts:

1. Preheat the oven to 400°F.

2. In a mixing bowl, mash the blue cheese with a fork. Then add the mascarpone and whisk until blended. Set aside.

3. Spread the hazelnuts on a baking sheet or in a baking dish and toast until lightly browned, 5 to 10 minutes. Reduce the oven temperature to 350°F.

4. Transfer the nuts to a folded kitchen towel; then fold the towel over them and rub well to remove their skins. Put the nuts in a food processor with the metal blade and pulse until coarsely chopped. Set aside.

For the butternut squash and pear soup:

1. Lightly butter a shallow baking dish and put the squash in it, seasoning to taste with salt and pepper. Cover with aluminum foil and bake until tender, about 45 minutes.

2. Shortly before the squash is done, melt 2 tablespoons of butter in a large soup pot over medium heat. Add the onion and sage and cook, stirring, until the onion is translucent, 4 to 5 minutes. Add the squash, pears, and stock and simmer until the pears are tender, about 20 minutes.

3. In a blender or food processor, puree the soup in batches. Return it to the pot and, over low heat, stir in the remaining butter. Adjust the seasoning to taste with salt and pepper.

4. Ladle the soup into 8 warm bowls. Top each with a generous spoonful of blue cheese cream and sprinkle with hazelnuts. Serve immediately.

Corn Soup with Petit Vegetables

Jean-Louis Palladin, Jean-Louis at the Watergate Hotel, Washington, D.C.

Serves 4

"I have soup running through my veins," declares Jean-Louis Palladin. "My mother taught me to love it. My father, an Italian, was a very hard worker, and if he didn't have a pot of soup every day, he was the most unhappy guy in the world." This elegant yet easy version of corn chowder will keep any soup-lover happy.

1 carrot, peeled and cut into 1/4- to 1/2-inch dice

1 turnip, peeled and cut into 1/4- to 1/2-inch dice

1 zucchini, peeled and cut into 1/4- to 1/2-inch dice

1 rib celery, peeled and cut into 1/4- to 1/2-inch dice

5 ears corn

2 cups heavy cream

Salt

Pepper

1. Bring a large saucepan of lightly salted water to a boil over high heat. One at a time, add the diced vegetables and boil until tender-crisp: 3 to 5 minutes for the carrot and turnip, 1 to 2 minutes for the zucchini and celery. As soon as each vegetable is done, remove the dice with a slotted spoon or small wire strainer and transfer to a bowl of ice water to stop cooking; drain well and set aside.

2. Add the corn to the boiling water and cook until tender, 5 to 7 minutes. Drain and transfer the ears to a large bowl of ice water. When the corn is cool, use a sharp knife to cut the kernels from each ear. Set aside 2 tablespoons of the kernels.

3. Put the remaining corn kernels in a food processor and process the corn until pureed.

4. In the saucepan, stir together the corn puree and the cream and bring to a boil over medium heat. Press the soup through a fine strainer, return it to the pan over medium heat, and season to taste with salt and pepper.

5. In individual soup bowls, arrange the vegetable dice and reserved corn kernels. Ladle the hot soup into each bowl. Serve immediately.

Asparagus Soup with Crabmeat

Georges Perrier, Le Bec-Fin, Philadelphia, Pennsylvania

Serves 4 to 6

One of springtime's greatest pleasures, fresh asparagus is highlighted here in a simple pureed soup lightly enriched with cream and garnished with fresh crabmeat. The recipe doubles easily.

2 tablespoons unsalted butter

1 rib celery, thinly sliced

1 medium-size onion, thinly sliced

1 small carrot, peeled and thinly sliced

2 bunches asparagus, trimmed and thinly sliced

2 cups chicken stock

1/2 bunch Italian parsley, stemmed

1 clove garlic, finely chopped

1/2 cup heavy cream

Few drops hot pepper sauce

Salt

Pepper

1/2 pound fresh-cooked lump crabmeat, picked over to remove any bits of shell or cartilage

Garlic croutons (optional)

1. In a medium-size saucepan, melt the butter over medium heat. Add the celery, onion, and carrot and cook, stirring, until tender, about 5 minutes. Add the asparagus and stock, bring to a boil, reduce the heat to low, and simmer gently for 30 minutes.

2. Meanwhile, bring a small saucepan of water to a boil. Add the Italian parsley. As soon as the water returns to a boil, drain well, rinse the Italian parsley under cold running water, and drain again. Puree in a blender or food processor and set aside.

3. Stir the garlic, cream, and hot pepper sauce into the pan of asparagus. After the soup returns to a simmer, carefully puree, in batches if necessary, in the blender or food processor. Pour and press through a fine strainer set over a bowl. Return the soup to the pan and stir in the parsley puree to intensify its color. Warm gently over low heat until hot and season to taste with salt and pepper.

4. Ladle the soup into warm bowls. Garnish with crabmeat and, if you like, garlic croutons. Serve immediately.

Chicken Vegetable Soup

Fernando Castillo, Project Open Hand, San Francisco, California

Serves 6 to 8

"Every time I make this soup, it reminds me of my three friends who were living with AIDS," says Fernando Castillo of this traditional Mexican-style recipe. "When I was taking care of them, I always served this soup because I knew they were getting a warm, nutritious, soothing meal." Robust and generous enough to be offered as a main course, the soup should be accompanied by French bread or tortillas.

1 1/3 gallons cold water

One 3 1/2-pound chicken, cut into serving pieces

2 chicken bouillon cubes

1 clove garlic, finely chopped

1/2 medium-size onion, diced

1/3 bunch fresh cilantro, coarsely chopped

1/2 cup white rice

1/2 tablespoon dried oregano

3 ribs celery, cut crosswise into 1/4-inch-thick slices

2 medium-size zucchini, cut crosswise into 1/4-inch-thick slices

2 medium-size carrots, peeled and cut crosswise into 1/4-inch-thick slices

2 medium-size potatoes, peeled and quartered

2 medium-size ears fresh sweet corn, quartered

Salt

Black pepper

2 lemons or limes, cut into quarters

1. In a large pot, bring the water to a boil over high heat. Add the chicken, bouillon cubes, garlic, onion, cilantro, rice, and oregano; reduce the heat to medium and simmer, skimming frequently, until the chicken is tender, 30 to 40 minutes.

2. Add the vegetables and simmer until tender, about 10 minutes more. Season to taste with salt and pepper.

3. Serve along with lemon or lime wedges to be squeezed in to taste.

Escarole Soup with Chicken and Meatballs

JoAnn diLorenzo, JoAnn's Cafe & Pantry, San Francisco, California
JoAnn's B Street Cafe, San Mateo, California

Serves 4 to 6

"I wish I was eating this right now," says JoAnn diLorenzo. "The aromas and textures remind me of cold childhood evenings when this soup was one of my favorite dinners. Sometimes Grandma would serve very hard cheese for us to break off and chew gently between bites of bread and soup."

One 3-pound stewing chicken, rinsed well

2 cloves garlic, peeled

1 carrot, peeled and cut into 1-inch pieces

1 rib celery, cut into 1-inch pieces

1 onion, quartered

1 bay leaf

1/4 teaspoon black peppercorns

1/2 pound lean ground beef

1 bunch escarole, thoroughly washed, thick outer stems trimmed off, leaves cut into 2-inch pieces

Salt

Pepper

Grated Parmesan cheese

1. Put the chicken, carrot, celery, onion, bay leaf, and peppercorns in a pot just large enough to hold them comfortably and add cold water to cover them well. Bring almost to a simmer over medium heat, skimming continuously; reduce the heat to low, cover, and barely simmer for 3 to 4 hours.

2. Line a strainer with cheesecloth and set it in a large bowl. Lift out the chicken and set it aside to cool. Strain the liquid into the bowl, cover, and refrigerate.

3. When the chicken is cool enough to handle, remove and discard the skin and fat. Pull or cut the meat from the bones and, with your fingers, shred the meat. Cover and refrigerate.

4. Skim all fat from the surface of the chilled broth. Put the broth in a medium-size soup pot and bring it to a boil over medium heat. Reduce the heat to a simmer and, with your hands, shape the beef into 1-inch meatballs, dropping them into the broth. Simmer gently for about 1 hour.

5. Add the escarole and shredded chicken to the pot and simmer gently just until the escarole turns bright green, about 6 minutes more. Season to taste with salt and pepper.

6. Serve the soup hot in warmed bowls, and pass the grated Parmesan cheese for each person to add to taste.

Pasta e Fagioli

Joyce Goldstein, Square One, San Francisco, California

Serves 8 first courses or 6 main courses

"Some of my happiest days have been spent in Italy," says Joyce Goldstein, "so most Italian food is comforting to me. I like to make this soup when the weather is somewhat nippy, and I feel like holing up and reading and eating at the same time."

Though the soup may be made in advance and reheated, Joyce points out that the pasta will become soft as it sits. If you like your pasta firm, she suggests cooking it as needed and adding it to the made-in-advance soup base.

2 cups dried cranberry, cannelini, or small white beans, picked over to remove any stones or impurities and rinsed well

5 cups cold water

3 tablespoons olive oil

1/4 pound pancetta, finely chopped

4 large cloves garlic, finely chopped

2 medium-size carrots, peeled and finely chopped

2 medium-size ribs celery, finely chopped

1 medium-size onion, finely chopped

1 1/2 cups canned diced plum tomatoes

8 cups chicken stock or water

Salt

Black pepper

1/2 pound small dried pasta shapes such as shells or ditalini

Virgin olive oil

Grated Parmesan cheese

1. Put the beans in a large saucepan and add the cold water. Bring the water to a boil over high heat; reduce the heat to medium and simmer about 5 minutes. Turn off the heat and leave the beans to sit for 1 hour. Drain them and set aside.

2. In the saucepan, heat the olive oil over medium heat. Add the pancetta and cook, stirring frequently, for 5 minutes. Add the garlic, carrots, celery, and onion and cook, stirring, for 5 minutes more. Add the beans, tomatoes, stock or water, and 2 teaspoons of salt. Bring to a boil, then reduce the heat and simmer, covered, until the beans are tender, about 1 hour.

3. To give the soup more body, remove about 1/2 cup of beans and vegetables and puree them in a food processor. Stir the puree back into the pot. Season to taste with salt and pepper. Keep warm.

4. Bring a separate large pot of salted water to a boil. Add the pasta and cook until al dente, tender but still chewy, following suggested cooking time on the package. Drain the pasta well and stir it into the soup. Simmer for 5 minutes more.

5. Ladle the soup into bowls and top with a swirl of virgin olive oil, some grated Parmesan, and a liberal grinding of black pepper. Serve immediately.

Black Bean Soup

Serves 6 to 8 *Kevin Taylor, Zenith American Grill, Denver, Colorado*

A robust tradition shared by the Southwest and the Caribbean, black bean soup here gets an up-to-date refinement from Kevin Taylor by being pureed until smooth and then seasoned with a lively tasting mixture of balsamic vinegar and lime juice.

1/4 pound bacon, diced

1 onion, diced

8 serrano chilies, stemmed

1 pound dried black beans, picked over for any stones or other impurities and thoroughly rinsed

1 1/2 gallons chicken stock

1 tablespoon ground cumin

1/4 cup balsamic vinegar

1/4 cup lime juice

Salt

1. Heat a large stockpot over medium heat. Add the bacon and cook, stirring constantly, for 5 minutes. Add the onion and chilies and cook, stirring occasionally, for 10 minutes. Add the beans, stock, and cumin. Bring to a boil, reduce the heat slightly to medium-low, and simmer briskly until the beans are very tender, about 2 1/4 hours.

2. In batches, carefully puree the soup until very smooth in a blender or a food processor. Return to the pot and stir in the vinegar and lime juice. Season to taste with salt. Serve immediately.

Hearty Black-Eyed Pea Soup

Elizabeth Terry, Elizabeth on 37th, Savannah, Georgia

Serves 6

"This is a hearty winter soup of the first dimension, featuring the rich meaty flavor of the black-eyed pea, of which Southerners are enamored," says Elizabeth Terry. "I think its flavor is enhanced by the similar, yet still distinct, sweet-salty tastes of the ham, sausage, and bacon." Because of this complex combination, she notes that no extra salt is needed.

2 cups dried black-eyed peas, picked over for any stones or other impurities and thoroughly rinsed (see Note)

2 1/2 cups water

4 strips bacon, cut crosswise into thin strips

1/4 pound spicy Italian-style sausage, casings discarded, meat finely chopped

2 cloves garlic, finely chopped

1 cup finely chopped onion

1/2 cup finely chopped carrot

1/4 cup finely chopped celery heart

2 tablespoons all-purpose flour

Two 14-ounce cans diced tomatoes in juice

1/4 pound country ham or prosciutto, finely chopped

4 cups chicken stock

1 tablespoon mild vegetable oil, such as peanut

1/4 cup stemmed, seeded, and finely chopped green bell pepper

1/4 cup trimmed and finely chopped green onion

1/4 cup finely chopped fresh thyme

1/4 cup dry sherry

Black pepper

1. Put the peas in a large soup pot and add the water. Over high heat, bring to a boil; lower the heat to medium-low and simmer for 25 minutes. Turn off the heat and set aside, but do not drain.

2. In a large skillet over medium heat, cook the bacon, stirring, until crisp. Add the sausage and continue cooking, stirring, until the sausage is browned. Carefully pour off all but about 3 tablespoons of the fat. Then, add the garlic, onion, carrot, and celery and cook, stirring, until all the vegetables are lightly browned. Stir in the all-purpose flour and continue cooking and stirring until the flour is lightly browned, about 2 minutes more. Whisk in the tomatoes.

3. Stir the cooked vegetable mixture into the pot of black-eyed peas. Add the ham and stock. Over medium heat, simmer the soup, stirring occasionally, for 45 minutes.

4. Just before serving, heat the oil in a medium-size skillet over medium heat. Add the bell pepper, green onion, and thyme and cook, stirring, until they soften and begin to turn golden. Stir the mixture into the soup along with the sherry. Add pepper to taste. Serve immediately.

NOTE • *If you can't find black-eyed peas in your grocery store or in a Latin American market, substitute dried black beans.*

Navy Bean Soup with Shallots and Ham

Jimmy Schmidt, The Rattlesnake Club, Detroit, Michigan

Serves 6 to 8

"With its smoky flavor, this traditional soup satisfies right down to your soul," says Jimmy Schmidt.

1 pound dried navy beans, picked over for any stones or other impurities and thoroughly rinsed

2 tablespoons plus 1 teaspoon virgin olive oil

2 cups chopped shallots

1 gallon low-salt vegetable or chicken stock

1 whole smoked ham hock

1 tablespoon salt

Black pepper

4 cloves garlic, peeled

1/2 cup cider vinegar

1/2 cup finely chopped fresh chives or green onion tops

1. The night before you make the soup, put the beans in a large bowl and cover generously with cold water. Leave to soak overnight.

2. The next day, heat the 2 tablespoons of olive oil in a large soup pot over high heat. Add the shallots and cook, stirring, until tender, about 3 minutes. Drain the beans and add them to the pot with the stock and ham hock. Stir in the salt and add pepper to taste. When the liquid begins to simmer, reduce the heat to medium and cook, covered, until the beans are tender, 3 1/2 to 4 hours.

3. While the beans cook, preheat the oven to 350°F.

4. To roast the garlic, coat the peeled cloves with the remaining oil. Wrap securely in aluminum foil and bake until the cloves are soft, about 30 minutes. Leave them to cool, then chop finely, and set aside.

5. When the beans are tender, remove the ham hock. Cut the meat from the bones, coarsely chop the meat, and return it to the pot. Stir in the roasted garlic and the vinegar. Taste and add more salt and pepper if necessary.

6. Just before serving, stir in the chives. Ladle into warmed bowls. Serve immediately.

Stracciatelle with Sorrel

 Serves 4 *Judy Rodgers, Zuni Cafe & Grill, San Francisco, California*

Stracciatelle—"rags," in Italian—describes the wisps of cooked egg in this popular Roman soup. "I find it a light but restorative dish," says Judy Rodgers. "It is very easy to digest and a perfect meal when you're feeling under the weather." If you like, you can leave out the pleasantly sharp-tasting sorrel leaves. "But I often add them to the traditional formula," Rodgers adds, "because I like their flavor with the eggs and they cook instantly."

4 cups chicken stock

Salt

1 large egg

5 teaspoons freshly grated Parmigiano-
  Reggiano cheese

1 tablespoon semolina flour

2 ounces tender sorrel leaves, stemmed
  and washed

1. In a medium-size saucepan, bring the stock to a simmer over medium heat. Add salt to taste.

2. In a small mixing bowl, use a fork or wire whisk to beat together the egg, cheese, and semolina just until smoothly blended. With a knife, cut the sorrel into wide ribbons.

3. At the same time, add the egg mixture and the sorrel leaves to the simmering stock. Wait about 5 seconds; then, with a fork, stir vigorously but briefly. Reduce the heat to low and cook about 1 minute more.

4. Ladle instantly into warmed bowls.

Strawberry Soup

The Haussner Family, Haussner's Restaurant, Baltimore, Maryland

Serves 4 to 6

An elegant yet totally indulgent start to a summer lunch or dinner, this old Eastern European recipe would be equally good served at brunch—or even as an unusual dessert.

1 pint fresh strawberries

2 cups plain yogurt

3/4 cup sour cream

1/4 cup honey

1 ounce strawberry schnapps

1. Wash and hull the strawberries. Reserve 4 for a garnish.

2. Put the berries, yogurt, 1/2 cup of the sour cream, the honey, and schnapps in a food processor and process until smoothly pureed.

3. Transfer the puree to a mixing bowl, cover, and refrigerate until thoroughly chilled and thickened, 2 to 3 hours.

4. Neatly slice the reserved berries. Ladle the soup into chilled cups or bowls. Garnish with the strawberry slices and dollops of the remaining sour cream. Serve immediately.

Papa's Parsley Salad

Serves 4 to 6   *Jesse Cool, Flea Street Cafe, Menlo Park, California*

"My Italian grandfather handed down this heirloom recipe to me," says Jesse Cool. "When I was a child in western Pennsylvania, he'd forage for wild dandelion leaves." Though the bitter greens here are more readily accessible Italian parsley and radicchio, this version nonetheless, says Jesse, "conjures up memories of lessons he taught me about eating foods indigenous to where you live."

1/2 cup extra-virgin olive oil

1/2 cup grated Parmesan or other hard Italian cheese, plus additional for garnish

1/4 cup balsamic vinegar

3 large hard-boiled eggs, peeled and grated

2 cloves garlic, finely chopped

2 bunches Italian parsley, stemmed, washed, dried, and torn into small bite-size clusters

3 or 4 leaves radicchio, washed, dried and torn into small bite-size pieces

Salt

Black pepper

1. In a large mixing bowl, stir together the olive oil, 1/2 cup cheese, the vinegar, eggs, and garlic. Add the Italian parsley and radicchio and toss well. Season to taste with salt and pepper.

2. Leave the salad to marinate at room temperature for about 15 minutes. Taste and adjust the seasonings. Offer the additional cheese and pepper for each person to add to taste.

Heirloom Tomato Salad with Toasted Garlic-Miso Vinaigrette and Basil Oil

Bruce Hill, Oritalia, San Francisco, California

Serves 4

In his signature style, combining Italian and Asian ingredients and techniques, Bruce Hill adds the smooth, rich flavor of miso paste to the dressing for an anything-but-classic tomato salad. Heirloom tomatoes, colorfully striped old-fashioned varieties, may be found in good produce and farmers' markets, but you can substitute any sun-ripened summer tomatoes that are available.

Garlic-Miso Vinaigrette:

1/3 cup pure olive oil

1 tablespoon finely chopped garlic

2 tablespoons mirin

1 tablespoon yellow miso (soybean paste) (see Note)

1 tablespoon rice wine vinegar

Salt

Black pepper

Basil Oil:

1 cup packed fresh basil leaves

1/4 cup pure olive oil

Tomato Salad:

4 medium-size heirloom (multicolored) tomatoes, peeled (see Box, page 3) and cut into 1/4- to 1/2-inch slices

Salt

Black pepper

8 cups loosely packed arugula leaves, washed, dried, and thinly sliced

1/2 medium-size red onion, thinly sliced

For the vinaigrette:

In a small skillet, heat the olive oil over medium heat. Add the garlic and cook, stirring, until golden brown, 5 to 7 minutes. Stir in the mirin and remove from the heat. In a small bowl, stir together the miso and vinegar. Stir in the garlic mixture and salt and pepper to taste. Set aside.

For the basil oil:

Fill a medium-size bowl with ice cubes and water and set aside. Bring a small saucepan of water to a boil. Add the basil leaves to the boiling water and blanch them for 30 seconds. Drain and immediately plunge the leaves into the ice water; leave them there for 2 to 3 minutes. Drain well and squeeze them firmly with your hands to remove excess liquid. Put the leaves and the olive oil in a blender or a food processor; puree until smooth. Strain the mixture through a fine-mesh strainer set over a small bowl. Discard the solids and set the oil aside.

For the tomato salad:

1. Neatly arrange the tomatoes on 4 individual serving plates and season to taste with salt and pepper.

2. In a large mixing bowl, toss the arugula and red onion with 1/4 cup of the reserved vinaigrette until evenly coated. Pile the greens in the center of each plate of tomatoes. Drizzle the basil oil and the remaining vinaigrette all over each plate. Serve immediately.

NOTE • *Miso is available in the refrigerated section of well-stocked supermarkets and Asian food stores.*

Panzanella with Teleme Cheese

Serves 6

Hiro Sone and Lissa Doumani, Terra, St. Helena, California

"In summer, when vine-ripened tomatoes are so good, we're always happy with this when we can't think of anything else we'd want to eat for lunch or dinner at home," say Hiro Sone and Lissa Doumani of this traditional Tuscan salad of garlic croutons, tomatoes, and cheese. "It's easy to make, and though you feel satisfied, you don't feel stuffed afterward."

1/2 small baguette loaf, about 12 inches long

1 large clove garlic, crushed with a garlic press

3/4 cup extra-virgin olive oil

6 medium-to-large sun-ripened tomatoes, cored and cut into large chunks

1/3 medium-size mild, sweet onion, finely chopped

3 tablespoons coarsely chopped fresh basil

1/4 cup balsamic vinegar

Salt

Black pepper

3/4 pound teleme cheese, cut into 1-inch squares (see Note)

Whole fresh basil leaves

1. Preheat the oven to 300°F.

2. Cut the baguette in half lengthwise. Rub the cut sides with the crushed garlic and brush them liberally with 1/4 cup of the olive oil. Cut each half lengthwise in half again down the middle of the cut side. Then cut the resulting strips crosswise into 3/4-inch-wide croutons. Spread the croutons on a baking sheet, crust sides down, and bake until dark golden brown, about 30 minutes.

3. In a large salad bowl, toss the croutons, tomatoes, onion, and basil. Add the vinegar, remaining olive oil, and salt and pepper to taste and toss again. Scatter the cheese on top and garnish with the basil leaves. Serve.

NOTE • *Teleme is a California cheese that actually evolved from feta but today more closely resembles a good mozzarella. You could substitute cubes of fresh mozzarella, jack cheese, or a mild, creamy feta.*

Mom's Stuffed Tomatoes with Grilled Tuna Salad

Derek Burns, Elka, San Francisco, California

Serves 6

"During summers in my childhood, a family weekend supper nearly always included this specialty of my mother's," says Derek Burns. Of course, he has taken some liberties with the original. "I remember something about opening cans," he adds. If you can't find fresh ahi tuna, feel free to revert to his mom's option.

1 1/2 pounds fresh skinless ahi tuna fillets

1/2 cup plus 2 tablespoons extra-virgin olive oil

Salt

Black pepper

6 large vine-ripened summer tomatoes, peeled (see Box, page 3)

1/4 cup finely chopped shallots

1/4 cup finely chopped French cornichons (pickled baby cucumbers) or dill pickles

2 tablespoons drained capers, finely chopped

2 tablespoons finely chopped Italian parsley

1 teaspoon grated lemon zest

2 tablespoons lemon juice

6 cups mixed salad greens of your choice, washed and dried

1. Preheat a grill or broiler.

2. Brush the tuna fillets with 2 tablespoons of the olive oil and season to taste with salt and pepper. Grill or broil until rare, 2 to 3 minutes per side. Remove from the heat and chill in the refrigerator 1 to 2 hours.

3. Before serving, cut a 1/2-inch-thick slice from the stem ends of the tomatoes. With a sharp-edged spoon, scoop out the tomatoes, leaving a shell of their outer flesh.

4. With your fingers, break the tuna into large flakes and small chunks, putting them in a medium-size mixing bowl. Add 1/4 cup more of olive oil along with the shallots, cornichons, capers, Italian parsley, lemon zest, and salt and pepper to taste. Toss well and stuff the mixture into the tomatoes.

5. In a small bowl, season the lemon juice with salt and pepper to taste, stirring until the salt dissolves. Stirring briskly, pour in the remaining olive oil to make a vinaigrette.

6. In a salad bowl, toss the salad greens with the vinaigrette to coat them lightly.

7. Arrange the greens on individual salad plates and top each bed of greens with a stuffed tomato. Serve immediately.

Marinated Cauliflower Salad

Sanford D'Amato, Sanford Restaurant, Milwaukee, Wisconsin

"The original olive salad on which this is based was sold in my father's grocery store around the holidays," recalls Sanford D'Amato. "My grandfather prepared it next door in his house." Today, Sanford's restaurant stands on the site of his father's store.

Serve this fragrant salad as part of an hors-d'oeuvre or antipasto tray or as an accompaniment to sandwiches such as Sanford's Sicilian Burgers (page 115).

Marinade:

2 cups water

1 cup red wine vinegar

1/3 cup sugar

1 tablespoon kosher salt

20 black peppercorns, slightly crushed

4 cloves garlic, peeled

3 allspice berries, slightly crushed

2 whole cloves

2 bay leaves

2 sprigs fresh rosemary

2 sprigs fresh thyme

Vegetables:

1 cup small cauliflower florets

1/2 cup peeled and thinly sliced carrots

1/4 cup finely diced red onion, rinsed with warm water

1/4 cup thin matchstick strips red bell pepper

1/2 cup pitted green Sicilian-style brine-cured olives, each cut into 6 pieces

1/4 cup seeded and thinly sliced Italian green pickled peppers (pepperoncini)

1/4 cup capers, rinsed

1/2 cup extra-virgin olive oil

1/4 cup finely shredded fresh basil leaves

Salt

Pepper

For the marinade:

Put all the ingredients in a nonreactive medium saucepan and bring to a boil, stirring occasionally, over medium heat. Cover, remove from the heat and leave to steep for about 30 minutes. Pour through a fine strainer and set aside.

For the vegetables:

1. Put the cauliflower, carrots, onion, and red bell pepper in a medium-size saucepan. Add the reserved marinade. Bring to a boil over medium heat. Remove the pan from the heat and stir in the olives, pepperoncini, and capers.

2. Transfer the mixture to a nonreactive container. When the mixture has cooled to room temperature, close the container and refrigerate overnight.

3. The next day, drain the vegetables. Toss them with the olive oil, basil, and salt and pepper to taste and serve.

Tuna Salad with Apple and Onion

Anne Rosenzweig, Arcadia, New York, New York

You'll find evidence of Anne Rosenzweig's culinary talent in the way she transforms a basic tuna salad into a fresh-tasting combination of flavors. You could also use the tuna mixture as a sandwich filling with good-quality white, egg, or whole-wheat bread.

Three 7-ounce cans chunk-style tuna packed in water or oil, drained

1 large eating apple, halved, cored, peeled, and cut into 1/2-inch dice

1/2 medium-size red onion, finely chopped

3/4 cup loosely packed chopped fresh basil

3/4 cup mayonnaise

2 tablespoons grated lemon zest

2 tablespoons lemon juice

1 head Romaine or butter lettuce, washed, dried, and torn into bite-size pieces

1. In a large mixing bowl, toss together the tuna, apple, onion, and basil. In a small bowl, stir together the mayonnaise and lemon zest and juice. Add the mayonnaise to the tuna mixture and toss well to coat.

2. Arrange the lettuce in beds on 6 serving dishes. Spoon the tuna mixture on top and serve.

Spinach, Radicchio, and Warm Goat Cheese Salad

Jimmy Schmidt, The Rattlesnake Club, Detroit, Michigan

Serves 4

1 medium-size red bell pepper

3 tablespoons balsamic vinegar

Salt

Black pepper

1/4 cup extra-virgin olive oil

2 tablespoons finely chopped fresh chives

1/2 pound soft goat cheese

2 cups packed small fresh spinach leaves, stemmed, thoroughly washed, dried, and torn into bite-size pieces

1 small head radicchio, washed and dried, 4 outer leaves reserved, remainder cut crosswise into thin strips

1 cup packed arugula leaves, washed and dried

1 small red onion, very thinly sliced

1/2 cup Kalamata or other black brine-cured olives, pitted and halved

1. Preheat the oven to 500°F.

2. Put the bell pepper on a foil-lined baking sheet and roast it, turning occasionally, until its skin is evenly blistered and blackened, about 25 minutes. Remove it from the oven and cover with a kitchen towel.

3. When the pepper is cool enough to handle, pull out the stem, peel off the skin, and remove the seeds and white ribs from inside. Cut the pepper into 1/4-inch dice and set aside.

4. In a small bowl, stir the vinegar with salt and pepper to taste. Stir in the olive oil, then the chives. Set aside.

5. Place the goat cheese on a microwave-safe plate. Set the microwave oven to medium and cook the cheese in the oven until warmed through, 1 to 2 minutes, depending on the strength of your oven.

6. In a large mixing bowl, toss together the spinach, radicchio, arugula, and onion. Add the olives and bell pepper. Pour in the dressing and toss until the leaves are evenly coated.

7. On each serving plate, place 1 reserved radicchio leaf to form a cup shape. Fill the leaves to slightly overflowing with the salad. Spoon the warm goat cheese onto each salad and dust lightly with black pepper. Serve immediately.

Dungeness Crab Salad
with Citrus and Fennel

Cory Schreiber, Wildwood, Portland, Oregon

Serves 4 to 6

Sweet herbs, spices, citrus fruits, and fennel highlight the natural sweetness of crabmeat in Cory Schreiber's easily prepared salad, a delightful dish to serve on a warm summer's day.

1 tablespoon whole fennel seeds

1 tablespoon whole coriander seeds

1 pound fresh cooked Dungeness crabmeat, picked over to remove any bits of shell or cartilage

1 medium-size red onion, halved and thinly sliced

1 medium-size fennel bulb, trimmed, halved, cored and thinly sliced

1/4 cup Italian parsley leaves

1/4 cup small fresh basil leaves

1/4 cup fresh tarragon leaves

1/4 cup coarsely chopped fresh fennel leaves

1/2 cup extra-virgin olive oil

Juice and grated zest of 2 lemons

Juice and grated zest of 1 orange

Salt

Cayenne pepper

1. In a small, dry heavy skillet over medium heat, toast the fennel and coriander seeds until they color slightly and give off an aroma, 1 to 2 minutes. Put them in a spice mill and coarsely grind them. Set aside.

2. Put the crabmeat in a medium-size mixing bowl and add the onion and fennel bulb. Add the herb leaves, ground fennel and coriander seeds, olive oil, and lemon and orange juices and zests. Toss well and season to taste with salt and cayenne. Serve immediately.

Field Greens with Shrimp, Corn, and Ginger

Michel Richard, Citrus, Los Angeles, California; Citronelle, Santa Barbara, California, Baltimore, Maryland, and Washington, D.C.; Michel's Bistro, Philadelphia, Pennsylvania; and Bistro M, San Francisco, California

Serves 4 to 6

Ginger Dressing:

3 tablespoons mayonnaise

3 tablespoons champagne vinegar or white wine vinegar

1 tablespoon orange juice or water

3 tablespoons olive oil

One 2-inch piece fresh ginger, peeled and thinly sliced crosswise

Salt

Black pepper

Salad:

1 large ear white or yellow corn, husked, kernels cut off

1 tablespoon olive oil

24 large raw shrimp, shelled and deveined

7 cups packed bite-size mixed baby salad greens, washed and dried

2 tablespoons trimmed and finely chopped green onion or chives

For the dressing:

In a small bowl, stir together the mayonnaise, vinegar, and orange juice or water. Whisking continuously, pour in the olive oil in a slow, thin stream. Use a garlic press, held over a small cup, to press the ginger slices, yielding about 2 teaspoons of juice. Stir the ginger juice, to taste, into the dressing. Season to taste with salt and pepper and set aside.

For the salad:

1. Bring a small saucepan of water to a boil over high heat. Reduce the heat to medium, add the corn kernels, and simmer for 5 minutes. Drain well and set aside.

2. Heat a small, heavy nonstick skillet over medium heat. Add the olive oil and cook the shrimp, turning them once with tongs, just until they turn pink, about 1 minute per side. Remove from the skillet and set aside.

3. To serve the salad, put the greens and corn in a large mixing bowl and toss well. Gently toss again with enough of the dressing to coat the greens lightly. Mound the greens in the centers of 4 or 6 large plates.

4. Toss the cooked shrimp with several tablespoons of the remaining dressing to coat them lightly. Arrange them around the greens. Garnish the salads with green onion or chives and serve immediately.

Tandoori Shrimp Over Spring Greens

Serves 4 — *Irene Trias, Appam—Cuisine of Old India, San Francisco, California*

Seafood, poultry, or meat cooked in the Indian tandoor, a jar-shaped charcoal-heated oven, develop a crisp exterior and succulent interior that make it irresistible and intensely satisfying—and all the more so for the spiced yogurt in which the food marinates before cooking.

Here, Irene Trias has lightened the traditional Indian barbecue and adapted it for the western kitchen, marinating shrimp in low-fat yogurt, grilling or broiling them, and serving them over baby salad greens. "Our customers love this as an appetizer or as a light main course," she says, "especially when they eat it during summer in our outdoor courtyard."

1 cup plain low-fat yogurt

1/4 cup lemon juice

2 tablespoons finely chopped garlic

2 tablespoons finely chopped fresh ginger

1 tablespoon ground turmeric

2 teaspoons paprika

6 whole green cardamom pods, crushed

1/4 teaspoon cayenne pepper (optional)

1 1/2 pounds shrimp, rinsed, peeled, and deveined

Salt

1/4 pound mixed baby salad greens, washed and dried

1 lemon, cut in half

1. In a mixing bowl, stir together the yogurt, lemon juice, garlic, ginger, turmeric, paprika, and cardamom; if you'd like the shrimp slightly hotter, add the cayenne as well. Transfer half the mixture to another bowl, add the shrimp, and toss well. Cover and marinate in the refrigerator for 1 hour.

2. Meanwhile, preheat a charcoal grill or broiler.

3. Remove the shrimp from the marinade, season with salt, and grill or broil, basting liberally with the reserved yogurt mixture, until firm and cooked through, 4 to 5 minutes per side.

4. Meanwhile, put the salad greens in a medium-size bowl, squeeze the lemon juice over them, and toss well. Arrange the greens on individual serving plates. The moment the shrimp are done, place them on top of the greens and serve immediately.

Pan-Seared Sea Scallop Salad with Bing Cherry Chutney

Bruce Hill, Oritalia, San Francisco, California

Serves 4

The tang of good, spicy-sweet fruit chutney is one of the great pleasures of Asian cooking. Bruce Hill's recipe forgoes the need to make a big batch of the Indian preserves by simply combining fresh summer cherries with a quickly prepared syrup that transforms them into a chutney to accompany a salad of seared sea scallops.

Bing Cherry Chutney:

- 1 tablespoon unsalted butter
- 1 tablespoon peeled and finely chopped fresh ginger
- 1 teaspoon finely chopped shallots
- 1/2 teaspoon finely chopped garlic
- 1 tablespoon wildflower honey
- 1 tablespoon sugar
- 1/4 cup champagne vinegar
- 2 teaspoons balsamic vinegar
- Juice and grated zest of 1 lime
- 1 cup fresh Bing cherries, washed and pitted

Pan-Seared Sea Scallop Salad:

- 1 tablespoon champagne vinegar
- Salt
- Black pepper
- 2 tablespoons olive oil
- 2 teaspoons whole coriander seeds
- 1 teaspoon whole Szechwan peppercorns
- 12 medium-size sea scallops, trimmed, rinsed, and patted dry
- 2 tablespoons mild vegetable oil, such as peanut
- 2 cups mixed baby salad greens, washed and dried

For the Bing cherry chutney:

In a medium-size sauté pan or skillet over medium heat, melt the butter. Add the ginger, shallot, and garlic and cook, stirring, for 2 minutes. Add the honey and sugar and cook, stirring, until the sugar turns golden brown, 3 to 5 minutes more. Stir in the vinegars and cook, stirring, until they reduce to form a very thick syrup, about 5 minutes more. Stir in the lime juice and zest and continue cooking for 1 minute more. Add the cherries, stir well to coat, and immediately transfer the mixture to a bowl. Set aside.

For the pan-seared sea scallop salad:

1. In a small mixing bowl, prepare a vinaigrette by stirring the champagne vinegar with salt and pepper to taste until the salt dissolves. Stirring continuously, pour in the olive oil. Set the dressing aside.

2. In a small, dry heavy skillet over medium heat, toast the coriander seeds and Szechwan peppercorns until they color slightly and give off an aroma, 1 to 2 minutes. Put them in a spice mill and grind them.

3. Season the scallops on both sides with the spice mixture and salt to taste.

4. In a medium-size sauté pan or skillet over medium heat, heat the vegetable oil. Add the scallops and cook until seared golden, about 2 minutes per side. Remove from the pan and set aside.

5. In a medium-size mixing bowl, toss the salad greens with the prepared vinaigrette. Mound a small pile of salad greens on each of 4 serving plates. Place 3 spoonfuls of cherry chutney on each plate around the greens. Top each pile of greens with 3 scallops and serve immediately.

chapter

2

Main Courses

Meat, seafood, or poultry crisped in the pan or on the grill and bathed in its own juices. A stew or braise simmering over a low fire. Roasts or casseroles sending forth rich aromas from the oven. A mound of al dente pasta bathed in a fragrant sauce. A generous sandwich on good-quality bread. Egg and cheese dishes to make a breakfast or brunch extramemorable.

So many different main courses offer comfort. Part of the pleasure to be found on the following pages lies in that very variety. You'll find recipes for every taste, every eating style, and every budget—from vegetarian entrees to dishes for the confirmed carnivore, health-conscious preparations to once-a-month splurges, weeknight standards to special-occasion extravaganzas. All of them, however, share the ability to bring pleasure and promote a sense of profound well-being.

Shrimp with Walnuts

Alice Wong, Hong Kong Flower Lounge, Millbrae, California

Serves 4

In one of her most popular dishes, Alice Wong quickly deep-fries fresh shrimp, coats them with a mayonnaise-based sauce, and garnishes them with walnuts. The result is succulent, voluptuous, and intensely satisfying. Serve with steamed rice.

3/4 pound medium-size shrimp, peeled and deveined

1 large egg yolk

1/2 cup cornstarch

Salt

White pepper

3 cups mild vegetable oil

1/2 cup mayonnaise

1 tablespoon water

1/2 teaspoon sugar

1 cup shelled walnut halves

1. Rinse the shrimp. Using a small, sharp knife, slit them along their backs to open them partially. Pat dry with paper towels. In a medium-size bowl, stir together the egg yolk, cornstarch, and salt and pepper to form a paste. Add the shrimp and coat them well.

2. In a large wok or deep skillet, heat the oil over medium heat. When it is hot, drop in the shrimp one by one, cooking them in batches if necessary to prevent crowding; fry until golden brown, about 3 minutes. Remove them with a slotted spoon or wire skimmer and drain them on paper towels.

3. Carefully pour out the oil from the wok or skillet. Add the mayonnaise, water, sugar, and 1/4 teaspoon salt and stir well for a few seconds over medium heat. Add the shrimp and stir briefly for about 10 seconds more to coat them.

4. Mound the shrimp in the center of a platter or serving bowl and garnish with the walnuts.

Stir-Fried Shrimp in Black Bean Sauce

Andy Wai, Harbor Village Restaurants, San Francisco and Monterey Park, California

Serves 4

Andy Wai delivers a definitive, very quickly prepared home version of a Chinese restaurant dish that brings comforting memories to just about everyone. You'll find all the ingredients in a well-stocked supermarket or Asian food store. Serve over steamed white rice.

1 tablespoon fermented black beans, rinsed, drained well, and finely chopped

3 large cloves garlic, finely chopped

3 tablespoons water

2 teaspoons cornstarch

1 teaspoon oyster sauce

1 teaspoon sugar

1/2 teaspoon dark soy sauce

1/4 teaspoon Chinese sesame oil

1/8 teaspoon salt

2 tablespoons mild vegetable oil

1/2 pound medium-size shrimp, peeled and deveined

1 medium-size red bell pepper, halved, stemmed, seeded, and cut into 3/4-inch squares

1 medium-size green bell pepper, halved, stemmed, seeded, and cut into 3/4-inch squares

1 teaspoon cooking sherry

1. In a small bowl, thoroughly stir together the black beans, garlic, 2 tablespoons of the water, the cornstarch, oyster sauce, sugar, soy sauce, sesame oil, and salt. Set the mixture aside.

2. Heat the vegetable oil in a wok over high heat. Add the shrimp and quickly stir for 1 minute. Add the red and green bell peppers, cooking sherry, and remaining 1 tablespoon of water, stir well, cover, and cook for about 30 seconds more.

3. Quickly restir the seasoning mixture and add it to the wok. Continue stirring until the sauce thickens and coats the shrimp and peppers, 1 to 2 minutes more. Serve immediately.

Seared Rare Tuna with Olive-Tomato Ragout, Roast Potatoes, and Balsamic Butter

Kevin Taylor, Zenith American Grill, Denver, Colorado

Serves 4

At first glance, this recipe, with its 4 separate elements, may look a little complicated. But each part involves only a few ingredients and takes next to no time to accomplish. And those parts add up to an intoxicatingly aromatic main course that is likely to remind you of the south of France or coastal Italy, even if you've never been there.

Roast Potatoes:

8 medium-size Yukon gold or other yellow potatoes, cut lengthwise in halves

Olive oil

Salt

Pepper

Balsamic Butter:

1/2 cup (1 stick) unsalted butter, at room temperature

1/4 cup balsamic vinegar

1 teaspoon lemon juice

Salt

Pepper

Olive-Tomato Ragout:

Olive oil

1/2 medium-size onion, cut into olive-size dice

1/2 cup Niçoise olives, pitted

2 medium-size tomatoes, cored and cut into olive-size dice

4 fresh basil leaves, finely chopped

1/4 cup balsamic vinegar

Salt

Pepper

Seared Rare Tuna:

2 tablespoons olive oil

Salt

Four 6-ounce pieces sashimi-quality skinless tuna fillet, each about 1/2 inch thick

For the potatoes:

1. Preheat the oven to 400°F.

2. Put the potatoes in a shallow baking dish large enough to hold them in a single layer and bake until tender, about 45 minutes. When the potatoes are done, season with a little olive oil and salt and pepper. Set aside.

3. While the potatoes are baking, prepare the balsamic butter and the olive-tomato ragout.

For the balsamic butter:

Put the butter, balsamic vinegar, and lemon juice in a food processor. Process until smooth, then season to taste with salt and pepper. Remove from the bowl and set aside at room temperature.

For the ragout:

Heat a thin film of olive oil in a medium-size skillet over medium heat. Add the onion and cook, stirring, until translucent, about 3 minutes. Add the olives, tomatoes, and basil. Cook, stirring occasionally, for about 5 minutes. Stir in the balsamic vinegar and season to taste with salt and pepper. Cover and remove from the heat.

For the tuna:

1. In a large skillet, heat 2 tablespoons of olive oil over high heat until it begins to smoke. Sprinkle the skillet lightly with salt and add the tuna. Cook just until seared, about 30 seconds per side.

2. Spoon the olive-tomato ragout in the centers of 4 serving plates. Place the tuna on top and surround with the potatoes. Spoon a little balsamic butter on top of each piece of tuna and serve immediately. Pass any remaining balsamic butter separately.

Sautéed Trout with Pancetta, Garlic, and Parsley

Gary Danko, The Dining Room, The Ritz-Carlton Hotel, San Francisco, California

Serves 2

If you've ever caught your own trout and cooked it over a campfire, you'll understand how such a simple dish can soothe the soul. Gary Danko's recipe, prepared in just minutes, gives the fish a slight Italian accent, and the dish pleases all the more for its absence of bones. Ask your fishmonger to bone the trout for you.

2 ounces pancetta, cut into 1/4-by-1-inch strips

Two 6- to 8-ounce trout, cleaned, boned, and opened like a book; heads and fins trimmed and discarded

Salt

Black pepper

1/4 cup all-purpose flour

2 tablespoons mild vegetable oil

2 tablespoons unsalted butter

2 tablespoons finely chopped Italian parsley

1 tablespoon finely chopped garlic

1. In a large nonstick skillet, cook the pancetta over medium heat, stirring, until golden brown but not yet crisp, about 5 minutes. Transfer the pancetta to paper towels to drain. Discard the fat from the skillet.

2. Season the trout on both the skin and flesh sides with salt and pepper to taste. Sprinkle the all-purpose flour on a plate and lightly dredge both sides of each trout in it, shaking off the excess.

3. In the skillet, heat the vegetable oil over medium-high heat. Add the trout skin sides down and cook until golden brown and crusty, 3 to 4 minutes. With a spatula, turn them over and cook just until the fish is opaque through, 2 to 3 minutes more. Remove each trout to a heated serving plate. Pour off the oil and wipe out the skillet.

4. Return the skillet to the heat and add the butter. As soon as it begins to foam, add the parsley, garlic, and reserved pancetta and cook, stirring, for 30 seconds. Season to taste with a little salt and pepper and spoon the mixture, still sizzling, over the trout. Serve immediately.

Involtini of Swordfish and Shrimp with Vermouth Butter

Serves 4

Piero Selvaggio, Valentino, Los Angeles, California

Though this dish looks as elegant as can be, it has its origins in Italy's seaside trattorias, where rolls of swordfish and shrimp are quite popular. You could serve it as a main course over rice or thin fresh pasta; or in the spirit of Piero Selvaggio's Valentino restaurant, as a first course, perhaps on a bed of grilled radicchio.

12 medium-size shrimp, peeled and deveined

Juice of 1 lemon

1 bunch fresh thyme, leaves removed and finely chopped

3 medium-size shallots, finely chopped

9 ounces skinless swordfish fillet, cut into 12 long, thin strips

Salt

1/2 cup dry vermouth

1 tablespoon green peppercorns

1/2 cup (1 stick) plus 2 tablespoons unsalted butter, cut into pieces

1 medium-size tomato, peeled, seeded (see Box, page 3), and finely chopped

1. In a small mixing bowl, toss the shrimp with the lemon juice, thyme, 1 chopped shallot, and a pinch of salt. Then, neatly roll up each shrimp in a strip of swordfish, secure with a wooden toothpick, and leave the rolls to marinate, covered, in the refrigerator for about 30 minutes.

2. Shortly before you cook the shrimp, put the remaining shallots in a medium-size sauté pan or skillet with the vermouth and green peppercorns. Bring to a boil over medium heat, then reduce the heat to low and simmer for 3 minutes. A piece or two at a time, whisk in 1/2 cup of the butter to form a creamy sauce. Set aside. Cover and keep warm.

3. On a griddle or in a skillet or sauté pan large enough to hold the swordfish-and-shrimp rolls comfortably, melt the remaining butter over medium-high heat. Cook the rolls until cooked through and lightly browned, 1 1/2 to 2 minutes per side.

4. Serve immediately, topped with the sauce and garnished with chopped tomato.

Grilled Salmon and Shrimp with Smoked Ham and Vegetable Minestrone

Robert Calderone, Anago Bistro, Cambridge, Massachusetts

Serves 4

Rustic and robust, yet elegant, this main course from Robert Calderone recognizes culinary affinities that please people's palates, including the complementary flavors of shrimp, salmon, smoked pork, and dried beans; and the pleasing contrast of grilled seafood and broth. Though the recipe at first glance may appear a bit involved, it is easily prepared in stages, with the beans soaked and the ham broth made up to a day ahead, leaving only the easy simmering of the soup and the final quick grilling of the seafood.

2 cups navy, Great Northern, or other small white beans, picked over to remove any stones or impurities and rinsed well

2 pounds bone-in smoked pork shoulder

2 medium-size onions, quartered

2 ribs celery, cut into 1-inch pieces

2 carrots, cut into 1-inch pieces

4 sprigs fresh thyme

Olive oil

2 tablespoons finely chopped garlic

1 medium-size onion, finely chopped

1 cup coarsely chopped carrots

1 cup coarsely chopped celery

8 plum tomatoes, cored, halved, seeded, and coarsely chopped

1/2 pound small fresh spinach leaves, stemmed and thoroughly washed

2 teaspoons finely chopped Italian parsley

2 teaspoons finely chopped fresh oregano

2 teaspoons finely chopped fresh thyme

Salt

Black pepper

16 jumbo shrimp, peeled and deveined

Four (6-ounce) skinless salmon fillets

1. Put the beans in a large mixing bowl and cover generously with cold water. Leave overnight at room temperature to soak. Drain well and set aside.

2. Up to one day ahead, prepare a ham stock by filling a large stockpot with cold water and adding the smoked pork shoulder, quartered onions, celery and carrot pieces, and thyme sprigs. Bring to a boil over high heat, skimming occasionally. Then reduce the heat to low and simmer until the pork is tender enough to fall off the bone, about 2 hours. Leave at room temperature until cool. Then, strain the stock and reserve it, covered, in the refrigerator. With your fingers, pick the meat off the shoulder and shred it. Cover and refrigerate.

3. To make the minestrone, pour a thin film of olive oil in the bottom of a heavy, large saucepan. Heat over medium heat, add the garlic, and cook, stirring, until it begins to soften, 3 to 4 minutes. Add the finely chopped onion and cook, stirring, for 5 minutes more.

4. Pour in 10 cups of the reserved ham stock, adding water if necessary to make up the volume. Bring to a boil over high heat. Add the reserved beans, reduce the heat to low and simmer, uncovered, until the beans are tender, 45 minutes to 1 hour.

5. While the beans are cooking, preheat a charcoal grill or a broiler until very hot; if using wood skewers for the shrimp, soak them in cold water for at least 30 minutes.

6. Add to the saucepan the chopped carrots, celery, tomatoes, and 2 cups of the shredded pork. Continue simmering until the vegetables are tender, about 15 minutes more. Stir in the spinach leaves and herbs and season to taste with salt and pepper. Keep the soup warm.

7. Arrange the shrimp on 4 skewers, passing the skewers through the head and tail end of each shrimp. Brush the shrimp and the salmon fillets with olive oil and season lightly with salt and pepper. Grill or broil the seafood until the shrimp turn uniformly pink and opaque and the salmon is nicely seared and opaque through but still moist, 1 to 2 minutes per side for the shrimp and 3 to 4 minutes per side for the salmon fillets.

8. Ladle the minestrone soup into 4 large, shallow soup plates. Place a salmon fillet and shrimp skewer on top of the vegetables in each plate and serve immediately.

Grilled Salmon Kebabs with Lemon Rice

The Haussner Family, Haussner's Restaurant, Baltimore, Maryland

There's something very satisfying about eating a kebab: the colorful arrangements of ingredients, the pleasure of sliding the bite-sized pieces off the skewer, the smoky flavor that comes from grilling or broiling. This recipe makes use of everyday ingredients to achieve a surprisingly elegant effect.

3 pounds fresh salmon steaks, skinned, boned, and cut into 2 dozen 2-inch cubes

16 firm cherry tomatoes, stemmed

16 medium-size mushrooms, stems removed

1 medium-size green bell pepper, halved, stemmed, and seeded; each half cut into 8 squares

1 medium-size mild white onion, halved, each half cut into 8 chunks

1 bottle creamy Italian salad dressing

1 cup uncooked long-grain white rice

2 lemons, one halved, one cut into 8 wedges

1 teaspoon lemon-dill seasoning (see Note)

Pinch of white pepper

1. Soak 8 long bamboo skewers in water for about 30 minutes to prevent burning.

2. On each skewer, thread 3 salmon cubes, 2 cherry tomatoes, 2 mushrooms, and 2 pieces each of pepper and onion, arranging them in a colorful pattern. Place the skewers in a single layer in a baking pan and pour the Italian dressing over them. Cover and marinate in the refrigerator, turning occasionally, for 3 hours.

3. About 30 minutes before serving, preheat the broiler. Cook the rice, following package directions. Keep warm.

4. Transfer the kebabs to a broiler tray and cook, turning the kebabs about halfway through the cooking time, until the fish is opaque through, about 10 minutes.

5. Just before serving, squeeze the juice from the lemon halves over the rice and stir it in with the lemon-dill seasoning and white pepper. Mound the rice on 4 dinner plates and top each with 2 kebabs. Garnish each serving with 2 lemon wedges.

NOTE • *Lemon-dill seasoning mixes for seafood may be found in the herb and spice section of well-stocked markets.*

Sautéed Chicken Breasts with Ratatouille

 Serves 4

Grant Showley, Showley's at Miramonte, St. Helena, California

The aromatic flavors of ratatouille, the vegetable stew of southern France, penetrate the chicken breasts in this simple main course. "Served chilled," says Grant Showley, "it's our favorite picnic fare. But it's also great hot over fresh pasta or basmati rice." He also suggests reheating the chicken the next day for even fuller flavor.

1/2 cup olive oil

1 medium-size onion, coarsely chopped

4 plum tomatoes, cored and coarsely chopped

3 ribs celery, coarsely chopped

2 medium-size zucchini, cut into halves lengthwise and cut crosswise into 1/4-inch-thick slices

1 large Japanese eggplant, coarsely chopped (see Note)

1 green bell pepper, stemmed, seeded, and coarsely chopped

1 red bell pepper, stemmed, seeded, and coarsely chopped

1 yellow bell pepper, stemmed, seeded, and coarsely chopped

3 cloves garlic, finely chopped

2 teaspoons dried oregano

Salt

Pepper

4 whole boneless skinless chicken breasts

1. In a large sauté pan or saucepan, heat half the olive oil over medium to low heat. Add the onion and cook, stirring, until translucent, 3 to 5 minutes. Add the tomatoes, celery, and zucchini and continue to cook, stirring occasionally.

2. In a large skillet, heat 2 tablespoons more of the olive oil over medium heat. Add the eggplant and cook, stirring, until golden brown. Transfer the eggplant, bell peppers, garlic, and oregano to the pan with the other vegetables; season to taste with salt and pepper. Cook, stirring occasionally, for 10 to 12 minutes more.

3. Meanwhile, wipe out the large skillet and heat the remaining oil in it over medium heat. Lightly season the chicken breasts with salt and pepper and cook them in the skillet until lightly browned on both sides, 1 to 2 minutes per side. Pour the vegetable mixture over the chicken breasts and simmer until done, 6 to 8 minutes more.

NOTE • *Though the long, slender Japanese eggplant called for has a sweeter flavor than more widely available globe eggplant, the latter may be substituted.*

Herb-Crusted Chicken

Matthew Kenney, Matthew's, New York, New York

Matthew Kenney serves this simple, light, oven-fried chicken recipe over his Glazed Fennel Mashed Potatoes. "My mom used to make chicken and mashed potatoes any time I was feeling blue," he says. "Even now, when I feel down, I eat this combination at my restaurant."

1 cup fine dry bread crumbs

1 tablespoon finely chopped fresh thyme

1 tablespoon finely chopped fresh basil

1 teaspoon finely chopped fresh marjoram

1 teaspoon finely chopped fresh rosemary

1/4 teaspoon salt

Pinch of crushed red pepper flakes

Pinch of black pepper

4 medium-size boneless chicken breast halves

1 tablespoon olive oil

Glazed Fennel Mashed Potatoes (page 132)

1. Preheat the oven to 400°F.

2. In a mixing bowl, stir together the bread crumbs, herbs, salt, and red and black pepper until thoroughly mixed.

3. Spread the seasoned crumbs on a plate and press the chicken breasts firmly into them, skin sides down, to coat them generously.

4. In a large, ovenproof, nonstick sauté pan or skillet, heat the olive oil over medium-high heat. Add the chicken breasts, breaded sides down, and cook until the crust is golden brown, 3 to 4 minutes.

5. Carefully turn the breasts over and transfer the pan to the oven. Bake until the juices run clear when a breast is pierced in its thickest part, 15 to 20 minutes.

6. Cut each chicken breast crosswise into 1/2-inch-thick slices and serve over the Glazed Fennel Mashed Potatoes.

Steak with Shallot Sauce

Michel Richard, Citrus, Los Angeles, California; Citronelle, Santa Barbara, California, Baltimore, Maryland, and Washington, D.C.; Michel's Bistro, Philadelphia, Pennsylvania; and Bistro M, San Francisco, California

Serves 4

Michel Richard offers up a generous serving of classic French bistro fare, guaranteed to lift your spirits—especially if served with a pile of french fries or a mountain of his Garlic Mashed Potatoes Ali-Bab (page 130). The shallot glaze may be prepared in advance, allowed to cool, and left covered at room temperature for several hours or overnight in the refrigerator.

Shallot Glaze:

4 medium-large shallots, thinly sliced (about 1/2 cup)

2 tablespoons red wine vinegar

1/2 cup dry white wine

2/3 cup unsalted chicken stock

1 large garlic clove, finely chopped

1 teaspoon soy sauce

Salt

Black pepper

Steak:

1 1/2 to 1 3/4 pounds flank or skirt steak, trimmed and patted dry

Salt

Black pepper

2 tablespoons mild vegetable or olive oil

For the shallot glaze:

Put the shallots and vinegar in a small, heavy saucepan and cook over medium heat until the vinegar boils down to a glaze. Add the wine and continue boiling, stirring occasionally, until it reduces to a syrupy sauce. Add the chicken stock, garlic, and soy sauce and boil, stirring occasionally, until the liquid has reduced and thickened to a consistency that will coat a wooden spoon. Season the sauce to taste with salt and pepper, cover, and set aside.

For the steak:

1. Season the steak with salt and pepper. Heat a large, heavy, nonstick skillet over medium-high heat and pour in a film of oil. Add the steak and cook until evenly browned, about 5 minutes per side for medium.

2. Meanwhile, if you've made the shallot glaze in advance and allowed it to cool, gently reheat it.

3. With a carving knife, cut the steak crosswise and on the diagonal into slices about 1/2 inch thick. Overlap the slices on warmed serving plates and spoon the shallot glaze over them.

Beef Tenderloin Marinated in Molasses and Black Pepper

Dean Fearing, The Mansion on Turtle Creek, Dallas, Texas

Serves 4

Country barbecue meets sophisticated cuisine in Dean Fearing's incredibly easy pan-seared steak. He says the recipe also works well with venison. Allow for 24 hours of marinating time before cooking. Dean accompanies the meat with his Compote of Smoked Bacon, Wild Mushrooms, Glazed Sweet Potatoes, and Pecans.

One 2-pound piece center-cut beef tenderloin, trimmed of all fat and membrane

1 cup molasses

2 tablespoons balsamic vinegar

2 tablespoons cracked black peppercorns

2 cloves garlic, finely chopped

1 large shallot, finely chopped

2 teaspoons peeled and finely grated fresh ginger

1 teaspoon finely chopped fresh thyme

1/2 to 1 teaspoon crushed red pepper flakes

Salt

2 tablespoons mild vegetable oil

Compote of Smoked Bacon, Wild Mushrooms, Glazed Sweet Potatoes and Pecans (page 142)

4 sprigs fresh watercress

1. Put the beef tenderloin in a glass dish with sides.

2. In a small bowl, stir together the molasses, balsamic vinegar, black peppercorns, garlic, shallot, ginger, thyme, and red pepper flakes to taste. Pour the mixture over the meat. Cover the meat and marinate in the refrigerator for 24 hours, turning it occasionally.

3. Remove the meat from the dish and reserve 1/2 cup of the marinade for the Compote of Smoked Bacon and another 1/4 cup for deglazing the pan. Put the meat on a cutting board and, with a sharp knife, cut it into 8 equal portions (medallions). Season with salt.

4. Heat the oil in a large cast-iron skillet over medium-high heat. Place the beef medallions in the skillet and cook until their undersides are browned, 3 minutes. Turn them over and cook 2 minutes more for rare meat or until the desired degree of doneness is reached.

5. Just before removing the meat, add the reserved 1/4 cup marinade to the skillet and bring to a boil over the same heat, stirring and scraping to dissolve the browned pan juices as well as spooning the marinade over the medallions to glaze them. Quickly turn the meat over to glaze the other side, then remove from the skillet immediately.

6. Put 2 medallions overlapping each other near the center of each of 4 heated serving plates. Spoon the Smoked Bacon Compote next to the medallions, letting the sauce flow out onto the plate. Place a sprig of watercress between the meat and the compote. Serve immediately.

Filet of Beef with Three Mustards

 Serves 4

Georges Perrier, Le Bec-Fin, Philadelphia, Pennsylvania

There's something undeniably elemental and robust about the combination of beef and mustard, and this simple recipe from Georges Perrier elevates the relationship to its most refined.

Four 5-ounce beef filets	2 shallots, finely chopped
Salt	1 cup heavy cream
Black pepper	1 teaspoon Dijon mustard
1 tablespoon mild vegetable oil	1 teaspoon whole-grain mustard
1 tablespoon unsalted butter	1 teaspoon prepared English mustard
2 tablespoons cognac	

1. Season the beef filets to taste with salt and pepper.

2. In a large, heavy skillet, heat the oil and butter over medium to high heat. As soon as the butter melts, add the filets and cook until done to taste, about 3 minutes per side for rare, 4 for medium-rare.

3. Add the cognac to the skillet and carefully tilt the skillet toward the flame to ignite the cognac, flambéing the meat. (Or if using an electric stove, light carefully with a long kitchen match.) Remove the filets from the skillet and cover to keep warm.

4. Add the shallots to the skillet and cook, stirring, just until lightly browned. Add the cream and the three mustards and stir to blend. Reduce the heat to medium low, cook until heated through, season to taste with salt and pepper, and pour the sauce through a strainer.

5. Place the filets on warmed serving plates and pour the sauce over them.

Stir-Fried Filet Mignon with Shiitake Mushrooms

Serves 4   *Marc Glassman, Cafe Majestic, San Francisco, California*

"This dish, with its wealth of colors, textures, and flavors, requires a good deal of advance slicing and chopping," says Marc Glassman. "But it takes only a few minutes to bring together, making it ideal for entertaining." All of the Asian ingredients he calls for can be found in a well-stocked supermarket or Asian food store. Serve the stir-fry over steamed rice.

One 1-pound filet mignon, trimmed and cut into 1/2- to 3/4-inch cubes

1 tablespoon all-purpose flour

1/4 cup mild vegetable oil

1/4 pound fresh shiitake mushrooms, thinly sliced

1 medium-size carrot, cut into thin matchstick strips

1/2 medium-size red onion, thinly sliced

1 medium-size zucchini, cut into thin matchstick strips

1 medium-size red bell pepper, quartered, stemmed, and seeded, quarters cut crosswise into thin strips

1/4 cup trimmed and thinly sliced green onion

1 tablespoon finely chopped garlic

1 tablespoon peeled and finely chopped fresh ginger

2 tablespoons plum sauce

2 tablespoons oyster sauce

2 tablespoons hoisin sauce

1 tablespoon Chinese sesame oil

1 tablespoon soy sauce

1. In a small mixing bowl, toss the filet mignon cubes with the all-purpose flour to coat them evenly.

2. In a large wok or heavy skillet, heat the vegetable oil over medium to high heat. Add the filet mignon and cook, stirring briskly, for 2 minutes.

3. Add the shiitake mushrooms, carrot, red onion, zucchini, bell pepper, green onion, garlic, and ginger. Cook, stirring briskly, for 3 minutes more.

4. Add the remaining ingredients and cook, stirring, for 3 additional minutes. Serve over steamed rice.

NOTE • *You'll find Chinese sesame and plum, oyster, and hoisin sauces in well-stocked supermarkets or Asian food stores.*

Veal Fricadelles with Lingonberries

 Serves 6

Christer Larsson, Christer's, New York, New York

A specialty of Christer Larsson's native Sweden, these moist, subtly flavored meatballs may also be served as appetizers, and the recipe is easily doubled or tripled. For this main-course version, Christer suggests serving the fricadelles with mashed potatoes and a garnish of preserved lingonberries, available in most specialty food stores.

1 medium-size Idaho potato, peeled and cut into 2-inch chunks	Pinch of black pepper
2 tablespoons unsalted butter	Pinch of ground allspice
1 medium-size red onion, finely chopped	Pinch of ground nutmeg
2 pounds ground veal	1 large egg, lightly beaten
1 tablespoon salt	1/4 cup milk
	3 tablespoons all-purpose flour

1. Put the potato in a medium-size saucepan of cold water. Bring to a boil over medium-high heat and cook the potato just until tender, 12 to 15 minutes. Drain well, transfer to a bowl, cover with plastic wrap, and chill in the refrigerator for 1 hour. Then, with the large holes on a handheld grater, shred the potato.

2. Melt 1 tablespoon of the butter in a large skillet over medium heat. Add the onion and cook, stirring, until tender, 5 to 7 minutes.

3. Put the veal, onion, and shredded potato in a large mixing bowl and stir with a wooden spoon until well blended. Stir in the salt, pepper, allspice, and nutmeg. Add the egg, milk, and allpurpose flour and stir again until smooth. Cover the bowl and refrigerate for 1 hour.

4. Moisten your hands and use them to shape the veal mixture into fricadelles the size and shape of eggs, placing them on a plate.

5. Melt the remaining butter in the skillet over low heat. Add the fricadelles and cook until evenly browned on all sides, 15 to 20 minutes.

Scandinavian Salmon Stew with Dill

Robert Kinkead, Kinkead's, Washington, D.C.

Serves 4 to 6

You can easily imagine eating this dill-scented stew on a blustery evening in a seaside cottage in Norway or Sweden. If you wish, offer it as a first course.

2 medium-size potatoes, peeled and cut into 1/2-inch dice

3 tablespoons unsalted butter

1 small onion, cut into 1/4-inch dice

1 small leek, white part only, thoroughly washed and cut into 1/4-inch dice

1 ounce bacon, cut crosswise into 1/4-inch-wide strips

3 medium-size shallots, finely chopped

6 medium-size mushrooms, cut into 1/4-inch-thick slices

3/4 pound skinless salmon fillet, cut into 1-inch pieces

1/4 cup dry white wine

2 cups fish stock (see Note)

2 cups heavy cream

Sea salt

Coarsely ground black pepper

2 tablespoons coarsely chopped fresh dill

2 tablespoons coarsely chopped fresh chives

1. Bring a medium-size saucepan of water to a boil over medium-high heat. Add the potatoes. When the water returns to a boil, cook the potatoes for 2 minutes. Drain well and set aside.

2. Melt the butter in a large skillet over medium-high heat. As soon as it foams, add the onion and leek and cook, stirring, until transparent, 3 to 4 minutes. Remove them from the skillet and set aside.

3. Add the bacon to the skillet and cook over the same heat, stirring, until the fat has rendered and the strips are lightly browned, 3 to 4 minutes. Remove from the skillet and set aside. Pour off about half the fat from the skillet.

4. Add the shallots to the skillet and cook, stirring, until transparent, 2 to 3 minutes. Add the mushrooms and cook, stirring, until tender, 4 to 5 minutes. Add the salmon to the skillet and cook, stirring, until opaque through, about 4 minutes more. Remove from the skillet.

5. Add the wine to the skillet and bring to a boil over medium-high heat, stirring and scraping with a wooden spoon to dissolve the browned juices. Stir in the fish stock, cream, and potatoes and bring to a boil. Stir in the onion, leek, and bacon. Simmer briskly until the liquid reduces by about one-quarter, 7 to 10 minutes.

6. Season to taste with salt and pepper. Stir in the fish, dill, and chives and serve immediately in warmed bowls.

NOTE • *Good-quality fish stock (fumet) may be found frozen in well-stocked markets or seafood shops.*

Braised Tofu, Shrimp, and Crab Dumplings

Alice Wong, Hong Kong Flower Lounge, Millbrae, California

Serves 4

If you're a fan of dim sum, Alice Wong says you'll love these soft, tender seafood dumplings, full of flavor yet mild and soothing to eat. Serve them with steamed rice. You can also offer them as an appetizer.

Dumplings:

10 large egg whites

1/2 pound soft bean curd (tofu), well drained

1/4 pound medium-size shrimp, peeled, deveined, and finely chopped

1 ounce fresh crabmeat, picked over to remove any pieces of shell or cartilage

1 tablespoon cornstarch

1 tablespoon finely chopped cilantro (fresh coriander)

1/2 teaspoon salt

Dash of pepper

Dash of Chinese sesame oil

1/4 cup mild vegetable oil

5 heads baby bok choy, cut lengthwise in quarters

Sauce:

1 cup chicken broth

1/2 teaspoon oyster sauce

1/4 teaspoon sugar

1/4 teaspoon salt

3/4 teaspoon cornstarch, dissolved in 1 tablespoon cold water

For the dumplings:

1. Bring a large saucepan or pot of water to a boil and place a large flat-bottomed steamer basket on top.

2. In a mixing bowl, use your hands to mix together the egg whites, bean curd, shrimp, crabmeat, cornstarch, cilantro, salt, pepper, and sesame oil until they are thoroughly combined. Fill 12 to 16 Chinese soup spoons with the resulting paste and place them in the steamer basket, resting on their flat bottoms. Cover with the lid and steam until firm, about 5 minutes. Remove the basket, uncover it, and let the dumplings cool to room temperature. With a knife tip, loosen and remove them from the spoons and set aside.

3. In a wok or skillet, heat 2 tablespoons of the vegetable oil over medium-high heat. Add the bok choy, sprinkle lightly with salt, and stir-fry until tender-crisp, 5 to 7 minutes. Drain the bok choy and set aside.

4. In a large skillet, heat the remaining vegetable oil over medium heat. Carefully place the dumplings in the pan and cook until golden brown, 3 to 4 minutes per side, turning them gently.

5. Arrange the dumplings in rows on a serving platter, interspersed with rows of bok choy. Keep warm.

For the sauce:

In a saucepan, stir together the chicken broth, oyster sauce, sugar, and salt and bring to a boil over medium-high heat. Stir in the cornstarch mixture and boil, stirring, until the sauce thickens, 30 seconds to 1 minute. Pour over the dumplings and bok choy and serve immediately.

NOTE • *You'll find the special ingredients in well-stocked supermarkets or Asian food stores.*

King Crab and Sun-Dried Tomato Stew

Gary Danko, The Dining Room, The Ritz-Carlton Hotel, San Francisco, California

Serves 6 to 8

This rustic stew just begs you to pick up the crab legs with your fingers and suck out every last drop of meat and flavor. To soak up the juices, Gary Danko suggests serving it over polenta or steamed couscous or accompanying it with garlic croutons.

1/2 cup olive oil

4 garlic cloves, finely chopped

2 medium-size red bell peppers, halved, stemmed, seeded, and cut into 1/2-inch dice

2 medium-size yellow bell peppers, halved, stemmed, seeded, and cut into 1/2-inch dice

1 large onion, cut into 1/2-inch dice

1 medium-size fennel bulb, trimmed and cut into 1/2-inch dice

1 1/2 cups vacuum-packed sun-dried tomatoes, soaked in warm water to cover until soft, drained well, and cut into thin strips

1 cup dry white wine

5 cups bottled clam juice

1/2 teaspoon crushed red pepper flakes

1/2 teaspoon Hungarian paprika

1 teaspoon kosher salt

1 teaspoon black pepper

3 pounds crab legs, cut into 3-inch lengths

1. In a Dutch oven, heat the olive oil over medium heat. Add the garlic, bell peppers, onion, fennel, and sun-dried tomatoes and cook, stirring, until the vegetables are tender, about 10 minutes.

2. Add the wine, bring to a boil over medium-high heat and cook, stirring occasionally, until the liquid reduces to a glaze, 7 to 10 minutes. Stir in the clam juice, red pepper flakes, and paprika. Bring to a boil and cook, stirring occasionally, until the liquid reduces by half, 20 to 25 minutes.

3. Stir in the salt and pepper. Add the crab legs, cover, and steam until the crab legs are completely heated through, about 5 minutes. Serve immediately.

Steamed Clams with Saffron and Tomato

Cory Schreiber, Wildwood, Portland, Oregon

Serves 4

"For anyone who has grown up near the seaside," says Cory Schreiber, "nothing compares to the pleasure of eating roasted or steamed clams in their own juices." At Wildwood, he cooks them in their wood-burning brick oven. But the recipe works just as well on top of the stove.

1/2 cup chardonnay vinegar (see Note)	1/2 pound cherry tomatoes, cut into halves
Pinch of saffron threads	
1 1/2 cups extra-virgin olive oil	2 shallots, thinly sliced
Salt	1 tablespoon finely chopped garlic
Black pepper	2 large garlic cloves, cut into halves
8 slices good-quality sourdough bread	1 lemon, cut in half
6 pounds Manila or littleneck clams, thoroughly cleaned and soaked in water	1/2 cup finely chopped Italian parsley

1. Put the vinegar and saffron in a small, nonreactive saucepan and warm them over low heat to soften the saffron and develop its flavor. Remove the pan from the heat when the saffron begins to expand. When the vinegar is cool enough to touch, whisk in the olive oil and season to taste with salt and pepper.

2. Preheat the broiler removing the broiler tray. Arrange the sourdough slices in a single layer on the tray and set aside.

3. Put the clams in the largest pot or roasting pan you have, large enough to hold them in a single layer. Pour the vinaigrette mixture over them and scatter in the tomatoes, shallots, and finely chopped garlic. Cover the pot or pan and put it over high heat; as the clams open, after 7 to 10 minutes or so, remove them and keep them warm. Discard any clams that do not open.

4. While the clams cook, toast the bread on both sides under the broiler. As soon as the toast is done, rub one side of each piece with the cut side of a garlic half.

5. When all the clams are done, taste the liquid in the pot, squeeze in lemon juice to taste, and add the parsley.

6. Pile the cooked clams into 4 large serving bowls. Ladle the liquid and tomatoes over the clams and serve with the garlic toast.

NOTE • *Chardonnay vinegar is available in gourmet food shops.*

San Francisco Seafood Hot Pot

Barbara Figueroa, B Figueroa, Seattle, Washington

Serves 8

"Who in this world doesn't love the warm glow of a good soup or stew?" asks Barbara Figueroa. "This entree combines the characteristics of both in an Asian-style broth that marries lively, flavorful spiciness with an exhilaratingly healthy feeling." For the choice of seafood, she suggests a mixture of scallops, shrimp, mussels, salmon, and whitefish, and any other fish or shellfish you might like.

1 ounce dried black shiitake mushrooms

1 1/2 tablespoons mild vegetable oil

1 large carrot, thinly sliced

1 large onion, thinly sliced

1 scant teaspoon crushed red pepper flakes

4 cups fish stock (see Note)

2 cups chicken stock

1/4 cup soy sauce

1 1/2 tablespoons hoisin sauce

1 tablespoon peeled and grated fresh ginger

1 1/2 Chinese air-cured sausages, thinly sliced (see Note)

1 1/2 ounces Chinese-style barbecued pork, thinly sliced, slices cut crosswise into thin matchstick strips (see Note)

1/2 large head bok choy, thinly sliced on the diagonal

2 pounds assorted fresh seafood, small shellfish scrubbed and left whole, skinless fish fillets cut into large bite-size pieces

4 large green onions, green tops cut diagonally into diamond shapes

1. In a small bowl, cover the shiitake mushrooms with warm water and leave to soak until softened, about 30 minutes. Drain, straining the liquid through cheesecloth and reserving it. Trim off and discard the mushroom stems and cut the caps in half if small or into wide strips if large. Set aside.

2. In a large saucepan or stockpot, heat 1 tablespoon of the oil over medium heat. Add the carrot, onion, and red pepper flakes and cook, stirring occasionally, until they begin to soften, 3 to 5 minutes. Add the fish stock, chicken stock, soy sauce, hoisin sauce, ginger, sausage, and barbecued pork. Bring to a boil, reduce the heat, and simmer gently for about 45 minutes. Taste and if you feel the flavor needs to be richer, stir in some of the mushroom liquid.

3. In a separate, medium-size saucepan, heat the remaining oil over low to medium heat. Add the bok choy and cook, covered, stirring occasionally, until it is tender-crisp, 5 to 7 minutes. Take care not to let it brown. Set aside.

4. Add the seafood to the pot of simmering liquid and cook just until opaque through, 2 to 4 minutes. Distribute the bok choy among large, shallow serving bowls and ladle the seafood and liquid into each bowl. Garnish with the green onions.

NOTE • *Good-quality fish stock (fumet) may be found frozen in well-stocked markets or seafood shops. Chinese sausage and barbecued pork may be found in Chinese and other Asian markets.*

Chicken Breasts Masala with Fresh Tomatoes

Serves 4 *Irene Trias, Appam—Cuisine of Old India, San Francisco, California*

Slow, gentle cooking "infuses the chicken with deep flavor and aroma," says Irene Trias of her version of a traditional Indian curry. In authentic style, she blends spices individually, rather than using curry powder. Careful skimming away of most of the oil used at the beginning of the recipe, along with her choice of chicken breasts and low-fat yogurt, produces results that are notably lighter than the old-fashioned way. She suggests serving the chicken and sauce over steamed basmati or other long-grain white rice.

1 cup mild vegetable oil

2 medium-size onions, finely chopped

10 cloves garlic, finely chopped

2 inches fresh ginger root, peeled and finely chopped

1 tablespoon ground turmeric

1 teaspoon paprika

1 teaspoon ground cumin

1 teaspoon cayenne pepper (optional)

8 cardamom pods, crushed

4 bay leaves

Three 3-inch cinnamon sticks

Salt

1 cup plain low-fat yogurt

2 medium-size tomatoes, peeled, seeded (see Box, page 3) and finely chopped

1/4 cup coconut milk (optional)

1 1/2 pounds boneless skinless chicken breasts, each half breast cut crosswise into 4 pieces

2 tablespoons finely chopped cilantro (fresh coriander)

1. In a heavy medium-size saucepan, heat the oil over medium heat until it begins to shimmer. Add the onions and cook, stirring occasionally, until they turn translucent and the oil begins to bubble, about 5 minutes. Reduce the heat to low and continue cooking, stirring frequently, until the onions have begun to take on some color but have not yet turned golden brown, about 20 minutes more.

2. Stir in the garlic and cook, stirring occasionally, until it becomes very aromatic, about 5 minutes. Add the ginger, turmeric, paprika, cumin, cayenne (if you'd like somewhat hotter results), cardamom, bay leaves, cinnamon, and salt to taste; continue cooking, stirring constantly to prevent sticking, for another 10 minutes.

3. Raise the heat to medium and stir in the yogurt, tomatoes, and coconut milk (if you'd like somewhat richer results). Cook, stirring occasionally, until the sauce has thickened, about 15 minutes more.

4. Reduce the heat to low, add the chicken and cook, stirring occasionally, until the juices run clear yellow when pierced, 15 to 20 minutes more.

5. Remove the pan from the heat and let it sit someplace warm, covered, until the oil rises to the surface, 10 to 15 minutes. With a ladle or a baster, carefully remove the oil from the surface. Serve the curry immediately, garnished with the cilantro.

Braised Beef Short Ribs in Sweet and Sour Sauce

Todd Humphries, Campton Place Hotel, San Francisco, California

An intriguing blend of spicy, sweet, and sour flavors comes together in this hearty dish, prepared in Todd Humphries's "favorite style of cooking." He suggests serving them with mashed potatoes. He also recommends, for the best flavor, cooking the ribs one or two days in advance and refrigerating them in their sauce, then reheating just before serving.

2 cloves garlic, peeled

1 large onion, cut into chunks

One 1-inch piece fresh ginger, peeled

4 large tomatoes, peeled, seeded (see Box, page 3), and cut into chunks

1 ripe papaya, peeled, seeded, and cut into chunks

1/4 ripe pineapple, peeled, cored, and cut into chunks

1/2 cup mild vegetable oil

1/4 cup dark brown sugar

1/4 cup tamarind paste (see Note)

1 teaspoon ground coriander

1/2 teaspoon ground allspice

1/2 teaspoon ground cloves

1/4 teaspoon ground cinnamon

Salt

Black pepper

4 pounds beef short ribs, cut into 4 pieces and trimmed of excess fat

1. In a food processor, process the garlic, onion, and ginger until pureed. Remove from the work bowl and set aside.

2. Put the tomatoes, papaya, and pineapple in the processor and process until pureed. Remove from the work bowl and set aside.

3. In a medium-size saucepan, heat half the oil over medium-to-low heat. Add the garlic-onion mixture and cook, stirring, for 5 minutes. Stir in the tomato-papaya-pineapple puree, brown sugar, tamarind paste, coriander, allspice, cloves, and cinnamon; add salt and pepper to taste. Simmer, stirring occasionally, for 30 minutes.

4. Preheat the oven to 350°F.

5. In an ovenproof metal casserole, heat the remaining oil over medium-high heat. Season the short ribs with salt and pepper and cook until evenly browned on all sides. Carefully pour off excess fat. Pour the prepared sauce over the ribs, bring to a simmer, cover, and put in the oven. Bake until the meat is tender enough to cut with a fork, about 2 hours.

NOTE • *Tamarind paste is available in Indian groceries.*

Chicken and Autumn Vegetable Stew with Thyme

Sarah Stegner, The Dining Room, The Ritz-Carlton, Chicago, Illinois

Serves 4 to 6

Some of autumn's most colorful and flavorful ingredients join together to make this stew exceptionally comforting. Sarah Stegner suggests serving it over steamed couscous in shallow bowls; steamed rice would also be good for soaking up the juices.

Two 2 1/2-pound chickens, cut into pieces, rinsed, and patted dry

Salt

2 tablespoons finely chopped fresh thyme leaves

2 medium-size red onions

1 large butternut squash

1 large red bell pepper

2 tablespoons olive oil

4 large garlic cloves, finely chopped

4 cups chicken stock

1 tablespoon coarsely cracked black pepper

2 medium-size zucchini, cut into 1/2-inch dice

2 Granny Smith apples, halved, cored, peeled, and cut into 1/2-inch dice

1. Season the chicken pieces with salt and rub them all over with the thyme. Set aside to marinate at room temperature while you prepare the vegetables.

2. Peel the onions and cut each into 8 wedges. Cut the squash in half, peel it, and scrape out the seeds and fibers; cut the flesh into 1/2-inch dice. Halve, stem, and seed the bell pepper and cut it into 1/2-inch dice.

3. Heat the oil in a large skillet over medium-high heat. Add the chicken pieces, in batches if necessary to prevent overcrowding, and cook, turning them once, until evenly golden brown, 4 to 5 minutes per side. Remove the chicken and set aside.

4. Add the onions, squash, and bell pepper, season to taste with salt, and cook, stirring, until slightly browned, 5 to 7 minutes. Add the garlic and continue cooking, stirring, until it is tender, 4 to 5 minutes more. Add the stock and black pepper and return the chicken to the skillet, nestling it down in the liquid. Bring the liquid to a boil over high heat, then reduce the heat to low, and simmer gently until the chicken is cooked through and tender and the liquid has reduced by about half, 30 to 40 minutes more.

5. Add the zucchini and apples to the skillet and continue simmering until the zucchini is tender, 5 to 7 minutes more. Add salt and pepper to taste and serve.

Braised Lamb Shanks with New Potatoes and Carrots

The Haussner Family, Haussner's Restaurant, Baltimore, Maryland

Serves 6

Robust and aromatic, this traditional braise would go wonderfully with mashed potatoes or steamed rice. Francie George of Haussner's says the lamb tastes even better reheated the next day.

Six 1- to 1 1/2-pound pieces lamb shank

1 1/2 teaspoons salt

1 1/2 teaspoons white pepper

3 tablespoons mild vegetable oil

3 tablespoons flour

2 cups good beef stock

1 1/2 cups water

3 large ribs celery, coarsely chopped

3 medium-size tomatoes, peeled (see Box, page 3) and cut into wedges

1 medium-size onion, coarsely chopped

2 cloves garlic, finely chopped

1/4 cup finely chopped Italian parsley

12 red-skinned new potatoes

1 pound carrots, peeled and thickly sliced

1. Rub the lamb shanks with the salt and pepper.

2. In a Dutch oven, heat the oil over medium to high heat. In two or three batches if necessary to prevent crowding, add the lamb shanks and turn them in the oil until evenly browned. Remove from the Dutch oven and set aside.

3. With a wire whisk, stir the flour into the oil and continue stirring until the flour browns slightly. Whisking continuously, slowly pour in the stock and water. Bring the liquid to a boil.

4. Add the lamb shanks, celery, tomatoes, onion, garlic, and parsley. Reduce the heat to low, cover, and simmer gently until the lamb is very tender, about 1 1/2 hours. About 20 minutes before the lamb is done, add the potatoes and carrots. Taste the liquid and add more salt and pepper if necessary.

Osso Bucco al' Palio D'Asti

Craig Stoll, Palio D'Asti, San Francisco, California

Serves 4

One of the great glories of Milanese cooking, these veal shanks should be served atop soft polenta or risotto to soak up the juices. "This rich, belly-filling braise reminds me of long family meals on cold winter evenings," says Craig Stoll.

Gremolata:

1 lemon, scrubbed

2 garlic cloves, finely chopped

2 tablespoons finely chopped Italian parsley

Osso Bucco:

Four 1- to 1 1/2-pound pieces veal hind shanks, tied around their sides with kitchen string

Kosher salt

Black pepper

all-purpose flour

1 cup pure olive oil

1 medium-size onion, cut into 1/4-inch dice

1 medium-size carrot, peeled and cut into 1/4-inch dice

1 medium-size rib celery, cut into 1/4-inch dice

1/2 ounce pancetta, finely chopped

1 large garlic clove, finely chopped

1 teaspoon finely chopped Italian parsley

1 teaspoon finely chopped fresh sage

1 teaspoon finely chopped fresh rosemary

1 tablespoon tomato paste

One 28-ounce can peeled whole plum tomatoes with their juices

1 cup marsala

6 cups chicken stock

For the gremolata:

1. With a vegetable peeler, cut off the lemon's zest—the thin, yellow outermost layer of its peel—in thin strips. Cut the strips into thin 3/4-inch-long pieces. Bring a small saucepan of water to a boil, add the strips of lemon zest, and cook for 2 minutes. Drain well and dry on paper towels.

2. In a small bowl, toss the lemon zest together with the garlic and parsley. Cover and set aside.

For the osso bucco:

1. Preheat the oven to 325°F.

2. Season the veal shanks with salt and pepper and dust them generously with all-purpose flour.

3. In a Dutch oven just large enough to hold the veal shanks in a single layer, heat the 1 cup of olive oil over medium heat. Add the veal shanks and brown evenly, 4 to 5 minutes per side and on their edges as well. Remove them from the Dutch oven and set aside.

4. Add the onion, carrot, celery, and pancetta to the Dutch oven and cook, stirring, until the vegetables are just tender and the onion and celery are opaque, 2 to 3 minutes. Add the garlic, parsley, sage, and rosemary and cook, stirring, until the herbs release their aroma, 30 seconds to 1 minute. Reduce the heat to low, add the tomato paste, and cook, stirring slowly, for about 3 minutes more.

5. Add the canned tomatoes, breaking them up with your hands. Raise the heat to medium and cook, stirring occasionally, until their juices reduce to a thick consistency, 7 to 10 minutes. Add the marsala and cook, stirring occasionally, until the liquid again has all but evaporated, 7 to 10 minutes more.

6. Stir in the chicken stock, raise the heat to medium high, and bring the liquid to a boil. Reduce the heat to low to maintain a simmer and return the veal shanks to the Dutch oven. Cover and put it in the preheated oven.

7. Cook the veal shanks until the meat is very tender, about 2 hours. Remove them from the Dutch oven and, with a large spoon, skim the fat from the surface of the cooking liquid. If the liquid does not look thick enough, simmer it briefly, stirring, over medium heat to reduce it.

8. Cut and remove the veal shanks' strings and place each one on a serving plate. Spoon the sauce over the meat and top with gremolata.

Red Corn Posole with Grilled Pork

Kevin Taylor, Zenith American Grill, Denver, Colorado

 Serves 4

The southwestern roots of Colorado and of native-born chef Kevin Taylor show through in this contemporary version of the homey, heartwarming pork-and-hominy stew known as posole.

Look for red corn posole in specialty food stores or southwestern mail-order catalogs; more widely available blue or yellow posole may be substituted. Look in the same places for the habanero chili powder, made from the variety of pepper considered the hottest in the world; if you can't find it, substitute the hottest pure ground red chili you can find.

1 1/2 gallons chicken stock	One 3/4 pound loin of pork, trimmed
1/2 pound dried red corn posole	and cut into two 6-ounce pieces
1 pinch habanero chili powder	Pepper
Juice of 1 lime	4 sprigs cilantro (fresh coriander)
Salt	

1. In a large pot, bring the chicken stock to a boil over high heat. Add the posole, reduce the heat to low, and simmer, stirring occasionally, until the posole is tender and the stock has reduced to about one-quarter of its original volume, about 1 1/2 hours. When the posole is done, stir in the chili powder, lime juice, and salt to taste. Keep warm.

2. While the posole is cooking, preheat the grill or broiler.

3. Season the pork with salt and pepper. Grill or broil just until done, about 6 minutes per side. Remove the meat to a plate, let it rest for about 10 minutes, then cut it into 1-inch cubes. Stir the meat into the posole.

4. Serve the posole in warmed bowls and garnish with the cilantro.

Stewed Cabbage and Onions with Noodles and Paprika Sauce

Jesse Cool, Flea Street Cafe, Menlo Park, California

Serves 4 to 6

"This brothy stew of cabbage and onions, served over noodles, reminds me that food doesn't have to be overworked or expensive to be completely satisfying," says Jesse Cool. "Slow cooking brings out the sweetness of the vegetables. So before I go to work, I put the ingredients into a crockpot. Within minutes of returning home, a nurturing, warming meal is on the table."

The stew:
1 large onion, coarsely chopped

1/2 large green cabbage, coarsely chopped

2 carrots, peeled and cut into large bite-size chunks

6 black peppercorns

3 bay leaves

Salt

Black pepper

4 to 6 cups chicken stock, vegetable stock, or water

The paprika sauce and noodles:
1/2 cup sour cream or plain low-fat yogurt

2 tablespoons dry white wine

2 teaspoons sweet paprika

1/2 teaspoon salt

1/2 pound wide dry egg noodles

For the stew:

To make the stew, in a large pot or crockpot combine the onion, cabbage, carrots, peppercorns, bay leaves, and a little salt and pepper. Add enough stock or water to cover. Adjust the heat to very low, cover the pot and leave to cook until all the vegetables are very soft and the flavors have blended, 5 to 8 hours.

For the paprika sauce and noodles:

1. To make the sauce, in a small bowl, stir together the sour cream, wine, paprika, and salt. Cover and refrigerate until serving time.

2. Bring a large saucepan of lightly salted water to a boil. Add the noodles and cook until tender but still chewy, following the suggested cooking time on the package. Drain well.

3. Divide the noodles among 4 to 6 shallow soup bowls. Taste the stew and add salt and pepper to taste. Ladle the stew over the noodles and garnish with dollops of paprika sauce.

Portuguese Roast Monkfish with Clams and Chorizo

Robert Kinkead, Kinkead's, Washington, D.C.

Serves 6

Monkfish is often applauded as the poor man's lobster, and Robert Kinkead's robust interpretation of a traditional Portuguese peasant way of enjoying seafood does it proud. He suggests serving it with a gratin of potatoes and pimentos,

1/4 pound chorizo sausage

1 cup fish stock (see Note) or chicken stock

1 cup chicken stock

1 cup bottled clam juice

1/2 cup dry white wine

30 littleneck clams, cleaned

1/4 cup olive oil

1 medium-size onion, coarsely chopped

5 cloves garlic, finely chopped

2 medium-size tomatoes, peeled, seeded (see Box p. 3), and coarsely chopped

Six 5-ounce skinless monkfish fillets

Salt

Black pepper

12 medium-size shrimp, peeled and deveined, cut into 4 or 5 pieces each

1 lemon, zest grated and reserved, juice reserved

2 teaspoons drained capers

1/4 cup finely chopped Italian parsley

4 medium-size green onions, trimmed and coarsely chopped

2 canned anchovy fillets, drained

1. Preheat the oven to 450°F.

2. Bring a small saucepan of water to a boil over high heat. Add the chorizo, reduce the heat to low, and simmer until heated through, about 8 minutes. Drain and when it is cool enough to handle, slit and remove the casing and cut the meat into 1/2-inch pieces. Set aside.

3. In a large saucepan, bring the stocks, clam juice, and wine to a boil over medium-high heat. Continue boiling until it reduces by about one-third, 7 to 10 minutes. Add the clams, reduce the heat to medium, and cook, covered, until they open, 4 to 5 minutes. Remove the clams, discarding any unopened ones, and keep them warm. Pour the liquid through a cheesecloth-lined sieve, return it to the pan, and continue simmering very gently over low heat.

4. In a medium-size sauté pan or skillet, heat half the olive oil over medium heat. Add the onion and cook, stirring, about 3 minutes; add the garlic and cook, stirring, until the onion is transparent, about 2 minutes more. Add the chopped tomatoes and cook, stirring, until most of the juices have evaporated, 7 to 10 minutes.

5. Meanwhile, season the monkfish fillets with salt and pepper. In an ovenproof sauté pan or skillet large enough to hold the fillets in a single layer, heat the remaining olive oil over medium-high heat. Add the monkfish fillets and sear them until golden, about 1 minute per side. Then put the pan in the preheated oven and roast the monkfish until it is firm and opaque, about 5 minutes. Cover with aluminum foil and keep warm.

6. Stir the tomato mixture into the simmering stock along with the chorizo, clams, shrimp, lemon zest and juice, and the capers; uncover the monkfish and add its juices that have collected to the stock mixture. Bring back to a boil and stir in the parsley, green onions, and anchovies. Adjust the seasonings to taste with salt and pepper.

7. Spoon the sauce mixture, complete with the clams, shrimp, and chorizo, onto 6 warmed shallow soup plates. Place the monkfish fillets on top and serve immediately.

NOTE • *Good-quality fish stock (fumet) may be found frozen in well-stocked markets or seafood shops.*

Rock Shrimp Cassoulet

Allen Susser, Chef Allen's, North Miami Beach, Florida

Serves 4

You can clearly see the fundamental elements of Chef Allen's signature New World Cuisine in this quickly prepared, light yet still immensely soul-satisfying variation on the classic slowly cooked duck-and-sausage cassoulet of France. He suggests serving warm French bread on the side. Precook the white beans yourself, following package directions; or if you wish, take the shortcut of using canned white beans, rinsed and drained.

2 tablespoons olive oil	1 clove garlic, finely chopped
1/2 cup diced pancetta	1/4 teaspoon dried thyme
1/2 cup chopped shallots	Pinch of nutmeg
1 pound peeled rock shrimp, cleaned	3/4 cup fresh bread crumbs
Salt	2 tablespoons grated orange zest
Black pepper	2 tablespoons finely chopped cilantro (fresh coriander)
2 cups cooked white navy beans	
1 cup dry white wine	2 tablespoons finely chopped fresh chives

1. In a heavy-bottomed medium-size ovenproof skillet, heat the olive oil over low heat. Add the pancetta and cook, stirring, for about 5 minutes. Add the shallots and cook, stirring, until translucent. Add the rock shrimp, raise the heat to medium, season to taste with salt and pepper, and continue to cook, stirring, for 3 minutes more. Set aside.

2. Preheat the oven to 375°F.

3. In a small saucepan, combine the beans, wine, garlic, thyme, and nutmeg. Over medium heat, bring to a boil; reduce the heat and simmer for 5 minutes. Add the bean mixture to the rock shrimp, stirring them together gently but thoroughly.

4. In a mixing bowl, stir together the bread crumbs, orange zest, cilantro, and chives. Sprinkle the crumbs evenly over the rock shrimp in the skillet. Put the skillet in the oven and cook until the crumbs are golden brown, about 10 minutes.

Pot-Roasted Chicken with New Potatoes and Corn

Serves 4

Gary Danko, The Dining Room, The Ritz-Carlton, San Francisco, California

Without requiring any additional effort from the home cook, Gary Danko adds some subtly sophisticated touches to this home-style chicken dish by adding garlic and herbs. He suggests serving it with pickled beets and a coleslaw embellished with poppy seeds.

One 3 1/2-pound chicken, rinsed and patted dry

1 tablespoon kosher salt

1/4 cup mild vegetable oil

2 tablespoons unsalted butter

1 cup finely chopped onion

2 cloves garlic, finely chopped

2 tablespoons finely chopped Italian parsley

1/2 teaspoon dried thyme

1 bay leaf

1 cup chicken stock

1 1/2 pounds small red or white new potatoes (about 1 1/2 inches in diameter)

6 medium-size carrots, peeled and cut into 1/2-inch slices

3 ears fresh sweet corn, husked

2 teaspoons cornstarch, dissolved in 2 tablespoons cold water (optional)

1 tablespoon finely chopped fresh tarragon, or 1 teaspoon dried tarragon

Salt

Black pepper

1. Preheat the oven to 350°F.

2. With your fingers, rub the chicken inside and out with the kosher salt.

3. In a large nonstick skillet, heat the vegetable oil over medium heat. Add the chicken and brown it on all sides, using heavy tongs to turn it carefully, 10 to 15 minutes. Remove the chicken to a large plate and discard the oil.

4. In a Dutch oven large enough to hold the chicken and vegetables, melt the butter over medium heat. Add the onion and cook, stirring, until translucent, about 5 minutes. Stir in the garlic, parsley, thyme, and bay leaf and cook, stirring, 1 minute more.

5. Add 1/2 cup of the chicken stock to the Dutch oven and put the chicken inside, breast up. Cover tightly and bake for 45 minutes. Add the remaining stock and the potatoes and carrots. Cover again and bake until the potatoes are tender and the

Recipe continues • • •

juices run clear when the thickest part of the chicken's thigh is pierced with a long fork or skewer, about 30 minutes more; uncover the Dutch oven for the last 15 minutes or so.

6. While the chicken bakes, bring a medium-size saucepan of lightly salted water to a boil. Add the corn and cook for about 3 minutes. Drain, rinse under cold running water, and when the corn is cool enough to handle, use a sharp knife to cut the kernels from the ears. Set the corn kernels aside.

7. When the chicken is done, transfer it to a serving platter. Pour the contents of the Dutch oven through a strainer placed over a mixing bowl. Transfer the potatoes and carrots to the platter, discard the remaining solids in the strainer, and return the liquid to the Dutch oven.

8. Place the Dutch oven over medium heat and bring the liquid to a boil. If you'd like a thicker sauce, stir in the cornstarch mixture. Add the tarragon and season to taste with salt and pepper. Add the corn and cook until the kernels are heated through, 2 to 3 minutes more.

9. Carve the chicken and serve it with the new potatoes and carrots. Spoon the sauce and corn over each serving.

Lemon Herb Roasted Chicken Breasts with Orange

Serves 6 *Barr Hogen, Project Open Hand, San Francisco, California*

"Lemon is so good for enticing one's appetite," says Barr Hogen of the predominant flavor in this light yet satisfying main course. She likes to accompany it with Lemon Risotto (page 149).

4 tablespoons finely chopped garlic

Grated zest of 1 lemon

2 tablespoons herbes de Provence (see Note)

Salt

Black pepper

6 chicken breast halves, with bones and skin

2 oranges, peeled, white pith removed, cut crosswise into 12 slices and seeded

1 cup dry white wine

1. In a small bowl, mix together the garlic, lemon zest, herbes de Provence, and salt and pepper to taste.

2. Gently loosen the skin of each chicken breast half without removing it entirely. Under the skin of each breast half, rub the herb mixture and tuck 2 slices of the orange. Put the chicken breasts in an ovenproof glass dish large enough to hold them in an single layer, pour the wine over them, cover with plastic wrap, and marinate in the refrigerator for 20 minutes.

3. Meanwhile, preheat the oven to 400°F.

4. Turn the chicken breasts skin side down and roast them for 15 minutes. Turn over and continue roasting for 15 minutes more, until done. Let them sit at room temperature for a few minutes before serving.

NOTE • *Herbes de Provence may be found in the seasonings section of well-stocked markets or specialty food stores.*

Herb-Roasted Chicken with Cremini Mushrooms

Bob Calderone, Anago Bistro, Cambridge, Massachusetts

Serves 4

With just a few little flourishes, Bob Calderone transforms Sunday evening's heirloom roasted chicken into a fragrant, especially succulent main course. He advises that you can prepare the sauce for it up to three days ahead, storing it covered in the refrigerator. Start marinating the chicken the night before. For seasoning the chicken, try such fresh herbs as rosemary, thyme, oregano, basil, or savory. If you can't find meaty-flavored, brown-skinned cremini mushrooms, substitute regular white cultivated mushrooms.

Sauce:

3 1/2 pounds chicken necks or backs

1 tablespoon olive oil

4 cups canned low-salt chicken stock

1 1/2 cups dry red wine

4 plum tomatoes, sliced

2 ribs celery, sliced

1 onion, quartered

1 carrot, sliced

3 large garlic cloves, chopped

4 sprigs fresh thyme, or 1 teaspoon dried thyme

4 sprigs Italian parsley

2 tablespoons unsalted butter

Pot-Roasted Chicken and Mushrooms:

6 large garlic cloves, finely chopped

3 tablespoons finely chopped mixed fresh herbs, or 1 tablespoon dried

One 3 1/2-pound roasting chicken, rinsed and patted dry

3 tablespoons olive oil

Salt

Black pepper

1/2 pound cremini or white cultivated mushrooms, sliced

For the sauce:

1. Preheat the oven to 450°F. Put the chicken necks or backs in a roasting pan and coat them with the olive oil. Roast until browned, about 1 1/2 hours.

2. Transfer the roasted necks or backs to a stockpot. Add the chicken stock, wine, tomatoes, celery, onion, carrot, garlic, thyme, and parsley. Bring to a boil over high heat. Reduce the heat to low and simmer for 2 hours. Pour the liquid through a strainer into a medium-size saucepan. Discard the solids in the strainer. Return liquid to pot and boil over high heat until it reduces to 1 1/3 cups, about 20 minutes. Cool to room temperature and refrigerate, covered.

For the chicken:

1. Set aside 2 of the chopped garlic cloves in a small bowl. With one-third of the remaining garlic and one-third of the mixed herbs, rub inside the chicken cavity. From the neck opening, carefully slide your fingertips between the breast meat and the skin to loosen the skin from the meat. Rub half the remaining garlic and herbs between the breast meat and skin. Rub the remaining garlic and herbs all over the outside of the chicken. With kitchen string, tie the ends of the legs together. Cover the chicken with foil and refrigerate overnight.

2. Preheat the oven to 450°F.

3. In a large, heavy skillet over high heat, heat 1 tablespoon of the olive oil. Season the chicken with salt and pepper and brown it in the skillet on all sides, about 10 minutes.

4. Transfer the chicken, breast down, to a roasting pan. Roast for 10 minutes; then, turn the chicken breast up and roast 10 minutes more. Reduce the oven temperature to 350°F. Continue cooking until a roasting thermometer inserted into the thickest part of the thigh registers 175°F, about 35 minutes.

5. In another large, heavy skillet, heat the remaining oil over medium-high heat. Add the mushrooms and the reserved garlic and cook, stirring, until the mushrooms are tender and golden, about 7 minutes.

6. In a small saucepan, bring the sauce to a boil. Remove it from the heat and, with a wire whisk, briskly stir in the butter.

7. With a large, sharp knife, cut the chicken into 4 serving pieces. Place each on a heated serving plate. Spoon the sauce over the chicken and place the mushrooms on the side.

Chicken Pot Pie with Morels and Chervil

Serves 4 to 6

Todd Humphries, Campton Place Hotel, San Francisco, California

Think of chicken pot pie as a rich chicken casserole hidden beneath a quickly made pastry crust, and you'll begin to understand how easy it really is to make this impressive, satisfying main course. "It was one of the first dishes I ever learned how to successfully prepare when I started cooking," says Todd Humphries, who suggests serving it to friends and family on a cold day.

The wild mushrooms known as morels impart a distinctively rich, hearty flavor; if they're unavailable, leave them out or substitute another fresh wild mushroom such as chanterelles, cremini, or shiitakes.

One 3 1/2-pound chicken, rinsed and patted dry

1 quart chicken stock

Pie Pastry (recipe follows)

1/2 cup (1 stick) unsalted butter

1/4 cup all-purpose flour

1/2 cup heavy cream

1 parsnip, peeled and cut into 1/2-inch dice

1 large carrot, peeled and cut into 1/2-inch dice

1 rib celery, cut into 1/2-inch dice

1 leek, trimmed, cut in half lengthwise, thoroughly washed and coarsely chopped

1 onion, coarsely chopped

10 small button mushrooms, cut into quarters

1/4 pound fresh morels, trimmed and washed

1 bunch Italian parsley, finely chopped

1/4 cup packed fresh chervil leaves, finely chopped

Cayenne pepper

Lemon Juice

Salt

Pepper

1 tablespoon milk

1. Put the chicken in a large pot and add the stock and, if necessary, enough water to cover. Bring to a boil over medium heat, reduce the heat to low, and simmer for 50 minutes. Remove the chicken from the pot, reserving the cooking liquid. Let the chicken cool to room temperature.

2. While the chicken cools, prepare and chill the Pie Pastry.

3. Bring the chicken's cooking liquid back to a boil over high heat, skimming any froth from the surface. Continue boiling until the liquid reduces by half, 15 to 20 minutes. In a large saucepan, melt 2 tablespoons of the butter over low heat. Whisk

in the all-purpose flour until smooth. Whisking continuously to prevent lumps from forming, slowly pour in the hot stock. Stir in the cream and simmer briskly over medium heat, stirring frequently, until the sauce is smooth and thick enough to coat a spoon. Set aside.

4. In another saucepan, melt the remaining butter over low heat. Add the parsnip, carrot, celery, leek, onion, mushrooms, and morels and cook, covered, stirring occasionally, until tender. Set aside.

5. When the chicken is cool enough to handle, use a sharp knife and your fingers to remove the meat from the bones, discarding the bones and skin. Cut or tear the meat into bite-size pieces. Add them, along with the vegetables, parsley, and chervil, to the sauce. Add a little cayenne, lemon juice, salt, and pepper to taste.

6. Preheat the oven to 400°F.

7. Transfer the pie filling to a 1 1/2-to 2-quart round, deep baking dish. On a lightly floured work surface, roll out the Pie Pastry large enough to cover the dish. Place it on top. With a small, sharp knife, trim the edges; then, flute the edge of the pastry, pinching it with your fingertips. Lightly brush the top of the pastry with milk.

8. Bake the pie until the filling is hot and bubbly and the pastry is golden, about 25 minutes.

Pie Pastry

1 1/2 cups all-purpose flour
1/4 teaspoon salt
1/2 cup (1 stick) unsalted butter, chilled and cut into pieces
2 tablespoons cold water

In a mixing bowl, stir together the all-purpose flour and salt. With a pastry blender, a pair of knives, or your fingers, combine the flour and butter until the mixture resembles coarse crumbs. Stir in the water and gather the dough into a ball. Wrap in plastic wrap and refrigerate for 1 hour.

Mom's Meatloaf with Caramelized Onions

Jesse Cool, Flea Street Cafe, Menlo Park, California

Serves 4 to 6

A topping of onions cooked to a rich, sweet caramel-brown adds an extra touch of comfort to a classic meatloaf. This recipe makes enough to yield leftovers, which Jesse Cool suggests serving "between two slices of white bread, bringing back memories of Mom, home, and great American food."

Meatloaf:

1 pound ground beef

1 pound ground pork

2 large eggs

3/4 cup finely chopped onion

3/4 cup cocktail sauce

1/2 cup toasted bread crumbs, or
  2 slices bread, finely crumbled

2 tablespoons finely chopped fresh
  sage

1 tablespoon Dijon mustard

1 tablespoon Worcestershire sauce

1 teaspoon salt

1/2 teaspoon black pepper

3 strips bacon

Caramelized Onions:

2 large onions, thinly sliced

2 tablespoons mild vegetable oil

Salt

For the meatloaf:

1. Preheat the oven to 350°F.

2. In a large bowl, thoroughly combine the beef, pork, eggs, onion, 1/2 cup of the cocktail sauce, bread crumbs, sage, mustard, Worcestershire sauce, salt, and pepper.

3. Transfer the mixture to a 2-quart loaf pan, smoothing its surface. Spread on the remaining cocktail sauce, then top with the bacon strips. Bake for 1 hour.

For the caramelized onions:

1. While the meatloaf is baking, put the onions, oil, and salt to taste in a heavy-bottomed skillet. Cook over medium heat, stirring frequently, until the onions are soft and golden brown, about 30 minutes.

2. When the meatloaf is done, remove it from the oven and let it rest about 10 minutes. Then carefully pour off the excess fat. Unmold the meatloaf for slicing, or slice it in the pan, and serve smothered with the caramelized onions.

Eggplant Parmesan

Faz Poursohi, Circolo, Faz Cafe, and Cafe Latte, San Francisco, California

Eggplant, Faz Poursohi points out, has a sufficiently robust flavor to "satisfy even the most tenacious meat eaters." His simple method of preparing the classic Italian dish, which he suggests serving for a Sunday supper, makes it all the healthier still by skipping the breading and frying of the eggplant, baking it instead. Use your favorite recipe for the tomato sauce, or buy a ready-made version from the refrigerated case of your supermarket.

3 large eggplants, trimmed and cut lengthwise into slices 1/4 to 1/2 inch thick

Salt

Olive oil or mild vegetable oil

1/2 cup prepared tomato sauce

1 pound mozzarella cheese, thinly sliced or shredded

1/2 cup grated Parmesan cheese

1 bunch fresh basil, leaves cut into thin strips

1. Sprinkle the eggplant slices lightly with salt and layer them in a colander. Put a plate on top of them, weight them down with cans or other heavy objects, and leave in the sink to drain for about 30 minutes.

2. Preheat the oven to 350°F.

3. Rinse the eggplant slices with cold running water and pat them dry. Lightly oil a baking sheet and place the slices on it in a single layer. Bake until completely tender, 20 to 25 minutes. Let cool to room temperature.

4. In the bottom of a deep 2-quart ovenproof casserole, spread a very thin layer of the tomato sauce. Top with 1 layer of eggplant slices, and sprinklings of mozzarella, Parmesan, and basil. Repeat until the casserole is filled, ending with a layer of cheese, so no basil leaves will be exposed to burn.

5. Reduce the oven temperature to 325°F and bake the casserole until it bubbles and the cheese has melted and turned golden, about 25 minutes.

Springtime Angel Hair Pasta
with Roasted Garlic Sauce

Serves 4 to 6 *Barbara Figueroa, B Figueroa, Seattle, Washington*

"Ripe with sweetness and nuttiness, earthiness and pungency, this dish needs no long-winded intellectual description," says Barbara Figueroa.

Roasted Garlic Sauce:

9 cloves garlic, peeled

1 tablespoon olive oil

2 cups chicken stock

2 small shallots, finely chopped

1/4 cup garlic oil (see Note)

3/4 tablespoon unsalted butter

Salt

Black pepper

Springtime Angel Hair Pasta:

1/4 cup shelled unsalted pistachio nuts

2/3 cup thinly sliced young carrots, halved lengthwise and cut on the diagonal

2/3 cup thinly sliced asparagus, cut on the diagonal

1 pound fresh angel hair pasta

2 tablespoons unsalted butter

1 cup corn kernels, fresh or frozen thawed

2/3 cup stemmed, seeded, and thinly sliced red bell pepper

1/4 cup grated Parmesan cheese

For the roasted garlic sauce:

1. Preheat the oven to 350°F.

2. In a small ovenproof skillet or shallow baking dish, toss the garlic cloves with the 1 tablespoon of olive oil. Cover with aluminum foil and roast until the garlic is soft and golden in color, about 30 minutes. Remove from the oven and reduce the oven temperature to 325°F.

3. Meanwhile, put the chicken stock and shallots in a medium-size saucepan over medium heat. Bring to a boil and cook until the liquid reduces to about 3/4 cup, 10 to 12 minutes.

4. Put the chicken stock and shallots in a blender or a food processor. Add the roasted garlic and puree. With the motor running, pour in the garlic oil in a thin, steady stream; then add the butter. Season to taste with salt and pepper. Press this sauce through a fine-meshed strainer held over a bowl. Cover and keep warm.

For the springtime angel hair pasta:

1. Put the pistachios on a baking sheet or in a small shallow baking dish and roast them, stirring once, in the oven until they look lightly toasted, 5 to 7 minutes. Remove them from the oven and coarsely chop them.

2. Bring a large pot of salted water to a boil. Add the carrots and cook until tender crisp, 1 to 2 minutes; remove them with a wire skimmer or a slotted spoon and set aside. Add the asparagus and cook until tender crisp, about 1 minute. Remove with the skimmer or slotted spoon and set aside.

3. Add the angel hair pasta to the water and cook until al dente, tender but still slightly chewy, 3 to 5 minutes, depending on how dry it is before cooking; take great care not to overcook. Drain well.

4. While the pasta is cooking, melt the butter in a medium-size skillet over medium heat. Add the corn and bell pepper and cook, stirring, until the pepper is tender-crisp, 3 to 5 minutes. Add the asparagus and carrots and cook, stirring, just to warm them, about 1 minute more. Season to taste with salt and pepper.

5. In a serving bowl, toss the pasta with the garlic sauce and vegetables. Transfer to serving plates and sprinkle each with pistachios and Parmesan cheese.

NOTE • *For the garlic oil, use one of the commercial flavored olive oils now widely available in specialty food stores. Or you can easily make just enough for this recipe by putting 1/4 cup of olive oil in a small saucepan with 3 or 4 whole peeled garlic cloves and heating the mixture over medium heat until the oil is hot but not yet smoking; then remove it from the heat and let the garlic infuse in the oil for 1 hour or more. Strain out the garlic before using the oil.*

Pasta with Garlic and Parsley

Alice Waters, Chez Panisse, Berkeley, California

Serves 2

"I eat this when I come home from a trip," says Alice Waters. "It's a comfort to always find pasta in the cupboard and garlic and parsley in the garden." Sometimes she substitutes leaves of rocket (arugula) or basil for the parsley or adds Parmesan cheese, chopped anchovies or olives, fresh tomatoes, and pine nuts or walnuts.

4 ounces linguine, spaghettini, or other pasta

1/4 cup olive oil

3 small cloves (or more) garlic, chopped

3 to 4 tablespoons chopped Italian parsley

Salt

Black pepper

1. Bring a large pot of water to a boil over high heat. Add some salt and the pasta. Cook until al dente, following suggested cooking time on the package.

2. When the pasta is almost done, heat the olive oil in a large sauté pan or saucepan over medium-to-low heat. Add the garlic and cook, stirring, until it sizzles, taking care not to let it brown, less than 1 minute.

3. Drain the pasta. Remove the pan from the heat and add the pasta, tossing it with the oil and garlic. Add the parsley and salt and pepper to taste and mix again.

Linguine with Hazelnuts and Anchovies

JoAnn diLorenzo, JoAnn's Cafe, South San Francisco, California

Serves 4

"This was a specialty of my father's, who was especially fond of the spicier food of southern Italy and was confident that the more anchovies and red pepper flakes, the better," says JoAnn diLorenzo. "To go with this, my mother always made a simple lettuce and tomato salad dressed with oil and vinegar. Sometimes the sauce was so spicy that the salad was a welcome alternative to the fire."

JoAnn recommends using the best-quality dried linguine you can find. She also points out that this kind of sauce is traditionally served without cheese but that you could add a garnish of finely chopped parsley if you like.

1 pound linguine	1 cup hazelnut pieces
1/2 cup fragrant olive oil	1/4 teaspoon crushed red pepper flakes
3 cloves garlic, finely chopped	
1 can oil-packed anchovy fillets, drained, 1 tablespoon oil reserved from can	

1. Bring a large saucepan of water to a boil and cook the linguine until al dente, following suggested cooking time on the package. When the pasta is done, drain it, reserving 1/2 cup of its cooking water.

2. While the pasta is cooking, heat the olive oil and garlic in a medium-size skillet over medium heat. When the garlic begins to sizzle, add the anchovies and the reserved oil from their can, stirring with a wooden spoon to crush the anchovies.

3. Add the hazelnuts and red pepper flakes, reduce the heat to low, and cook, stirring occasionally, for 10 minutes.

4. Stir the reserved pasta water into the sauce, add the linguine, and toss thoroughly.

Macaroni with Four Cheeses and Herbs

Jimmy Schmidt, The Rattlesnake Club, Detroit, Michigan

Serves 4 main courses or 8 side dishes

"For me," says Jimmy Schmidt, "macaroni and cheese is the ultimate comfort food." Though his combination of 4 cheeses gives this recipe a contemporary twist, it satisfies just like the macaroni of childhood.

Salt

1/2 pound macaroni

1 cup shredded sharp cheddar cheese

1 cup grated Parmesan cheese

1 cup shredded fontinella or mozzarella cheese

1 cup finely chopped fresh chives or green onion tops

1/4 cup (1/2 stick) unsalted butter, at room temperature

3 large eggs, beaten

1 3/4 cups half-and-half

3/4 teaspoon coarsely ground black pepper

3/4 teaspoon paprika

1/2 cup fine fresh bread crumbs

1/4 cup grated Romano cheese

1. Preheat the oven to 375°F.

2. In a large pot, bring 2 quarts or more of water to a boil. Add 1 tablespoon salt, then stir in the macaroni. Cook until al dente, following suggested cooking time on the package. Drain, then rinse with warm running water.

3. In a large mixing bowl, stir together the cheddar, Parmesan, fontinella or mozzarella, and the chives. Add the macaroni and mix well.

4. With 1 tablespoon of the butter, grease a 2 1/2- or 3-quart deep baking dish. Add the macaroni mixture.

5. In the mixing bowl, stir together the eggs, half-and-half, pepper, paprika, and 1/2 teaspoon salt. Pour evenly over the macaroni.

6. In a small bowl, toss together the bread crumbs and Romano cheese. Sprinkle them evenly over the macaroni and dot with the remaining butter.

7. Bake the macaroni and cheese until bubbly and golden, about 30 minutes. Serve immediately.

Macaroni Gratin with Shiitake Mushrooms

Gerald Hirigoyen, Fringale, San Francisco, California

Serves 4 to 6

"Macaroni is such a traditional pasta that everyone can relate to it, so it's always apt to please," Gerald Hirigoyen observes. His robust, rapidly prepared take on macaroni and cheese makes use of fresh shiitake mushrooms, "which add an intense, earthy flavor," and two kinds of cheese.

If you can't find shiitake mushrooms, substitute another wild variety; or use good, ordinary cultivated mushrooms if necessary.

1 1/2 cups elbow macaroni

2 tablespoons unsalted butter

2 tablespoons finely chopped shallots

1 1/4 pounds fresh shiitake mushrooms, trimmed and thinly sliced

Salt

Black pepper

1 tablespoon finely chopped Italian parsley

1 tablespoon finely chopped fresh chives

3/4 pound mild Cheddar cheese, finely shredded

1/4 pound Parmesan cheese, freshly grated

1. Preheat the broiler.

2. In a large saucepan, bring 2 quarts of water to a boil. Add the macaroni and cook until al dente, following suggested cooking time on the package.

3. While the pasta is cooking, in a large skillet, melt the butter over medium heat, add the shallots, and cook, stirring, until translucent. Add the shiitake mushrooms and salt and pepper to taste. Cook, stirring, until they are tender and their edges slightly browned, 2 to 3 minutes.

4. As soon as the pasta is done, drain it well and add it to the mushrooms, stirring to mix them well. Stir in the parsley and chives and, if necessary, more salt and pepper to taste.

5. Pour the mixture into a 2-quart shallow baking dish and sprinkle the cheeses evenly over the top. Put under the broiler just until the cheese melts, about 2 minutes. Serve immediately.

Gnocchi ai Pepe con Piselli Burro Salvia (Black Pepper Gnocchi with Peas and Sage Butter)

Serves 4 *Craig Stoll, Palio D'Asti, San Francisco, California*

"Its simplicity is very comforting," says Craig Stoll of this dish's appealing combination of fresh peas, brown butter, sage leaves, and potato–and–black-pepper gnocchi.

Gnocchi:

2 1/2 pounds russet potatoes, scrubbed

3 large eggs, lightly beaten

2 cups all-purpose flour

1 cup grated Parmesan cheese

1 tablespoon salt

1 tablespoon coarsely ground black pepper

Peas, Sage, and Cheese:

1 pound fresh peas, shelled

1/4 cup (1/2 stick) unsalted butter

Salt

Grated Parmesan cheese

12 whole fresh sage leaves

White pepper

For the gnocchi:

1. Put the potatoes, whole and unpeeled, in a large saucepan and add cold water to cover. Bring to a boil over medium-high heat; immediately reduce the heat to low to help prevent the potatoes' skins from rupturing, and simmer until just tender, 20 to 30 minutes, depending on size. Drain the potatoes well and let them cool slightly just until you can handle them. Peel the potatoes while still warm, then use a ricer, food mill, or meat grinder to puree them.

2. Transfer the potatoes to a floured work surface and form a well in their center. Put the eggs, all-purpose flour, Parmesan, salt, and pepper in the well. With your fingers, working from the edges of the well into the center, gradually combine the ingredients just until they come together into a dough with the consistency of soft, pliable cookie dough; take care not to overwork the dough, and add a little extra flour if the dough seems too moist.

3. Cut off one-quarter of the dough and cover the rest with a damp kitchen towel to keep it from drying.

4. Dust your hands with flour and, on a lightly floured surface, gently roll the one-quarter portion of dough with your hands to form a log about 3/4 inch in diameter. Keep flouring your hands if necessary to prevent sticking.

5. Cover a sheet pan or baking sheet with parchment paper or waxed paper and dust lightly with flour. Set aside.

6. With a pastry scraper or a knife, cut the log of dough into 3/4-inch-long pieces. With your thumb, gently press down on the top side of each piece to indent it. As each gnocchi is formed, transfer it to the lined sheet pan. Cut another one-quarter of the dough and repeat the procedure until all the gnocchi dough is used up. (If you'd like to reserve the gnocchi for later use, transfer the sheet pan to the freezer, uncovered; when the gnocchi are frozen solid, pack them in an airtight container or freezer bag.)

For the peas, sage, and cheese:

1. Put the shelled peas, 1/2 tablespoon of the butter, and a little salt in a medium-size sauté pan or saucepan; add just enough cold water to cover. Bring the water to a boil over high heat and simmer briskly until the peas are tender and most of the water has evaporated, 5 to 7 minutes.

2. Meanwhile, bring a large pot of salted water to a boil over high heat. Add the gnocchi and cook until they all rise to the surface, float, and are tender, 1 to 2 minutes.

3. Drain the gnocchi well, reserving just a splash of their cooking water, and add them and the splash of water to the pan with the peas. Raise the heat to high and cook, tossing or stirring gently, until the liquid in the pan evaporates and the gnocchi are glazed. Transfer the gnocchi and peas to a large serving bowl and top with grated Parmesan.

4. At the same time the gnocchi and peas are cooking together, put the remaining butter and the sage leaves in a small saucepan over medium heat and season to taste with salt and pepper. Cook, swirling the pan, until the butter turns golden brown and the sage leaves turn crisp, 3 to 5 minutes. Quickly spoon the hot butter and sage leaves over the gnocchi, causing the cheese to bubble. Serve immediately.

Gnocchi with Rock Shrimp and Ginger Cream Sauce

Bruce Hill, Oritalia, San Francisco, California

Makes 2 main courses or 4 appetizers

Though the ingredients may at first glance seem exotic, this dish—one of the most popular on the menu at Oritalia—is incredibly soothing and satisfying. If you can't find rock shrimp, substitute the smallest fresh raw shrimp available.

Gnocchi:

2 medium-size white potatoes, peeled and cut into 1-inch chunks

1/4 cup all-purpose flour

2 tablespoons grated Parmesan cheese

1 large egg yolk

Salt

White pepper

Rock Shrimp and Ginger Cream Sauce:

1 teaspoon mild vegetable oil

1/2 pound fresh rock shrimp, peeled and deveined

1/2 cup dry white wine

3 tablespoons finely chopped fresh ginger

1/2 teaspoon finely chopped garlic

2 teaspoons tomato paste

1/2 cup heavy cream

1/2 cup crème fraîche

Garnish:

2 tablespoons tobiko (flying fish roe) (see Note)

2 tablespoons finely chopped cilantro (fresh coriander)

2 tablespoons finely chopped fresh chives

For the gnocchi:

1. Put the potatoes in a medium saucepan of cold water. Bring to a boil over high heat and boil until the potatoes are tender, 10 to 15 minutes. Drain well and press them through a potato ricer or a fine sieve to puree them.

2. Measure out 1 cup of the potatoes, reserving any leftovers for another use. In a medium-size mixing bowl, combine the potatoes, all-purpose flour, Parmesan, egg yolk, and salt and pepper to taste; with your hands, mix them thoroughly to form a soft, smooth dough.

3. On a lightly floured work surface, divide the dough into 3 or 4 equal portions. With your hands, roll each portion into a log about 1/2 inch in diameter. Use a small, sharp knife to cut each log into 1-inch-long gnocchi. Place them on a floured cookie sheet and set aside.

4. Bring a large pot of water to a boil while you prepare the rock shrimp and sauce.

For the rock shrimp and ginger cream sauce:

1. In a large skillet, heat the vegetable oil over high heat. Add the rock shrimp and cook, stirring, until they are opaque but not quite cooked through, about 1 minute. Remove from the skillet and set aside.

2. In the same skillet, add the white wine, ginger, and garlic and cook over high heat, stirring, until the liquid reduces by about half, 2 to 3 minutes. Reduce the heat to medium-high and stir in the tomato paste until it dissolves. Pour in the cream and crème fraîche and continue simmering until the liquid reduces to a thick sauce consistency, about 2 minutes more. Add the rock shrimp and cook, stirring, about 1 minute more.

3. When the pot of water has reached a rolling boil, add the gnocchi and cook until they rise to the surface and float, 1 to 2 minutes. Drain well and transfer to a large serving bowl.

4. Pour the shrimp and sauce over the gnocchi and stir gently to coat. Spoon the gnocchi, shrimp, and sauce onto 2 or 4 individual serving plates. Garnish with tobiko, cilantro, and chives.

NOTE • Tobiko *is the Japanese term for flying fish roe, the tiny, sweet, bright orange-pink eggs commonly used as a garnish or ingredient in sushi. It's available in Japanese markets; or try buying a little to go from your favorite local sushi bar.*

Vegetable Tamales

Lisa Hemenway, Lisa Hemenway's, Santa Rosa, California

Makes 1 dozen tamales

Lisa Hemenway's recipe for the traditional, home-style cornmeal dumplings of Mexican cooking infuses them with a California sensibility, mixing a colorful assortment of diced fresh vegetables with the tamale dough. These are great served at an informal party, whether as a vegetarian main course or as a side dish to meat, poultry, or seafood.

Adobado Sauce:

1 tablespoon olive oil

1 medium-size onion, finely chopped

1 medium-size garlic clove, finely chopped

4 medium-size tomatoes, coarsely chopped

1/2 cup orange juice

1/2 cup water

1/4 cup packed dark brown sugar

3 small dried chilies

1/2 teaspoon ground allspice

1/2 teaspoon ground cinnamon

1/2 teaspoon ground cumin

1/2 teaspoon ground coriander

1/2 teaspoon salt

1/2 teaspoon black pepper

Vegetable Tamales:

1 cup (2 sticks) unsalted butter

1 medium-size carrot, peeled and cut into 1/4-inch dice

1 medium-size rib celery, cut into 1/4-inch dice

1 medium-size zucchini, cut into 1/4-inch dice

1 medium-size yellow summer squash, cut into 1/4-inch dice

1/2 medium-size red onion, cut into 1/4-inch dice

1/2 cup corn kernels, fresh or frozen thawed

1/2 medium-size russet potato, boiled until tender, peeled, and cut into 1/4-inch dice

2 tablespoons finely chopped cilantro (fresh coriander)

1 teaspoon dried oregano

1 teaspoon salt

1/4 teaspoon ground cumin

2 cups masa harina (Mexican-style cornmeal) (see Note)

1/2 teaspoon baking powder

1/4 cup warm water

14 dried corn husks, soaked in water until pliable, about 1 hour, then drained and patted dry (see Note)

3/4 pound cheddar or Monterey Jack cheese, cut into 12 thin slices

For the adobado sauce:

In a medium-size saucepan, heat the oil over medium heat. Add the onion and garlic and cook, stirring, until translucent, 4 to 5 minutes. Add the tomatoes, orange juice, water, brown sugar, and chilies. Bring to a boil, reduce the heat, and simmer for 30 minutes. Stir in the spices, salt, and pepper. Transfer to a processor or blender and puree; then pour through a sieve set over a bowl. Set the sauce aside.

For the vegetable tamales:

1. Melt the butter in a large skillet or sauté pan over medium heat; pour off and reserve 2/3 cup of the butter. Add the carrot, celery, zucchini, squash, red onion, and corn to the remaining butter and cook, stirring, until tender, 7 to 10 minutes. Stir in the potato, cilantro, oregano, 1/2 teaspoon of the salt, and the cumin. Set aside.

2. In a medium-size mixing bowl, stir together the masa harina, baking powder, and remaining salt. Add the reserved melted butter and warm water and knead by hand until the mixture forms a soft, smooth dough. Add the vegetables and mix until combined.

3. In the center of a corn husk, spread a generous 1/2 cup of the tamale-vegetable mixture. Top with a slice of cheese and 1 tablespoon of the adobado sauce. Then roll up the husk to enfold the cheese and sauce inside the dough and to fully enclose the tamale. Tear 2 thin strips from one of the soaked corn husks and use them to tie each end of the rolled tamale. Repeat with the remaining ingredients.

4. Bring several inches of water to a boil in a large saucepan with a steamer placed on top. Put the tamales in the steamer and cook until firm, 30 to 45 minutes. Serve immediately, along with remaining adobado sauce.

NOTE • *Masa harina and dried corn husks may be found in well-stocked supermarkets and Mexican food stores.*

Ma Po Tofu Noodles

Andy Wai, Harbor Village, San Francisco, and Monterey Park, California

This Chinese mixture of noodles, soft bean curd cubes, meat, and mild yet well-seasoned sauce is one of the cuisine's most comforting home-style creations. Look for the sesame oil, chili bean sauce, and oyster sauce in well-stocked supermarkets or Asian food stores. If you like, substitute ground pork or even ground chicken or turkey for the beef.

1 cup water

2 tablespoons tomato paste

1 tablespoon cornstarch

2 teaspoons Chinese sesame oil

1 to 2 teaspoons Chinese chili bean sauce

1 teaspoon sugar

1/2 teaspoon salt

1/4 teaspoon Szechwan peppercorns, crushed (optional)

3 whole medium-size green onions, trimmed and cut crosswise into thin slices

1 pound soft bean curd (tofu), drained well and cut into 1/4-inch cubes

1 tablespoon mild vegetable oil

1/2 pound lean ground beef

2 large cloves garlic, finely chopped

1/2 pound linguine

1 tablespoon oyster sauce

1. In a medium-size mixing bowl, stir together the water, tomato paste, cornstarch, 1 teaspoon of the sesame oil, chili bean sauce to taste, sugar, salt, peppercorns, and green onions until well blended. Gently fold in the bean curd cubes to coat them completely. Set aside.

2. Heat a heavy medium-size saucepan over medium heat. Add the vegetable oil and swirl the pan to coat its bottom; then add the beef and garlic, raise the heat to high, and cook, stirring to break up the beef, until it is uniformly browned, about 3 minutes. Pour in the prepared sauce mixture with the tofu, stirring gently to mix it with the beef; reduce the heat to low, cover the pan, and cook, stirring occasionally, to prevent sticking, until the mixture is thick, 15 to 20 minutes.

3. While the tofu-beef mixture is cooking, prepare the noodles. Bring a large saucepan or pot of water to a boil and cook the linguine until al dente, tender but still chewy, following suggested cooking time on package.

4. When the noodles are done, drain them well, rinse quickly under hot running water, and drain well again. Put them on a warmed serving platter or in a warmed bowl and toss with the remaining sesame oil and the oyster sauce.

5. Spoon the tofu-beef mixture and sauce over the noodles and serve immediately.

Risotto

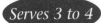

Serves 3 to 4

Alice Waters, Chez Panisse, Berkeley, California

"Risotto has so many variations," says Alice Waters. "It's comforting to have this base to which I can add whatever is ripe and fresh—sweet peas with ham, wilted greens, mushrooms, leftover bits of roasted chicken or grilled vegetables. Try adding a pinch of saffron threads to the onions for a golden risotto." Or you can take comfort in the utter simplicity of this plain risotto on its own.

4 cups chicken broth	1 sprig fresh thyme
Salt	1 cup Arborio rice or short-grain white rice
1 small onion, finely chopped	
2 tablespoons olive oil	Black pepper
1 tablespoon unsalted butter	Freshly grated Parmesan cheese
1 bay leaf	

1. In a medium-size saucepan, bring the broth just to a boil over medium heat. Taste it: It should taste salty, so add some salt if needed.

2. Put the onion, 1 tablespoon of the olive oil, the butter, bay leaf, and thyme in a heavy-bottomed, medium-size saucepan. Cook, stirring, over medium heat until the onion is soft and translucent, 4 to 5 minutes.

3. Add the rice and cook, stirring often, for another 5 minutes. Then ladle into the pan enough hot chicken broth to just cover the rice. Stir, then reduce the heat to low to maintain a very gentle simmer. Cook, uncovered, for about 10 minutes, until almost all the broth has been absorbed.

4. Add the remaining hot broth and continue cooking at a gentle simmer until the rice is tender but just a little chewy at the center, another 10 minutes or so. Near the end of cooking, stir in the remaining olive oil. Taste and add more salt if necessary. Serve immediately with pepper and Parmesan cheese to taste.

Risotto with Mushrooms, Peas, and Gremolata

Joyce Goldstein, Square One, San Francisco, California

Serves 4

"Risotto is the ultimate comfort food," says Joyce Goldstein. "It is warm, slightly soupy, and can be eaten with a soup spoon if you're feeling too lazy to eat it with a fork." She also finds that the ritual of slow, patient stirring it requires when cooking "is just as comforting as eating it."

To achieve the right creamy consistency, use only the short, plump-grained, starchy Italian varieties of rice known as Arborio or Carnaroli, available in well-stocked supermarkets and Italian food stores. In this version, she suggests using fresh peas, precooked in boiling water just until tender, only if you can find ones that are flavorful and unstarchy; if not, substitute frozen baby peas. Though you can use ordinary cultivated mushrooms, she recommends throwing in a few wild ones if you can. The gremolata, a traditional Italian garnish, adds a finely aromatic burst of parsley, garlic, and lemon zest.

6 cups chicken or vegetable stock

6 tablespoons unsalted butter or olive oil

3/4 cup finely chopped onion

1 1/2 cups Arborio or Carnaroli rice

1 pound assorted mushrooms, trimmed and cut into 1/4-inch-thick slices

1 cup cooked shelled fresh or thawed frozen baby peas

6 tablespoons finely chopped Italian parsley

2 tablespoons grated lemon zest

1 1/2 tablespoons finely chopped garlic

Salt

Black pepper

Grated Parmesan cheese

1. In a medium-size saucepan, bring the chicken or vegetable stock to a boil over high heat. Reduce the heat to low and keep the stock at a bare simmer.

2. In a large skillet with high sides or a shallow saucepan, melt 2 tablespoons of butter over medium heat. Add the onion and cook, stirring frequently, until tender, about 8 minutes. Add the rice and cook, stirring frequently, until it looks opaque, about 3 minutes.

3. Ladle in about 1 cup of the hot stock, reduce the heat to low, and simmer, stirring occasionally, until the stock has been absorbed, about 5 minutes. Add about 1 cup more stock and continue to cook, stirring occasionally, until the stock is absorbed. Continue the process until the rice is almost tender but still chewy, about 30 minutes total.

4. While the rice is cooking, melt the remaining butter in a large skillet over high heat and cook the mushrooms, stirring, until they cook down to about half their original volume, about 4 minutes.

5. When the rice is almost done, add the cooked mushrooms and the peas and continue to cook until most of the liquids have been absorbed, the mixture has a creamy consistency, and the rice is al dente, tender but still slightly chewy in the center. Stir in the parsley, lemon zest, and garlic and adjust the seasoning to taste with salt and pepper. Stir in some Parmesan cheese to taste, if you like, or pass it separately for each person to add individually.

Grilled Onion and Cheese Sandwiches

Carlo Middione, Vivande, San Francisco, California

Serves 4

Caramelized sweet onions, aromatic balsamic vinegar, and fragrant fresh basil make these grilled cheese sandwiches an extraordinarily satisfying experience. Carlo Middione suggests accompanying them with "thick-sliced tomatoes, plenty of anchovies, and a stout red wine."

4 to 5 tablespoons extra-virgin olive oil

4 large red onions, cut into 1/4-inch-thick slices

3/4 pound Fontina Val D'Aosta cheese or Asiago fresco or Gruyère, shredded

12 large, fresh basil leaves

3 tablespoons balsamic vinegar, preferably aged

Sea salt

Black pepper

8 slices Italian bread (not sourdough), each about 3/4 inch thick

1. Heat 2 tablespoons of the olive oil in a large skillet over high heat. Add the onions, reduce the heat to medium, and cook, stirring frequently, until they are soft and dark golden in color, about 12 minutes.

2. Put the onions in a large mixing bowl and add the cheese, basil, balsamic vinegar, sea salt to taste, and lots of black pepper. Toss well.

3. Divide the mixture evenly among 4 slices of bread. Top with the remaining slices and press down firmly to seal. With the remaining olive oil, brush the tops and bottoms of the sandwiches.

4. In the same skillet you used to cook the onions, grill the sandwiches until the cheese melts and the bread is golden, turning them carefully. Cut in halves and serve immediately.

Warm Brie Sandwiches with Marinated Peppers, Onions, and Roasted Garlic

Jesse Cool, Flea Street Cafe, Menlo Park, California

Serves 2

"My mother loves anything that has lots of gooey cheese melted over it," says Jesse Cool. "I presented her with this California-sounding sandwich, and she responded by saying it was even better than her favorite food, pizza." Jesse suggests serving the sandwiches with plenty of napkins.

1 medium-size tomato, cored, seeded, and coarsely chopped

1/2 red or yellow bell pepper, stemmed, seeded, and very thinly sliced

1/4 cup extra-virgin olive oil

1 tablespoon balsamic vinegar

Salt

Black pepper

8 cloves garlic, peeled

1/4 cup mayonnaise

2 pieces baguette loaf, each 8 inches long, split into halves lengthwise

6 fresh basil leaves

3 ounces ripe Brie cheese, at room temperature, rind removed

1. Preheat the oven to 350°F.

2. In a small bowl, combine the tomato, bell pepper, 3 tablespoons of the olive oil, and the vinegar. Add a pinch each of salt and pepper, stir well, and set aside to marinate.

3. To roast the garlic, coat the peeled cloves with the remaining oil. Wrap securely in aluminum foil and bake until the cloves are soft, about 30 minutes. Transfer the garlic to a small bowl, add the mayonnaise, and mash with a fork.

4. Spread the mayonnaise generously on one-half of each baguette piece. Place 3 basil leaves on top. On the other half, spread the Brie. Top with the marinated tomato and pepper. Close the sandwiches and cut each in half crosswise.

Pan Bagnat

Jean-Louis Palladin, Jean-Louis at the Watergate Hotel, Washington, D.C.

Serves 4

Literally "bathed bread," pan bagnat is the signature sandwich of southern France. "It always reminds me of home," says Jean-Louis Palladin. Comforting thoughts, indeed.

2 medium-size plum tomatoes, peeled (see Box, page 3) and cut into 1/4-inch-thick slices

1/4 medium-size bulb fennel, trimmed and very thinly sliced

2 ounces canned anchovy fillets, drained

1/2 cup Niçoise-style black olives, pitted and cut into thin strips

1 cup olive oil

Salt and black pepper

1/4 cup balsamic vinegar

Two 6-ounce cans tuna, drained

8 leaves Romaine lettuce, cut crosswise into thin strips

4 French rolls (see Note)

1. In a medium-size mixing bowl, toss together the tomatoes, fennel, anchovies, and olives with 2 tablespoons of the olive oil and salt and pepper to taste. In a separate bowl, stir together 2 more tablespoons of oil with 2 tablespoons of the vinegar; add the tuna, breaking it into coarse chunks. Leave both bowls to marinate at room temperature about 30 minutes.

2. Before serving, in another bowl, season the remaining vinegar to taste with salt and pepper and stir in 1/4 cup of the oil. Toss with the lettuce.

3. With a bread knife, split each roll in half horizontally. With your fingertips, pull out the crumb from each half, leaving a shell 1/4 to 1/2 inch thick. Liberally brush the inside of each half with the remaining olive oil. In the bottom half of each roll, layer the lettuce, then top with the marinated vegetables and anchovies and the tuna. Place the top halves on each sandwich and cut crosswise into halves.

NOTE • *A French roll looks like a stunted baguette, 6 to 8 inches long, with tapered ends.*

Sicilian Burgers

Serves 6

Sanford D'Amato, Sanford Restaurant, Milwaukee, Wisconsin

"I used to eat these at my grandfather's house, next door to my father's grocery store, where I worked as a youth," says Sanford D'Amato. "Today, my restaurant stands on the site of that grocery store."

Old-world Italian seasonings add evocative memories to these pan-fried burgers, which Sanford says may also be charcoal-grilled on your barbecue. He suggests serving the burgers with his Marinated Cauliflower Salad (page 40).

1/4 cup plus 2 tablespoons olive oil

1 large onion, finely chopped

2 tablespoons kosher salt

1/2 tablespoon black pepper

3 cloves garlic, finely chopped

1 small bay leaf

1/2 cup dry white wine

1 cup dry bread crumbs

1 cup moderately packed finely chopped Italian parsley

1/2 cup moderately packed finely chopped fresh basil leaves

1/4 cup marsala

1 pound ground chuck

1/2 pound ground pork shoulder

1/4 pound grated imported Romano cheese

1 large egg

1 large egg yolk

6 good-quality sandwich buns, split

1. Heat a large skillet over medium heat and add the 1/4 cup of olive oil. Add the onion and cook, stirring, until translucent, 3 to 5 minutes. Add the salt, pepper, garlic, and bay leaf and cook, stirring, for about 30 seconds. Add the white wine and cook, stirring occasionally, until it evaporates.

2. Remove the skillet from the heat and stir in the bread crumbs. Then stir in the parsley, basil, and marsala. Transfer the mixture to a large mixing bowl, cover, and refrigerate until cool.

3. Remove and discard the bay leaf. Add the ground chuck and pork, Romano cheese, egg, and egg yolk to the bowl, and with your hands, mix well until fully incorporated. Divide and loosely pat the mixture into 6 individual patties slightly bigger than the diameter of the buns.

4. In a large skillet, heat the remaining 2 tablespoons of olive oil over medium-high heat. Add the patties and cook until done medium-well, about 8 minutes per side; do not cook any longer or they will dry out.

5. Serve on buns with your choice of condiments.

Molasses Barbecued Pork Sandwiches

Michael McCarty, Michael's, Santa Monica, California, and New York, New York

Serves 6

"This is one of my favorite home recipes, adapted from one my parents made," says Michael McCarty of these wondrously succulent barbecued sandwiches. He recommends starting with a really good commercial tomato-molasses barbecue sauce—they use KC Masterpiece's Original Recipe at the restaurant—and then building on it with other additions. "I marinate the pork in it overnight—though you can get away with as little as 45 minutes of marinating and still get good results—and then baste the pork with the sauce as it grills." More sauce goes on the sandwiches themselves, along with Michael's signature jalapeño-cilantro-lime salsa.

2 1/2 pounds pork tenderloin

4 cups tomato-molasses-based commercial barbecue sauce

3/4 cup molasses

1/4 cup strong black coffee

Juice of 1 lime

1 small Maui, Walla Walla, Vidalia, or red onion, finely chopped

2 medium-size garlic cloves, finely chopped

1 small red bell pepper, finely chopped

1 small yellow bell pepper, finely chopped

2 medium-size jalapeño chilies, roasted in a 400°F oven until the skins blacken, about 20 minutes, then peeled, stemmed, seeded, and finely chopped

Salt

White pepper

1 medium-size Maui, Walla Walla, Vidalia or red onion, cut into 1/4-inch thick slices

3/4 cup (1 1/2 sticks) unsalted butter, melted

1/2 cup extra-virgin olive oil

1 tablespoon finely chopped cilantro (fresh coriander) leaves

2 sourdough baguettes, each about 18 inches long, or 6 sourdough rolls, each about 6 inches long

2 bunches watercress leaves, coarsely chopped

1 lime, cut in half

1. As early as the night before, but no later than 45 minutes before cooking, start marinating the pork. In a medium-size mixing bowl, stir together 3 cups of the barbecue sauce, the molasses, coffee, lime juice, chopped onion, garlic, bell peppers, and one of the roasted jalapeños. Put the pork in the bowl and turn to coat it well. Cover with plastic wrap and leave in the refrigerator to marinate until cooking time.

2. Before cooking, preheat the grill or broiler until very hot. Wipe the marinade from the pork, reserving the marinade; lightly season the meat with salt and white pepper. Grill or broil the pork, basting frequently with the marinade until no longer pink in the center, 5 to 7 minutes per side.

3. About 3 minutes before the pork is done, lightly brush the sliced onion with some melted butter, sprinkle with salt and white pepper, and grill or broil until lightly golden, about 1 1/2 minutes per side.

4. Prepare the salsa by stirring together the olive oil, the other roasted jalapeño, and the cilantro. Season to taste with salt and white pepper and set aside.

5. Cut each sourdough baguette crosswise into three 6-inch pieces and cut the pieces—or individual rolls—into halves lengthwise. Brush the cut sides with butter and toast them on the grill or broiler as the pork finishes cooking. Lightly brush the bottom halves of the toasted bread with some of the remaining 1 cup of barbecue sauce and arrange the watercress leaves on top.

6. Cut the roast pork diagonally into 1/4-inch-thick slices and place them on top of the watercress. Squeeze the lime into the reserved salsa, stir, and spoon it over the pork. Arrange the grilled onions on top and spoon more barbecue sauce over the onions and pork. Top with the remaining bread halves, and cut each sandwich in half before serving.

Paper-Thin Blueberry Pancakes

Michael McCarty, Michael's, Santa Monica, California, and New York, New York

Serves 6

"When I was a kid," says Michael McCarty, "my mother used Bisquick all the time to make great peach cobbler. I loved its flavor. When I lived in Brittany, I discovered their paper-thin crepes, made from a thin, creamy batter. So when I set out to make blueberry pancakes, it seemed logical to cross Bisquick with French crepes; this is the result." Though these pancakes have a great all-American taste, they're indeed as light as crepes.

Michael cautions that the best way to show off their flavor is to cast self-restraint to the wind and drench them with warm syrup and melted butter before serving. "Don't make the mistake of serving the toppings on the side," he says. Accompany the pancakes with grilled sausage or bacon if you like.

2 cups packed Bisquick

2 1/3 cups milk

1/2 cup (1 stick) unsalted butter, chilled

2 cups blueberries, fresh or frozen (no need to thaw)

1 1/2 cups (3 sticks) salted butter, melted

1 1/2 cups Vermont grade A maple syrup, heated

1. Put the Bisquick in a medium-size mixing bowl and make a well in the center. Pour in all the milk and stir with a wire whisk until just blended. Do not overwork the batter; lumps are okay. Let the batter rest for about 30 minutes at room temperature.

2. Preheat an electric griddle to 400°F or a regular stovetop griddle until very hot.

3. Pour the batter through a fine sieve to strain out any lumps. The batter should have the consistency of heavy cream.

4. With the end of the chilled stick of unsalted butter, quickly grease the hot griddle for each batch of pancakes. Using a 2-ounce (1/4-cup) ladle (or measuring with a measuring cup), pour the batter onto the griddle to form paper-thin, 5- to 6-inch round pancakes; if the first one is too thick to spread evenly, stir a little more milk into the batter. Scatter a few blueberries on top of each pancake, patting them into the batter with a large spatula.

5. When the edges of the pancakes are brown, after about 1 minute, very carefully flip the pancakes with a spatula; tuck any stray berries back under the pancakes. Cook for about 30 seconds more, then carefully transfer to a large heated serving plate, overlapping them. Repeat with the remaining batter and berries.

6. Pour about 1/4 cup each of melted butter and maple syrup over each serving of pancakes.

Savory Crepes with Tomato Filling

Sylvie Le Mer, Ti-Couz, San Francisco, California

Serves 12

"Cooking, smelling, and tasting these crepes takes me home to Brittany," says Sylvie Le Mer, who also contributes sweet dessert crepes on page 220. Prepare them at home in casual style as Sylvie does in her restaurant, one crepe at a time, delivering each one at its hot, crisp best. You could also fill them with any other savory filling or combination of fillings that takes your fancy: plain or garlic butter, fried or scrambled egg, cheese, ham, sautéed mushrooms, smoked salmon, and so on.

To get the right consistency with easy measurements, the batter quantities given below yield enough for twice as many crepes as you'll need. But the batter keeps well, covered in the refrigerator, for 2 days or so. Sylvie also points out that the unfilled crepes, once cooked, will keep fresh in the refrigerator, covered, for 2 to 3 days and that they freeze well.

The crepes:

4 1/2 cups water

1 1/2 cups milk

1 large egg, lightly beaten

2 1/2 cups buckwheat flour

1/2 cup all-purpose flour

1 tablespoon salt

1/2 cup (1 stick) salted butter, at room temperature

The filling:

2 tablespoons unsalted butter

6 medium-size yellow onions, cut into 1/4-inch dice

1/4 cup hard apple cider

15 medium-size tomatoes, peeled, seeded, and chopped (see Box, page 3)

5 cloves garlic, finely chopped

1 sprig fresh thyme

1 bay leaf

Salt

Black pepper

1 1/2 cups crème fraîche or sour cream, for garnish

For the crepes:

1. In a large mixing bowl, use a wire whisk to stir together the water, milk, and egg until well blended. Whisk in the buckwheat and all-purpose flours and the salt until a smooth batter forms. Cover with plastic wrap and let the batter rest in the refrigerator for at least 1 hour.

2. While the batter rests, prepare the filling. Reserve salted butter.

For the filling:

1. In a large skillet, melt the unsalted butter over medium heat. As soon as it foams, add the onions and cook, stirring, until they are lightly browned, 7 to 10 minutes. Stir in the cider and bring it to a simmer. Stir in the tomatoes and garlic and add the thyme and bay leaf. Cook, stirring occasionally, until the mixture reduces to a thick sauce consistency, 20 to 25 minutes. Remove and discard the thyme and bay leaf, season to taste with salt and pepper, and set aside.

2. To prepare the crepes, swirl about 1 teaspoon of salted butter in a 12-inch nonstick skillet over medium heat to coat its bottom. Gently stir the batter. Ladle about 3 ounces (measuring with a measuring cup) of the batter into the skillet and swirl it around to coat the bottom and sides, then place it on the heat. When the crepe's edges start turning light brown, after 1 to 2 minutes, use a spatula to peel it from the skillet and flip it over. Cook 1 minute more, then flip it over again.

3. With a rubber spatula, spread the crepe with about 1 teaspoon of salted butter. Still over the heat, spread a generous 1/4 cup of the tomato filling in the center of the crepe. Fold the bottom edge, sides, and then the top edge of the crepe over the filling to enclose it in a square package. Continue cooking until the bottom is crisp and brown, about 1 minute more. With a spatula, flip the crepe over onto a heated serving plate and garnish with a dollop of crème fraîche or sour cream.

4. Repeat the procedure with the remaining batter and filling.

Strawberry French Toast with St. Andre Cheese

Gary Danko, The Dining Room at The Ritz-Carlton Hotel, San Francisco, California

Serves 4

The simple step of melting St. Andre cheese in between slices of French toast transforms this dish into a showstopper for a weekend brunch. Substitute another favorite creamy cheese for the St. Andre if you like.

2 large eggs

1/2 cup heavy cream

1/2 cup milk

2 tablespoons confectioners' sugar, plus additional for dusting

1/2 teaspoon pure vanilla extract

1/8 teaspoon grated nutmeg

Pinch of salt

1 tablespoon unsalted butter

Eight 3/4-inch-thick slices brioche or pullman loaf

1 pound St. Andre cheese, rind removed, cheese cut into 8 slices

1 cup pure maple syrup

1/4 cup Courvoisier

2 pints strawberries, hulled and cut into 1/4-inch-thick slices

1. Preheat the oven to 350°F.

2. Put the eggs, cream, milk, 2 tablespoons of confectioners' sugar, vanilla, nutmeg, and salt in a blender or food processor and process until smooth. Pour into a wide, shallow bowl or soup plate.

3. In a large nonstick pan or griddle, melt the butter over medium-high heat. While it melts, dip a slice of bread in the egg mixture for 10 to 15 seconds on each side. Place it in the pan or griddle and repeat with the remaining bread. Cook until golden brown, 2 to 3 minutes per side.

4. As each slice is done, place it partially overlapping the others on an ovenproof platter, alternating the bread slices with slices of St. Andre cheese. When the platter is completed, put it in the oven until the cheese melts, 7 to 10 minutes.

5. While the platter is in the oven, stir together the maple syrup and Courvoisier in a small saucepan and warm over low heat.

6. Dust the French toast and cheese with additional confectioners' sugar. Serve on individual plates, topped with sliced strawberries. Pass the warm syrup-Courvoisier mixture on the side.

Sweet Matzoh Brei

 Serves 4

Anne Rosenzweig, Arcadia, New York, New York

A breakfast specialty of the Jewish Passover season, when only the unleavened bread known as matzoh is eaten, matzoh brei—a dish akin to French toast—may be found on delicatessen breakfast menus year round. Anne Rosenzweig's version gains extra tang and mellowness from buttermilk and brown sugar—untraditional additions that seem as if they were always meant to be a part of the dish. Anne suggests serving the matzoh brei with applesauce or strawberry jam—both traditional accompaniments.

8 whole matzohs, broken into
  2-inch pieces

4 extra-large eggs, lightly beaten

1/2 cup buttermilk

1/4 cup packed light brown sugar

1/4 teaspoon ground cinnamon

Pinch of salt

3 tablespoons unsalted butter

1. Bring a kettle of water to a boil. Put the matzoh pieces in a large mixing bowl and pour boiling water over them to cover. Leave them to soak for 5 minutes, then drain well in a sieve or strainer.

2. In the bowl, whisk together the eggs, buttermilk, brown sugar, cinnamon, and salt. Add the drained matzohs and toss gently to coat them evenly.

3. In a large, heavy skillet, melt the butter over medium heat. As soon as it begins to foam but before it browns, pour in the matzoh mixture and cook, gently stirring and turning the matzoh pieces with a spatula, until golden brown on both sides, 5 to 7 minutes. Serve immediately.

Savory Matzoh Brei

Anne Rosenzweig, Arcadia, New York, New York

Serves 4

Though less common, savory matzoh brei may be found in some Jewish delicatessens. Anne Rosenzweig adds slowly caramelized onion, and for an interesting contrast she suggests serving it with unsweetened applesauce. "For a very, very unconventional version," says Anne, "add 1/3 cup smoked salmon cut into thin strips to the egg mixture and serve with sour cream and chives."

5 tablespoons unsalted butter	8 whole matzohs, broken into
1 medium-size onion, finely chopped	2-inch pieces
Salt	4 extra-large eggs, lightly beaten
Black pepper	1/2 cup buttermilk

1. Heat a medium-size skillet over medium heat. Add 2 tablespoons of the butter, reduce the heat to low, and add the onion. Cook, stirring occasionally, until the onion is golden, about 1/2 hour. Remove from the heat, season to taste with salt and pepper, and leave to cool at room temperature.

2. Bring a kettle of water to a boil. Put the matzoh pieces in a large mixing bowl and pour boiling water over them to cover. Leave them to soak for 5 minutes, then drain well in a sieve or strainer.

3. In the bowl, whisk together the eggs, buttermilk, and onions. Add the drained matzohs and toss gently to coat them evenly, adding salt and pepper to taste.

4. In a large, heavy skillet over medium heat, melt the remaining butter. As soon as it begins to foam but before it browns, pour in the matzoh mixture and cook, gently stirring and turning the matzoh pieces with a spatula until golden brown on both sides, 5 to 7 minutes. Serve immediately.

Creamy Polenta

 Serves 4   *Margaret Fox, Cafe Beaujolais, Mendocino, California*

"I think of this as cornmeal mush," says Margaret Fox of this soothing morning or late-night treat. "When I was little my dad used to take my sister and me swimming at night. We'd come back really late, about 8 o'clock, completely famished. My dad would make cornmeal mush and we'd have it with milk and brown sugar on it. I still remember how delicious it was, in that time and place."

3 to 5 cups milk, plus additional for serving

3/4 teaspoon salt

1 cup polenta (see Note)

Maple syrup or dark brown sugar

1. In a medium-size heavy-bottomed saucepan, bring 3 cups of the milk to a simmer over medium heat. Add the salt. Whisking constantly, pour in the polenta in a steady stream; continue cooking, whisking constantly, for 5 minutes, adding more milk if the polenta gets too thick too quickly.

2. Pour into warmed bowls and top with maple syrup or brown sugar and more milk.

NOTE • *Polenta, Italian-style cornmeal, is available in well-stocked supermarkets and Italian delicatessens.*

Corned Beef Hash

George Mahaffey, The Little Nell, Aspen, Colorado

With his precise cubing of the ingredients and the hint of fresh thyme he includes, George Mahaffey adds an easily achieved touch of elegance to this American diner classic. His recipe may sound more complicated than some, but the results are worthy of the effort. You can, if you wish, start with whole cooked corn beef from the deli. Serve the hash on its own, as the recipe describes, or top with poached or fried eggs.

Corned Beef:

2 pounds uncooked corned beef

1 small rib celery, coarsely chopped

1 small onion, coarsely chopped

1 small carrot, coarsely chopped

1 bay leaf

1 tablespoon pickling spices

Hash Mixture:

1 pound Idaho or other baking potatoes, peeled and cut into 3/8-inch dice

Mild vegetable oil

2 medium-size red, yellow, or green bell peppers, halved, stemmed, seeded, and cut into 3/8-inch squares

1 small white onion, cut into 1/4-inch dice

1 rib celery, cut into 1/4-inch dice

2 tablespoons finely chopped Italian parsley

1 teaspoon finely chopped fresh thyme

1 teaspoon black pepper

Italian parsley sprigs

1 cup tomato ketchup

For the corned beef:

1. Put the beef, celery, onion, carrot, bay leaf, and spices in a 5-quart pot or Dutch oven. Add cold water to cover completely. Bring to a boil, then reduce the heat to a simmer. Cover and cook until the beef is tender enough for a sharp, thin-bladed knife to be inserted in its thickest part without the slightest resistance, 2 1/2 to 3 hours. Halfway through the cooking, carefully turn over the meat so it will cook evenly. Check the water level occasionally and top it up as necessary to keep the meat covered.

2. Let the beef cool to room temperature in its broth. Reserve and strain 3/4 cup of the cooking liquid. Refrigerate the beef overnight.

To make the hash:

1. First remove the beef from the refrigerator and trim off all traces of fat from its outside and between the muscles. With a sharp knife, cut the beef across the grain into 3/8-inch-thick slices. Cut the slices into 3/8-inch-wide strips; then cut across the strips to make 3/8-inch dice. The yield should be approximately 4 cups; reserve any extra for another use.

2. Bring a medium-size saucepan of water to a boil. Add the potatoes and cook just until tender. Drain and reserve.

3. In a medium-size skillet, heat a thin film of the vegetable oil over medium heat; add the peppers, onion, and celery and cook, stirring, for 2 minutes.

4. Put the corned beef cubes, potatoes, peppers, onion, celery, parsley, thyme, and pepper in a large mixing bowl. Toss them together until well mixed. Pour the reserved cooking liquid over them and toss again.

5. Preheat the oven to 300°F.

6. In a 10-inch nonstick skillet, heat a film of vegetable oil over medium heat. Evenly spread half the hash mixture in the skillet and cook, without stirring, until the bottom is crisp and lightly browned, about 5 minutes.

7. Invert a large, ovenproof platter over the skillet and, carefully holding the platter and skillet together, invert them to unmold the hash onto the platter. Set aside.

8. In the same way, cook the remaining hash mixture and invert it onto another platter. Put the platters in the preheated oven and bake for about 5 more minutes.

9. While the hash finishes cooking, warm the ketchup in a small saucepan and transfer to a sauceboat.

10. Garnish the platters of hash with parsley and serve them family style, passing warm ketchup on the side.

Fried Mush

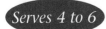

Margaret Fox, Cafe Beaujolais, Mendocino, California

Margaret Fox recalls that her mom would turn any leftover Creamy Polenta (page 125) into fried mush for breakfast, "which we'd drown in maple syrup." This version of the polenta, made with water instead of milk, holds out the versatile option of serving the fried mush either sweet or savory—topped with syrup or with tomato sauce and melted cheese.

5 cups water

1 teaspoon salt

1 2/3 cups polenta (see Note)

1/2 cup (1 stick) plus 2 tablespoons unsalted butter

1/2 cup yellow cornmeal

1. Put the water and salt in a heavy-bottomed medium-size saucepan over medium heat. Bring to a boil and, stirring constantly, slowly sprinkle in the polenta. Reduce the heat and continue stirring; after 15 minutes, the mixture will be very thick. Stir in the 2 tablespoons of butter.

2. Pour the polenta into a buttered 8-by-4-by-3-inch loaf pan. Cover with plastic wrap and refrigerate at least 8 hours or overnight.

3. Dip the pan into a larger pan or sink filled with hot water to loosen the polenta loaf. With a knife, gently loosen the sides and invert the pan onto a flat surface. Lift off the pan. Cut the loaf crosswise into 1/2-inch-thick slices. Dredge them in the yellow cornmeal.

4. In a large skillet over medium heat, melt the remaining butter. Add the polenta slices and cook until golden brown, about 10 minutes per side.

NOTE • *Polenta, Italian-style cornmeal, is available in well-stocked supermarkets and Italian delicatessens.*

chapter

3

Side Dishes and Breads

Often it's the little things—the potatoes and other vegetables, the beans and rices, the sauces and pickles, the hot-from-the-oven breads—that truly make a meal seem special. In the realm of comforting food, their importance grows even greater.

Try to think of a satisfying dinner, for example, that *didn't* have some form of potato or other starchy accompaniment. Picture the pleasure that comes from a smoothly pureed vegetable or a scoop of savory slow-cooked beans. Imagine butter melting into a just-baked muffin or a slice of crusty bread. Such mental images make you feel better just by bringing them to mind.

Some of the recipes that follow take a relatively short while to prepare; others—particularly the yeast-leavened breads—call for longer, more attentive preparation. All hold forth the opportunity to bring satisfaction to every meal.

Creamy Mashed Potatoes

Faz Poursohi, Circolo, Faz Cafe, and Cafe Latte, San Francisco, California

Serves 4 to 6

"The warm, creamy texture of these mashed potatoes complements virtually all foods," says Faz Poursohi. "And they also taste great on their own."

4 large baking potatoes, peeled and
  cut into quarters

1/4 cup (1/2 stick) unsalted butter,
  cut into small pieces

1/2 cup sour cream

Salt

Pepper

1. Put the potatoes in a medium-size saucepan with cold, salted water to cover. Bring to a boil over high heat. Reduce the heat to medium and simmer until the potatoes are tender, about 20 minutes. Holding the lid of the pan ajar to hold in the potatoes, carefully drain them.

2. With a potato masher, mash the potatoes in the pan until no lumps remain. Add the butter and beat it in with a wooden spoon. Beat in the sour cream and salt and pepper to taste. Serve immediately.

Garlic Mashed Potatoes Ali-Bab

Michel Richard, Citrus, Los Angeles, California; Citronelle, Santa Barbara, California, Baltimore, Maryland, and Washington, D.C.; Michel's Bistro, Philadelphia, Pennsylvania; and Bistro M, San Francisco, California

Serves 4

Boiling and rinsing garlic cloves four times in the preparation of the garlic cream makes them taste mild and sweet, adding beguiling flavor and richness to this exceptional recipe for mashed potatoes. Try them with Michel Richard's Steak with Shallot Sauce (page 61).

Michel points out that much of the work can be done in advance: The garlic cream may be prepared well ahead and refrigerated. The potatoes can be pureed and left in their pan, covered, at room temperature, for an hour or more. Or the full recipe may be completed up to 1 hour before serving and kept warm by setting its cooking vessel in a larger pan of gently simmering water and stirring the potatoes occasionally.

Garlic Cream:

8 large cloves garlic, peeled

1/4 cup heavy cream

Potato Puree:

1 pound russet potatoes, peeled and quartered

1/4 cup heavy cream

6 tablespoons (3/4 stick) unsalted butter, at room temperature, cut into pieces

Salt

Black pepper

For the garlic cream:

1. Put the garlic in a medium-size heavy saucepan. Add 3 inches of cold water. Bring to a boil over medium heat. Drain the garlic and rinse with cold water. Repeat the boiling, draining, and rinsing two more times.

2. Coarsely chop the garlic and return it to the saucepan, adding 1/4 cup cream. Bring to a boil over medium heat; then lower the heat to low and simmer gently, stirring occasionally, until the cream has reduced by half to a thick, saucelike consistency, 3 to 5 minutes.

For the potato puree:

1. Put the potatoes in a medium-size saucepan with cold, salted water to cover. Bring to a boil over high heat. Reduce the heat to low and simmer until the potatoes are tender, about 20 minutes. Drain well and remove the potatoes from the pan.

2. Set a large-holed sieve or a food mill with the coarse disk over the same pan. Press the potatoes through the sieve or work through the food mill.

3. Before serving, put the garlic cream in a small saucepan. Stir in the other 1/4 cup of cream and place over medium-low heat, stirring occasionally, until warmed, 2 to 3 minutes.

4. Put the pan of pureed potatoes over medium-high heat and stir with a wooden spatula until they are warmed through and dried out, 3 to 5 minutes. Several pieces at a time, stir in the butter. Stirring constantly, pour in the warm garlic cream in a slow stream. Season to taste with salt and pepper and serve immediately.

Glazed Fennel Mashed Potatoes

Matthew Kenney, Matthew's, New York, New York

Matthew Kenney imaginatively adds color to classic mashed potatoes, while subtly emphasizing their mellow sweetness, by combining them with green fennel stalks from the herb, not from its close cousin, bulb fennel—that have been quickly glazed with butter and a little sugar.

Serve them with Matthew's Herb-Crusted Chicken (page 60), or as a side dish to any poultry, meat, or seafood.

Mashed Potatoes:

2 pounds Idaho potatoes, peeled
  and cut into 2-inch chunks

1/2 cup heavy cream

1/2 cup milk

1/4 cup (1/2 stick) unsalted butter

Salt

White pepper

Glazed Fennel:

3/4 pound fresh fennel stalks and fronds

2 tablespoons unsalted butter

2 tablespoons sugar

1 teaspoon grated lemon zest

Salt

White pepper

For the mashed potatoes:

1. Put the potatoes in a medium-size saucepan with cold salted water to cover. Bring to a boil over high heat. Reduce the heat to medium low and simmer until the potatoes are tender, about 20 minutes.

2. Meanwhile, in a separate medium-size saucepan, bring the cream and milk to a boil over medium heat and simmer briskly until they reduce to 3/4 cup, about 5 minutes.

3. When the potatoes are done, drain them well and add them to the hot cream-and-milk mixture with the butter and salt and pepper to taste. Pass them through a food mill to puree. Return the puree to the saucepan, cover, and keep warm.

For the glazed fennel:

1. Prepare the fennel while you are cooking the potatoes. Remove and reserve the feathery fronds from the fennel, leaving about 1/2 pound of stalks. Coarsely chop the stalks.

2. Melt the butter and sugar in a medium-size nonstick skillet over medium heat. Add the fennel stalks and cook, stirring, until the sugar begins to caramelize and coat the fennel, 3 to 5 minutes. When the caramel turns brown, a minute or so more, stir in the lemon zest and remove the skillet from the heat. Season to taste with salt and pepper. Keep warm.

3. When both the fennel and the potatoes are ready, stir the glazed fennel stalks into the mashed potatoes over medium-low heat until warmed through. Transfer to a serving dish or individual plates and garnish with the reserved fennel fronds. Serve immediately.

Potato Pancakes

Serves 4 to 6   *The Haussner Family, Haussner's Restaurant, Baltimore, Maryland*

These traditional potato pancakes, excellent with any roast or braised meat or poultry, may also be served as a breakfast or brunch main course. Francie George of Haussner's suggests accompanying them with both applesauce and cranberry sauce.

1 teaspoon lemon juice

1 pound Idaho or other baking potatoes, scrubbed

1 large egg, lightly beaten

3/4 cup all-purpose flour

2 tablespoons finely chopped onion

Salt

White pepper

Mild vegetable oil

1. Fill a large mixing bowl with cold water and add the lemon juice. Peel the potatoes and, as each is peeled, put it in the water.

2. One by one, remove each potato, pat it dry, and finely grate it, using a handheld grater or the grating disk of a food processor. Put the grated potatoes in a large, clean, dry mixing bowl with the egg, all-purpose flour, onion, salt, and pepper to taste and 1 tablespoon of the vegetable oil. Mix well.

3. In a large, nonstick skillet, pour in enough oil to cover the bottom. Heat over medium to high heat. When the oil is hot, form each pancake by spooning 2 tablespoons of the potato mixture into the skillet and lightly flattening it to a 3-inch circle; take care not to crowd the skillet. Cook the pancakes until golden brown, 3 to 4 minutes per side. Drain on paper towels and keep warm while cooking the remaining batter. Serve as soon as possible.

Roast Potatoes with Garlic Mayonnaise

Alice Waters, Chez Panisse, Berkeley, California

"Garlic, they say, is as good as 10 mothers," says Alice Waters of this recipe. She advises making this in early summer, when little new potatoes are young and small and suggests trying this recipe with Yellow Finnish, Rose Fir, or Fingerling varieties.

Roast Potatoes:

20 to 24 small new potatoes, scrubbed and patted dry

1 1/2 tablespoons olive oil

Salt

Black pepper

2 or 3 sprigs each thyme and rosemary

2 bay leaves

Garlic Mayonnaise:

1 large egg yolk, at room temperature (see Note)

Salt

1 cup light olive oil or mild vegetable oil

1 teaspoon warm water

1/2 clove garlic

1/4 to 1/2 teaspoon white or red wine vinegar or lemon juice

Pepper

For the potatoes:

1. Preheat the oven to 375°F.

2. If the potatoes are very small, don't cut them; otherwise, cut them into halves or quarters. Put them in an earthenware or ceramic ovenproof dish. Pour the olive oil over them and season to taste with salt and pepper. Add the herbs and stir to coat the potatoes with the oil.

3. Bake, uncovered, stirring occasionally, until the potatoes are tender and browned, 50 to 60 minutes.

For the mayonnaise:

1. While the potatoes are baking, make the mayonnaise. Put the egg yolk in a medium-size mixing bowl and season with a good pinch of salt. Set the bowl on a damp dish towel so it won't slip and slide while you're mixing.

2. Put the oil in a container with a pour spout. With a whisk, mix the egg yolk and salt together. Whisking all the time, slowly add the oil to the egg yolk *drop by drop*. It will thicken gradually as the egg absorbs the oil.

3. The mayonnaise will start to get quite thick after you have mixed in about 1/4 cup oil. Thin it by adding 1/2 teaspoon of the warm water; then continue to add the oil in a thin, steady stream. It will be quite thick again after you have mixed in about 3/4 cup oil. Thin again with 1/2 teaspoon warm water, and whisk in the remaining oil in a steady stream.

4. Make a puree of the garlic by pounding it in a mortar with a pestle until smooth and juicy; or rub it against the tines of a fork held against the bottom of a small mixing bowl. Add about half the puree to the mayonnaise.

5. Finish the seasoning by adding about 1/4 teaspoon vinegar or lemon juice and a pinch of salt and pepper. Taste and add more vinegar, lemon juice, or salt if needed and more garlic puree if you like.

6. When the potatoes are done, serve them hot with the garlic mayonnaise alongside for dipping.

NOTE • *If you are concerned about the question of possible salmonella contamination in raw eggs, substitute a good-quality commercial mayonnaise as the base of the garlic mayonnaise in this recipe.*

Potato Leek Gratin

Maria Helm, The Sherman House, San Francisco, California

If you really want to indulge yourself, suggests Maria Helm, you can "eat a big bowl of this warm, rich, earthy gratin all by itself." More conventionally, serve it with a meatloaf, a stew, or grilled or broiled poultry, seafood, or meat.

1/4 cup unsalted butter

1 large leek, white and light green parts only, halved lengthwise, thoroughly washed and coarsely chopped

5 large white or baking potatoes, peeled and thinly sliced

2 1/2 cups heavy cream

1 1/2 cups milk

Dash of grated nutmeg

Salt

Pepper

1. In a large saucepan, melt half the butter over medium heat. Add the leek and cook, stirring, until tender, about 5 minutes.

2. Preheat the oven to 400°F. With the remaining butter, grease a 9-inch gratin dish.

3. Add the potatoes, cream, and milk to the saucepan. Stir in the nutmeg and the salt and pepper to taste. Continue cooking, stirring gently from time to time, until the liquid thickens, 15 to 20 minutes. Taste and add a little more salt and pepper if necessary.

4. Pour the potato-leek mixture into the gratin dish and smooth its surface. Bake until the potatoes are tender and the top of the gratin is golden brown, about 30 minutes. Serve immediately.

Baked Eggplant with Fresh Oregano and Balsamic Vinegar Glaze

Bobby Flay, BOLO, New York, New York

Serves 8

"The combination of flavors, the sweetness of the balsamic glaze, and the richness of the cheese make this dish a natural heartwarmer," says Bobby Flay. Serve the eggplant with roasted or grilled meat or poultry.

8 medium-size globe eggplants, peeled and cut lengthwise into 1/4-inch-thick slices

1/4 cup olive oil

Salt

Pepper

Paprika

8 cups good-quality balsamic vinegar

1 pound Manchego or Parmesan cheese, cut into 20 thin slices

1 bunch fresh oregano, leaves coarsely chopped

1. Preheat the oven to 375°F.

2. Place the eggplant slices in a single layer on one or more greased baking sheets. Brush both sides of each slice with olive oil and season to taste with salt, pepper, and paprika. Bake until tender and lightly browned, about 25 minutes. Remove from the oven and let cool.

3. Meanwhile, prepare the balsamic vinegar glaze. Put the vinegar in a medium-size saucepan and bring to a slow boil over medium heat. Reduce the heat to maintain a simmer and cook the vinegar until it reduces by about three-quarters to a syrupy consistency, 30 to 40 minutes.

4. When the eggplant slices are cool, stack them on one of the baking sheets. Begin with a slice of eggplant. Top it with cheese and some oregano. Repeat until you've formed 5 layers of eggplant, finishing with a slice of eggplant without the cheese or oregano. Repeat with the remaining eggplant, cheese, and oregano, making 8 rustic stacks in all. Return the stacks to the oven and bake them until they are heated through and the cheese has melted, about 10 minutes more.

5. Cut each eggplant stack crosswise in half. Spoon the vinegar glaze over the eggplant and top with oregano. Serve immediately.

Pureed Pumpkin or Banana Squash

Carlo Middione, Vivande, San Francisco, California

Serves 6

Carlo Middione finds amazing versatility in this simple puree of winter squash. "It is a fine accompaniment to roasted chicken or roasted or grilled meats," he begins. "It is also terrific for breakfast and makes a super snack. If you have any left over—and I always make extra because it's cheap and so easy—you can add enough tasty chicken stock to make a nice, glossy soup, adding some diced potatoes or a little rice if you want to."

Carlo cautions that so many pumpkins sold around Halloween are thin-fleshed to make carving into jack-o'-lanterns easy. If you can't find a choice, fleshy pumpkin, he suggests substituting the widely available banana squash, also known as Hubbard squash.

2 1/2 pounds thick-fleshed pumpkin or banana squash, thoroughly peeled and cut into 1 1/2-inch cubes

4 or more tablespoons extra-virgin olive oil

3/4 cup water

2 whole heads garlic, unpeeled

14 fresh mint leaves, finely chopped

Sea salt

Black pepper

1. Preheat the oven to 375°F.

2. Put the pumpkin cubes in a roasting pan and toss them with about 2 tablespoons of the olive oil. Add the water to the pan. Cover with aluminum foil or a lid and bake for 1 1/4 hours.

3. Raise the oven temperature to 425°F.

4. Rub the whole heads of garlic with some of the olive oil and place them on a pie pan. Put the pan in the oven with the pumpkin. Uncover the pumpkin. Continue baking until the garlic heads feel nicely soft when squeezed and the pumpkin is tender and slightly browned, 40 to 45 minutes more.

5. Transfer the pumpkin to a large, warmed mixing bowl. Protecting your hands with a folded kitchen towel and using a serrated knife, carefully cut the garlic heads horizontally in halves. Squeeze the roasted garlic out of the heads into the bowl with the pumpkin. Add the mint, sea salt to taste, and plenty of black pepper.

6. Mash thoroughly with a potato masher or ricer, stirring in a little more olive oil if necessary to give it a moist, smooth consistency and adding more salt and pepper to taste. Serve hot.

Summer Mediterranean Gratin

Gary Danko, The Dining Room at The Ritz-Carlton Hotel, San Francisco, California

Serves 12 side dishes, 6 main courses

Think of this fragrant gratin as a cross between ratatouille and eggplant parmigiana. Like both of those dishes, the gratin may be served either as a side dish to roasted or grilled meats or as a vegetarian main course. Either way, Gary says, "The gratin tastes best if allowed to mellow at least half an hour after cooking."

One 1 1/2-pound eggplant, peeled and cut crosswise into 1/4-inch-thick slices

1 cup olive oil

Salt

Black pepper

1 1/2 pounds zucchini, trimmed and cut crosswise into 1/4-inch-thick slices

3 medium-size onions, finely chopped

1 1/2 pounds bulb fennel, trimmed and cut into 1/4-inch-thick slices

1 cup grated Parmesan cheese (preferably Parmigiano-Reggiano)

1/2 cup dry bread crumbs

1/4 cup coarsely chopped fresh basil leaves

1/4 cup coarsely chopped fresh chervil leaves

1/4 cup coarsely chopped Italian parsley

1/4 cup coarsely chopped fresh chives or green onion tops

2 tablespoons coarsely chopped fresh thyme leaves

1 1/2 pounds firm ripe tomatoes, cut into 1/4-inch-thick slices

1. Preheat the oven to 450°F.

2. Put the eggplant slices in a single layer on a heavy baking sheet and lightly brush both sides with olive oil. Bake until their undersides are golden brown, about 10 minutes. Turn them over and bake about 5 minutes more. Remove them from the oven and let cool. Season lightly with salt and pepper and set aside.

3. Heat a large skillet over medium-high heat. Add 3 tablespoons of the olive oil and the zucchini slices. Raise the heat to high and cook, stirring, until lightly browned on both sides, about 4 minutes. Sprinkle lightly with salt and transfer the zucchini to a colander in the sink to drain.

4. In the same skillet over medium heat, add 3 more tablespoons of olive oil and the onions. Cook, stirring, until the onions start to turn translucent, about 4 minutes. Add the fennel, reduce the heat to low, and cook, stirring occasionally, until the fennel is tender, about 30 minutes. Season to taste with salt and pepper and let cool.

5. Preheat the oven to 400°F.

6. In a medium-size mixing bowl, toss together the Parmesan cheese, bread crumbs, herbs, and salt and pepper to taste.

7. To assemble the gratin, lightly brush a gratin dish measuring about 16 inches by 10 inches with olive oil. Spread a third of the onion-fennel mixture on the bottom. Sprinkle with some of Parmesan–bread crumb mixture and a little salt and pepper. Cover with one layer of sliced tomatoes, slightly overlapping, then a layer of zucchini, then eggplant slices, sprinkling each vegetable layer with more of the Parmesan bread crumbs. Repeat the layering, ending with a layer of tomatoes and topping with the remaining Parmesan bread crumbs. Drizzle lightly with olive oil.

8. Bake the gratin until bubbly and lightly browned, 30 to 40 minutes. Remove the dish from the oven and let the gratin rest for at least 30 minutes. Serve warm or at room temperature.

Compote of Smoked Bacon, Wild Mushrooms, Glazed Sweet Potatoes, and Pecans

Serves 4

Dean Fearing, The Mansion on Turtle Creek, Dallas, Texas

Filled with rich autumnal flavors, this side dish accompanies Dean Fearing's Beef Tenderloin Marinated in Molasses and Black Pepper. The compote is also excellent with other meats or poultry, especially for a festive holiday dinner; if you wish to serve it apart from the beef, prepare half the marinade mixture given in that recipe for use in the compote's preparation.

The quantities given below for the glazed pecans, by the way, will yield about twice as much as you'll need for the recipe, but that's all for the best: They make a delicious little snack.

Glazed Pecans:

1/2 cup water

1/2 cup sugar

2 small dried red chilies

1 cup shelled pecan halves

2 tablespoons molasses

Compote:

1/2 cup reserved molasses marinade from Beef Tenderloin Marinated in Molasses and Black Pepper (page 62)

4 cups veal or chicken stock, boiled briskly until reduced to 1 cup total, 25 to 30 minutes

1/2 pound slab bacon, cut into 1/2-inch dice

1 tablespoon mild vegetable oil

1/2 pound fresh wild mushrooms of any type, trimmed, large ones cut into halves or quarters

2 tablespoons unsalted butter

One 1/2-pound sweet potato, peeled and cut into balls with a melon baller

1/2 pound pearl onions, peeled

1 tablespoon brown sugar

2 teaspoons cider vinegar

Salt

Lemon juice

For the glazed pecans:

1. Preheat the oven to 250°F.

2. In a small saucepan, stir together the water, sugar, and chilies. Bring to a boil over high heat and stir in the pecans. Bring the mixture back to a boil, then reduce the heat to low and simmer, stirring occasionally with a wooden spoon, for 10 minutes.

3. Carefully drain the pecans over the sink and spread on a small baking sheet or baking dish in a single layer. Bake for 45 minutes, stirring occasionally.

4. Remove the pecans from the oven and empty into a small mixing bowl. Add the molasses and toss to coat the pecans evenly. Return them to the baking sheet or dish and bake until very crisp and crunchy but not yet burned, about 45 minutes more. Set aside.

For the compote:

1. Put the marinade in a small saucepan and boil over medium-high heat until reduced by half, about 5 minutes. Stir in the reduced stock and bring the mixture back to a boil. Reduce the heat to low and simmer until the mixture is thick enough to coat the back of a spoon, about 5 minutes more. Remove from the heat, cover, and keep warm.

2. In a small sauté pan or skillet, cook the bacon over medium-high heat, stirring, until it is golden brown and its fat has been rendered, 5 to 7 minutes. Drain off the fat and reserve the bacon.

3. Heat the oil in a medium-size sauté pan or skillet over medium-high heat. Add the mushrooms and cook them, stirring, until tender and lightly browned, about 3 minutes. Remove from the pan and set aside.

4. Preheat the oven to 350°F.

5. In a medium-size ovenproof sauté pan or skillet, melt the butter over medium heat. Add the sweet potato balls and pearl onions and cook, stirring, for 3 minutes. Stir in the brown sugar and cider vinegar and cook, stirring, for 2 minutes more.

6. Put the pan in the oven and cook, stirring occasionally, to glaze the ingredients evenly until the sweet potatoes and onions are tender, 7 to 10 minutes more. Remove from the oven and stir in the bacon, mushrooms, reduced marinade, and 1/2 cup of the glazed pecans. Season to taste with salt and lemon juice and serve immediately.

Spiced Cranberry Sauce

Cory Schreiber, Wildwood, Portland, Oregon

About 4 cups

No food at traditional holiday meals probably excites more passionate feelings than the cranberry sauce, with camps clearly divided between jellied and whole berries and whether or not they should be embellished or eaten straight from the can.

Cory Schreiber's recipe adds a new twist to the debate, combining fresh or frozen whole cranberries with an assortment of sweet and sour liquids and a wide spectrum of spices. The effect is incredibly aromatic—and unlike any cranberry sauce you've tasted before. Multiply the quantities, depending on how many people you'll be feeding.

1 1/2 pounds whole cranberries, fresh or frozen (no need to thaw)

1 1/4 cups red wine

3/4 cup plus 1 tablespoon balsamic vinegar

3/4 cup plus 1 tablespoon frozen orange juice concentrate

3/4 cup plus 1 tablespoon sugar

1 cinnamon stick

2 teaspoons fennel seeds

2 teaspoons black peppercorns

1 teaspoon juniper berries

1 teaspoon whole cloves

1. Put the cranberries, wine, vinegar, orange juice concentrate, and sugar in a large nonreactive saucepan. Add the cinnamon stick.

2. Put the fennel seeds, black peppercorns, juniper berries, and cloves in a spice mill and grind them coarsely. Add them to the pan.

3. Bring the ingredients to a boil over medium-high heat. Then, reduce the heat to low and simmer, stirring occasionally, until the mixture is thick and the cranberries are very soft, 30 to 40 minutes. Let cool to room temperature. Transfer to a bowl, cover, and chill in the refrigerator before serving.

Bread and Butter Pickles

 8 pints

Peter Harvey, Lake Merced Golf and Country Club, Daly City, California

Peter Harvey finds these sweet-sour pickles reminiscent of a picnic lunch on a summer's afternoon. He cautions against overcooking them and spoiling their crispness. Be sure to follow all manufacturer's instructions for the canning jars you use. If you don't want to mess with the sterilizing and canning procedure, cut the quantities and just refrigerate the pickles, making sure you prepare only enough to eat within a few days.

25 large pickling cucumbers, washed and cut into 1/4-inch-thick slices

12 large onions, cut into 1/4-inch-thick slices

6 large red bell peppers, quartered lengthwise, stemmed and seeded, quarters cut crosswise into 1/4-inch-wide strips

1/2 cup kosher salt

1 quart champagne vinegar

2 cups sugar

1 cup water

2 teaspoons whole yellow mustard seeds

2 teaspoons whole celery seeds

2 teaspoons ground turmeric

2 whole cloves

1. Wash and sterilize 8 pint-sized canning jars, lids, and seals.

2. In a large mixing bowl, toss the cucumbers, onions, and peppers with the salt and leave at room temperature, loosely covered, for 2 hours.

3. In a large nonreactive saucepan, combine the vinegar, sugar, water, mustard, and celery seeds, turmeric, and cloves. Bring to a boil over medium-high heat; then reduce the heat to medium-low and simmer for 10 minutes.

4. Rinse and drain the cucumbers, onions, and peppers and stir them into the simmering brine mixture. Return the pan to medium-high heat and bring the mixture to a full rolling boil. Then remove it from the heat immediately and transfer the vegetables to the sterilized jars, pouring the brine over them. Seal the jars, turn them over, and let them stand overnight to cool. Refrigerate before serving and keep refrigerated after opening.

Fresh Pickled Tomatoes

Serves 8 to 12   *Cory Schreiber, Wildwood, Portland, Oregon*

With its surprising mixture of sweet, sour, spicy, and hot sensations, this recipe from Cory Schreiber matches the pleasures of painstakingly made preserved pickles without the bother of sterilizing or canning. Serve it alongside sandwiches or grilled foods for an outdoor summer lunch or dinner.

3 pounds firm, ripe tomatoes, cored and cut into 1/2-inch-thick slices

2 bunches green onions, trimmed and cut crosswise into 1/4-inch-thick slices

2 jalapeño chilies, halved, stemmed, seeded, and finely chopped

2 cups olive oil

1/2 cup peeled and grated fresh ginger

3 tablespoons ground cumin

2 tablespoons whole black or yellow mustard seed

1 1/2 tablespoons ground black pepper

1 tablespoon curry powder

1 tablespoon paprika

1 1/2 cups rice vinegar

1/2 cup red wine vinegar

3/4 cup packed light brown sugar

1 1/2 tablespoons salt

1. Put the tomatoes, green onions, and jalapeños in a large mixing bowl and toss together. Set aside.

2. In a medium-size saucepan, heat the olive oil over medium heat. When it just begins to get hot, remove the oil from the heat and stir in the ginger, cumin, mustard seed, black pepper, curry powder, and paprika. Set aside.

3. Put the vinegars, brown sugar, and salt in a small nonreactive saucepan and stir over medium heat until the sugar and salt dissolve and the mixture is warm.

4. When the olive oil is warm but no longer hot, stir the warm vinegar into it. Pour the mixture over the tomatoes and toss well. Serve warm or cover and refrigerate until cold.

Grandma Wetzler's Baked Beans

Serves 10   *Chris Schlesinger, East Coast Grill, Cambridge, Massachusetts*

"Made from my grandma's Pennsylvania Dutch recipe, these beans just can't be beat," says Chris Schlesinger. "They're filling, satisfying, and slightly sweet." He recommends this recipe as "a virtually indispensable accompaniment" to any picnic food or barbecue. The beans will keep well in the refrigerator, covered, for up to a week and only improve with reheating.

1/2 pound bacon, coarsely chopped

1 onion, finely chopped

1 gallon water

1/2 cup molasses

1/2 cup packed dark brown sugar

2 cups ketchup

2 tablespoons yellow mustard

1 1/4 pounds navy beans, picked over to remove any stones or impurities, thoroughly washed, and soaked overnight in cold water to cover

Salt

Black pepper

1. In a large pot, cook the bacon over medium heat, stirring, until browned. Add the onion and cook, stirring until browned, 5 to 7 minutes. Stir in the water, molasses, brown sugar, ketchup, and mustard. Bring to a boil.

2. Drain the beans and add them. Bring the mixture back to a full boil, then reduce the heat to low and simmer very gently until the beans are soft, 4 to 5 hours. Add water from time to time if necessary and stir often to prevent burning. Season to taste with salt and pepper.

Lentils with Crisp Bacon

Serves 4

Sarah Stegner, The Dining Room at The Ritz-Carlton, Chicago, Illinois

Try this earthy, aromatic side dish alongside roasted chicken or ham.

16 strips bacon

2 ribs celery, each cut into 4 pieces

1 medium-size carrot, cut into 4 pieces

1 medium-size onion, peeled and studded with 2 whole cloves

4 cups chicken stock or water

2 cups dried green lentils, picked over to remove any stones or impurities and rinsed well

8 cloves garlic, peeled

2 bay leaves

1 small bunch fresh thyme sprigs

Black pepper

2 tablespoons olive oil

4 medium-size shallots, thinly sliced

1/4 cup finely chopped Italian parsley

Salt

1. In a medium-size saucepan, cook the bacon over medium heat until crisp, 5 to 7 minutes. Remove the bacon from the pan and drain on paper towels.

2. In the bacon fat still over medium heat, cook the celery, carrot, and onion, stirring, until lightly browned, about 5 minutes. Add the stock or water, lentils, garlic, bay leaves, thyme sprigs, and pepper to taste. Bring to a boil, then reduce the heat to low and simmer, uncovered, until the lentils are tender, about 40 minutes; if necessary, add a little more stock or water to the pan during cooking to keep the lentils submerged.

3. With a large spoon, remove and discard the celery, carrot, onion, garlic, bay leaves, and thyme.

4. In a small skillet, heat the olive oil over medium heat. Add the shallots and cook, stirring, until brown and crisp, 5 to 7 minutes.

5. Add the shallots and parsley to the lentils, crumble in the bacon, and stir gently. Season to taste with salt and pepper and serve immediately.

Lemon Risotto

Barr Hogen, Project Open Hand, San Francisco, California

Serves 4

Barr Hogen suggests serving this creamy, citrusy side dish as an accompaniment to her Lemon Herb Roasted Chicken Breasts with Orange (page 89).

1 teaspoon finely chopped fresh mint	3/4 teaspoon salt
1 teaspoon finely chopped fresh sage	1 1/2 cups Arborio rice
Zest of 1 lemon	1/2 cup lemon juice
5 cups low-sodium chicken broth	1/2 cup grated Parmesan cheese
2 tablespoons unsalted butter	1/2 teaspoon white pepper
2 shallots, finely chopped	

1. In a small bowl, toss together the herbs and lemon zest.

2. Put the broth in a medium-size saucepan and warm over medium heat.

3. In a large nonreactive saucepan, melt the butter over medium heat. Add the shallots and 1/4 teaspoon of the salt and cook, stirring, until tender, about 3 minutes. Add the rice and stir to coat all the grains.

4. Stir in 1/2 cup of the broth and stir constantly until it is absorbed; continue this process until all the broth has been absorbed, about 20 minutes total. Toward the end, check the rice to make sure it is tender.

5. Stir in the herbs, lemon juice, Parmesan, remaining salt, and the pepper. Remove from the heat and let stand for 2 minutes before serving.

Three-Grain Risotto

Serves 4 *Ercolino Crugnale, Stouffer Stanford Court Hotel, San Francisco, California*

"A healthy combination of hearty grains, this dish satisfies generously," says Ercolino Crugnale. The key to achieving the risotto's complex texture comes in partially cooking each grain first separately, one after the other or at the same time, depending on how many pots and burners you have available; this step can be done in advance. Then, about half an hour before serving, the grains are cooked a final time all together.

Ercolino recommends serving the risotto as an accompaniment to grilled chicken, fish, or beef, and also suggests that you might like to try it as a simple appetizer.

Rice:

3/4 cup chicken stock

1/2 cup arborio rice

1 bay leaf

Pinch of salt

Quinoa:

1 1/2 cups chicken stock

1/2 cup quinoa, rinsed under cold running water until the water runs clear (see Note)

1 sprig fresh thyme (optional)

Pinch of salt

Barley:

3 cups chicken stock

1/2 cup pearl barley, rinsed under cold running water until the water runs clear

1 rib celery, cut into 4 pieces

Pinch of salt

Assembly:

1 tablespoon olive oil

2 tablespoons finely chopped garlic

1 cup diced fresh tomato

1 cup chicken stock

3 tablespoons unsalted butter

3 tablespoons grated Parmesan cheese

Salt

Black pepper

For the rice:

Combine the stock, rice, bay leaf, and salt in a small saucepan. Bring to a brisk simmer over medium heat. Reduce the heat to low, cover, and cook, stirring occasionally, for about 15 minutes. Spread the rice on a large plate to cool. Remove and discard the bay leaf.

For the quinoa:

Combine the stock, quinoa, thyme, and salt in a small saucepan. Bring to a brisk simmer over medium heat. Reduce the heat to low, cover, and cook, stirring occasionally, for about 15 minutes. Remove the pan from the stove and leave it, covered, for 10 minutes more. Strain off any unabsorbed liquid and spread the quinoa on a large plate to cool. Remove and discard the thyme.

For the barley:

Combine the stock, barley, celery, and salt in a small saucepan. Bring to a brisk simmer over medium heat. Reduce the heat to low, cover, and cook, stirring occasionally, for about 30 minutes. Remove the pan from the stove and leave it, covered, for 10 minutes more. Strain off any unabsorbed liquid and spread the barley on a large plate to cool. Remove and discard the celery.

For the final assembly:

1. In a medium-size sauté pan, heat the olive oil over medium-high heat. Add the garlic and cook, stirring constantly, for 1 minute. Stir in the tomato and cook, stirring occasionally, until most of their liquid has evaporated, 7 to 8 minutes.

2. Stir in the stock and partially cooked rice, quinoa, and barley. Reduce the heat to medium to maintain a brisk simmer and cook, stirring constantly, until all but a small quantity of liquid has been absorbed, about 10 minutes more.

3. Stir in the butter and Parmesan cheese, season to taste with salt and pepper, and serve immediately.

NOTE • *Quinoa, an ancient grain gaining in popularity today, may be found in most health food stores.*

Gratin of Polenta, Tomato Fondue, and Sonoma Jack Cheese

Gary Danko, The Dining Room at The Ritz-Carlton Hotel, San Francisco, California

Serves 6

Gary Danko's rich, savory gratin makes a fitting companion to grilled meat, poultry, or seafood. Or try it with eggs as a brunch dish. If you can't find Sonoma Jack cheese, use a good-quality Parmesan. The polenta and fondue may be prepared and refrigerated up to two days in advance.

Oven Polenta:

4 cups water

1/4 cup (1/2 stick) unsalted butter

1/2 medium-size onion, finely chopped

1 cup coarsely ground polenta (preferably Golden Pheasant brand)

1 tablespoon coarse or kosher salt

1 teaspoon coarsely cracked black peppercorns

Tomato Fondue:

1/4 cup extra-virgin olive oil

1 tablespoon unsalted butter

2 medium-size shallots, finely chopped

1 medium-size clove garlic, finely chopped

4 medium-size tomatoes, peeled, halved crosswise, seeded, and finely chopped (see Box, page 3)

1 tablespoon tomato paste

1 tablespoon sugar

1/4 bay leaf

Salt

Black pepper

Assembly:

6 ounces dry Sonoma Jack cheese, cut into thin shavings

1 1/2 cups heavy cream

For the oven polenta:

1. Preheat the oven to 350°F.

2. Bring the water to a boil in a kettle or large saucepan.

3. Meanwhile, in a medium-size ovenproof saucepan, melt the butter over low heat. Add the onion and cook, stirring, until translucent, 4 to 5 minutes. Remove the pan from the heat and stir in the polenta. Stir the coarse salt and cracked pepper into the boiling water; then pour the water over the polenta and stir lightly. Put the pan in the oven and bake the polenta until it is firm but still fluid enough to be spread, about 1 hour.

4. Lightly oil a 10-by-15-inch jelly roll pan. Spread in the polenta, smoothing its surface with a spatula to produce a layer about 1/2 inch thick. Cool to room temperature, then cover with plastic wrap and refrigerate until firm, at least 2 hours.

For the tomato fondue:

1. In a medium-size skillet, heat the olive oil and butter over medium heat. Add the shallots and garlic and cook, stirring, until translucent, 4 to 5 minutes.

2. Stir in the tomatoes, tomato paste, sugar, and bay leaf and cook, stirring occasionally, until the mixture reduces to a thick saucelike consistency, about 20 minutes. Remove and discard the bay leaf and season to taste with salt and pepper.

To assemble:

1. Preheat the oven to 350°F.

2. Butter an 8-inch-square gratin dish and smear the bottom with some of the tomato fondue.

3. Cut the chilled polenta into 8 pieces, each about 2 1/2 by 7 1/2 inches. Place one piece lengthwise up against one side of the gratin dish. Spoon tomato fondue all along the polenta, leaving a 1/2-inch-wide strip of the polenta next to the edge of the dish uncovered; then sprinkle the fondue with cheese. Place another piece overlapping that part of the first strip covered in tomato and cheese. Top it with tomatoes and cheese in the same way, leaving the 1/2-inch-wide uncovered strip. Continue until all the strips are used and the dish is full; you may have to push the strips more tightly together to make them all fit.

4. Drizzle the cream all over the dish and sprinkle with any cheese you might have left over. Bake until the gratin is bubbly and golden, 35 to 40 minutes. Serve hot.

Buttermilk Biscuits

1 dozen

Maria Helm, The Sherman House, San Francisco, California

"A warm buttered biscuit makes the perfect companion to a hot bowl of soup," says Maria Helm. Try these with her Butternut Squash Soup with Sage (page 20).

2 cups all-purpose flour

1 tablespoon baking powder

1 tablespoon sugar

1/2 teaspoon salt

1/2 cup (1 stick) unsalted butter, chilled and cut into chunks

1 cup cultured buttermilk

1 large egg, lightly beaten with 1 tablespoon water

1. Preheat the oven to 475°F.

2. In a large mixing bowl, stir together the all-purpose flour, baking powder, sugar, and salt. Add the butter and, with a pastry blender or a pair of knives, cut it into the dry ingredients until it resembles small peas. Add the buttermilk and stir the dough just until it comes together.

3. On a lightly floured surface, pat out the dough to a thickness of about 1 1/2 inches. With a floured 2-inch round biscuit cutter, cut the dough into individual biscuits; gather up the scraps, pat them, and cut again until no dough remains.

4. Place the biscuits on a greased baking sheet and lightly brush their tops with the beaten egg. Bake until puffed and golden on top, 10 to 15 minutes. Serve warm.

Doc's Cheddar Biscuits

Chris Schlesinger, East Coast Grill, Cambridge, Massachusetts

"I've imported this southern tradition to the North for my annual Christmas party," says Chris Schlesinger. "I like to serve them with grilled country ham. The biscuits should split at the center during baking, exposing the cheese and making a handy configuration for a sandwich." Don't wait for the holidays, though, to try this easy-to-make, savory treat.

5 cups all-purpose flour	1 cup heavy cream
2 tablespoons baking powder	1 cup buttermilk
1/4 cup sugar	1 cup (2 sticks) unsalted butter, melted
1/2 teaspoon salt	1 cup grated cheddar cheese

1. Preheat the oven to 350°F.

2. In a large mixing bowl, sift together the all-purpose flour, baking powder, sugar, and salt.

3. Using the paddle attachment of a mixer on low speed or working by hand with a wooden spoon, mix the cream, buttermilk, and three-fourths of the butter into the dry ingredients, beating only until the dough just pulls together but is still somewhat crumbly.

4. Turn out the dough onto a floured surface and gently knead by hand just until the dry ingredients are fully incorporated. Do not overwork the dough.

5. Pat the dough into a rectangular shape and roll out the dough to a 1/2-inch thickness, keeping the edges as straight as possible. Brush half the rectangle with the remaining melted butter and sprinkle the cheese over the butter. Using the edge of your hand, make an indentation in the middle of the dough along the edge of the butter; then fold the unbuttered half over the cheese-covered half. Press down evenly and firmly with your hands.

6. With the rolling pin, roll the dough to a 3/4-inch thickness. Wrap it in waxed paper and refrigerate until firm, about 1/2 hour.

7. With a 3-inch biscuit cutter or round cookie cutter, cut the dough into rounds and place them on an ungreased baking sheet. Bake until the tops are golden brown, about 40 minutes. Serve warm.

Beal's Cheese Crackers

Derek Burns, Elka, San Francisco, California

6 dozen

"My father, Beal Burns, would bake these whenever we entertained," says Derek Burns. "I was in charge of rolling the logs—and eating as many of the crackers as I could. The dough was pretty tasty, too!" Serve these crisp crackers as a snack on their own or as the base for ham or spreads. The recipe doubles easily. Store them in an airtight container.

2 cups (4 sticks) unsalted butter at room temperature

1 pound very sharp Cheddar cheese, grated

3 cups all-purpose flour

Pinch of cayenne pepper

1. In a large mixing bowl, stir together all the ingredients until they form a smooth dough. With your hands, shape the dough into logs 1 inch in diameter. Cover with plastic wrap and chill in the refrigerator until very solid, about 6 hours.

2. Preheat the oven to 350°F.

3. With a sharp knife, cut the logs crosswise into slices 1/8 inch thick and place them slightly apart on a nonstick baking sheet. Bake until crisp and golden brown, 10 to 12 minutes. Let them cool before serving.

Oat Scones

Ercolino Crugnale, Stouffer Stanford Court Hotel, San Francisco, California

About 8 scones

"A couple of these and a steaming cup of caffe latte will get your day off to a great start," says Ercolino Crugnale. You might also like to try them at brunch or tea time on the weekend.

1 cup quick-cooking rolled oats

1 cup all-purpose flour

1/2 cup golden raisins

1/4 cup sugar

1 tablespoon baking powder

1 teaspoon kosher salt

Grated zest of 1 orange

1/4 cup (1/2 stick) unsalted butter, chilled and cut into 1/2-inch pieces

1/4 cup half-and-half

1. In a large mixing bowl, thoroughly combine the oats, all-purpose flour, raisins, sugar, baking powder, salt, and orange zest. Add the butter and, with a pastry blender, a pair of knives, or your fingers, cut or rub it into the dry ingredients until the mixture resembles coarse crumbs. Add the half-and-half and stir until the dough gathers together. Form it into a ball, cover the bowl, and refrigerate for 30 minutes.

2. Preheat the oven to 350°F.

3. Turn out the dough onto a floured work surface and roll it out to a thickness of about 1/2 inch. With a 3-inch round biscuit cutter, cut the dough into individual scones; gather up the scraps, pat them, and cut again until no dough remains.

4. Place the scones on a nonstick baking sheet and bake until puffed and golden brown, 15 to 18 minutes. Let them cool on the pan for about 5 minutes before removing.

Scones with Currants

About 1 dozen

Maria Helm, The Sherman House, San Francisco, California

"The smell of warm scones," says Maria Helm, "cuts through the drowsiness of awakening." These come together so quickly that you'll probably be enjoying them before you've finished your first cup of coffee or tea.

2 cups all-purpose flour

2 tablespoons sugar

1 tablespoon baking powder

1/2 teaspoon salt

1/2 cup (1 stick) unsalted butter, cut into chunks

1/2 cup currants, or coarsely chopped seedless dark raisins

3/4 cup plus 3 tablespoons heavy cream

1. Preheat the oven to 475°F.

2. In a large mixing bowl, stir together the all-purpose flour, sugar, baking powder, and salt. Add the butter and, with a pastry blender, a pair of knives, or your fingertips, cut or rub it into the dry ingredients until the mixture resembles coarse crumbs. Add the currants or raisins and toss them together. Add the 3/4 cup of cream and, with a fork, spoon, or your fingertips, mix just until the dough comes together.

3. On a floured surface, pat out the dough to a thickness of about 1 1/2 inches. With a 2-inch round biscuit cutter, cut the dough into individual scones; gather up the scraps, pat them, and cut again until no dough remains.

4. Place the scones on a greased baking sheet and lightly brush their tops with the remaining cream. Bake until puffed and golden on top, 10 to 15 minutes. Serve warm or at room temperature.

Bran Muffins

1 dozen

Faz Poursohi, Circolo, Faz Cafe, and Cafe Latte, San Francisco, California

"Your grandmother would say you should eat these 'because they're good for you,'" says Faz Poursohi. "But the rich taste and satisfying texture of these muffins makes them a great way to start the day. And they mix up so quickly that you can enjoy them hot from the oven."

1 1/2 cups bran

1 1/2 cups all-purpose flour

1 cup currants or other dried fruit, chopped if large

2 teaspoons baking powder

1/2 teaspoon baking soda

1/2 teaspoon salt

1 cup milk

1/2 cup molasses

1/3 cup unsalted butter, melted

2 large eggs, lightly beaten

1. Preheat the oven to 375°F.

2. In a large mixing bowl, stir together the bran, all-purpose flour, currants or other dried fruit, baking powder, baking soda, and salt. In another medium-size bowl, stir together the milk, molasses, butter, and eggs. Add the wet ingredients to the dry and stir until completely mixed.

3. Spoon the mixture into greased muffin tins, filling the cups partially, and bake until a wooden toothpick inserted into the center of one comes out clean, 12 to 15 minutes. Serve warm or at room temperature.

Apple-Walnut Muffins

JoAnn diLorenzo, JoAnn's Pantry, South San Francisco, California

About 18 muffins

"I love apples and nuts," says JoAnn diLorenzo of these dense-textured, wholesome muffins. "So this is my healthy answer to a sweet tooth." She also adds that it's the first muffin recipe she ever developed professionally, which makes her especially partial to it.

3 extra-large eggs	1 teaspoon salt
1/2 cup mild vegetable oil, such as canola	3 cups unbleached flour
2 teaspoons pure vanilla extract	1 1/2 pounds apples, peeled, cored, and coarsely chopped
1 1/4 cups sugar	1 cup walnut pieces
1 teaspoon baking soda	1/2 cup currants or raisins

1. Preheat the oven to 300°F. Line a muffin tin with paper muffin cups.

2. In a medium-size mixing bowl, stir together the eggs, oil, and vanilla until thoroughly blended.

3. In another large bowl, thoroughly sift together the sugar, baking soda, and salt. Add the egg mixture and stir until thoroughly blended, scraping down the bowl and stirring again to make sure.

4. Add the flour to the bowl and stir until it is thoroughly blended in. Add the apples, walnuts, and currants or raisins and stir just until they are mixed in.

5. Spoon the batter into the prepared muffin cups, filling them close to the rim. Bake for 17 minutes; then raise the oven temperature to 350°F and bake until a toothpick inserted into the center of a muffin comes out clean, about 20 minutes more. Serve warm or at room temperature.

Smoky Bacon Spoonbread

Cory Schreiber, Wildwood, Portland, Oregon

1 loaf

A favorite old southern dish, spoonbread is halfway between cornbread and cornmeal pudding, soft enough to require serving with a spoon. Cory Schreiber embellishes it with bits of bacon, chopped green onions, and finely chopped jalapeño chilies.

Offer the spoonbread alongside breakfast or brunch eggs, or at lunchtime or dinner with grilled meat or poultry.

6 ounces bacon, cut into 1/4-inch dice

3 large eggs

3 tablespoons unsalted butter, melted

3 cups milk

2 1/2 tablespoons sugar

2 tablespoons plus 1 teaspoon white wine vinegar

3/4 teaspoon salt

1 1/2 cups all-purpose flour

1 cup plus 2 tablespoons yellow cornmeal

1/2 tablespoon baking powder

1 teaspoon cayenne pepper

3/4 teaspoon baking soda

3 jalapeño chilies, halved, stemmed, seeded and finely chopped

3 medium-size green onions, trimmed and cut crosswise into thin slices

1 1/2 cups heavy cream

1. Preheat the oven to 350°F. Butter a 2 1/2-quart shallow baking dish and bring a kettle of water to a boil.

2. In a medium-size skillet, cook the bacon over low heat until its fat is rendered and the bacon is crisp, 7 to 10 minutes. Remove the bacon with a slotted spoon and set aside; save the bacon fat.

3. In a medium-size mixing bowl, beat together the eggs, butter, and reserved bacon fat. Stir in the milk, sugar, vinegar, and salt.

4. In another medium-size bowl, stir together the all-purpose flour, cornmeal, baking powder, cayenne, and baking soda. Add them to the egg mixture and stir until smooth. Fold in the bacon, jalapeños, and green onions.

5. Pour the mixture into the prepared baking dish and pour the heavy cream over the surface. Place the baking dish inside a baking pan large enough to hold it. Place the pan on the oven shelf and pour into the pan enough boiling water to come halfway up the side of the baking dish.

6. Bake until the spoonbread is set and its surface is golden, 30 to 40 minutes. Serve immediately.

Red Chili Sopaipillas

John Sedlar, Abiquiu, Santa Monica, California

2 dozen

"One bite of these puffed, triangular 'sofa pillows' of deep-fried bread takes me back to my aunt's kitchen in the New Mexican town of Abiquiu," says John Sedlar. "And one taste brings immediate satisfaction." Here, John subtly elaborates on the basic recipe by adding a touch of powdered red chili (take care, though, to use pure red chili, rather than the spice blend known as chili powder).

He suggests serving them with appetizers or main courses. For dessert, leave out the chili, puncture the fried sopaipillas with a knife or fork, and drizzle with honey.

2 1/2 cups all-purpose flour

2 tablespoons baking powder

1 tablespoon pure red chili powder

1 teaspoon salt

1 teaspoon vegetable shortening or lard

1 cup warm milk

Mild vegetable oil

1. In a large mixing bowl, stir together 2 cups of the all-purpose flour with the baking powder, chili powder, and salt. Add the shortening or lard and, with your fingertips, rub it into the dry ingredients.

2. Make a well in the center and pour in the milk. Adding enough of the remaining flour as necessary to achieve the desired consistency and using your hands, mix the milk and dry ingredients together to make a soft but dry dough that comes away from the side of the bowl and can be gathered into a ball.

3. On a lightly floured work surface, gently knead the dough for a few minutes, just until smooth. Return the dough to the bowl, cover with a kitchen towel, and let it rest at room temperature for about 45 minutes.

4. On a lightly floured work surface, use your hands to roll the dough into an even rope about 1 inch thick. Cut the rope crosswise in half. Keeping the surface lightly floured, roll out half the rope into a long rectangle about 1/4 inch thick and 3 inches wide. With a sharp knife, cut the rectangle into triangles with sides about 4 inches long and place the triangles in single layers on waxed-paper–lined trays or baking sheets. Repeat with the remaining piece of dough.

5. In a deep fryer or a large, heavy skillet, heat several inches of oil to 375°F on a deep-frying thermometer. Drop 2 or 3 triangles of dough at a time into the oil; they'll sink to the bottom, then gradually rise to the surface. With a slotted spoon or wire skimmer, keep pushing them under. They will gradually puff up. Fry them, turning once, until golden brown, 1 to 1 1/2 minutes total. Remove from the oil and drain on paper towels; then transfer to a napkin- or towel-lined basket to keep warm while you fry the remaining sopaipillas.

Potato Bread

George Mahaffey, The Little Nell, Aspen, Colorado

"I remember my mother baking bread like this when I was a boy," says George Mahaffey. "It bakes up as a whole loaf, but because that loaf is formed from smaller balls of dough, you can pull it apart easily into individual pieces." He suggests substituting fresh dill for the chives for an equally nice flavor.

2 3/4 cups plus 1 tablespoon bread flour

6 tablespoons whole wheat flour

3 tablespoons nonfat dry milk powder

2 tablespoons sugar

2 teaspoons salt

2 packages active dry yeast

1/2 pound potatoes, peeled, boiled until tender, drained, and mashed

3 tablespoons finely chopped fresh chives

2 tablespoons unsalted butter, at room temperature

2 large egg yolks

3/4 cup water

1. In the bowl of an electric mixer fitted with a dough hook or in a large mixing bowl using a handheld electric mixer, combine the flours, milk powder, sugar, salt, and yeast. Add the potatoes, chives, butter, and egg yolks and mix briefly. Add the water and mix until the dough comes together in a ball.

2. Using the dough hook or working vigorously with your hands on a lightly floured surface, knead the dough until it is smooth and elastic, about 10 minutes. Transfer to a bowl, cover with a damp kitchen towel, and let rise at warm room temperature until doubled in volume, about 1 hour.

3. Turn out the dough onto a lightly floured work surface and divide it up evenly into balls 2 1/2 to 3 inches in diameter. Lightly flour a baking sheet and place the balls of dough on it, spacing 1/2 inch apart to cover a circular area. Cover with a damp kitchen towel and let rise at warm room temperature until doubled in volume again, about 1 hour more. As they rise, the dough balls will join together.

4. Preheat the oven to 375°F.

5. Bake the bread until well risen and golden brown, 30 to 40 minutes. Remove from the oven and let it cool a short while, then serve warm.

Tuscan Walnut Bread

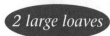

Grant Showley, Showley's at Miramonte, St. Helena, California

These rustic Italian-style loaves have an excellent crust. Grant Showley suggests slicing and toasting the bread for breakfast, thinly slicing and toasting it as a base for hors-d'oeuvres, or simply serving it alongside a lunch or dinner main course. If you like, make just half a recipe. The bread also freezes well.

2 packages active dry yeast

2 2/3 cups warm water

9 1/2 cups bread flour

2 tablespoons salt

1/3 cup coarsely chopped walnuts

1. In a small mixing bowl, dissolve the yeast in the water, about 5 minutes. Put the flour, salt, and walnuts in a food processor fitted with the dough blade and pulse to combine. (If your food processor is small, you will probably have to work in two batches.) With the machine running, add the yeast mixture and process until the mixture forms a ball that rides around the bowl on the blade.

2. Transfer the dough to a large bowl, cover with a damp kitchen towel, and let rise at warm room temperature until doubled in volume, about 1 hour.

3. Preheat the oven to 350°F.

4. On a lightly floured surface, divide the dough in half and shape each half into a long loaf 4 to 5 inches in diameter. Place the loaves on a bread-baking stone or heavy baking sheet and bake until they are nicely browned and sound hollow when their undersides are tapped, 45 minutes to 1 hour.

Raisin Walnut Bread

Michel Richard, Citrus, Los Angeles, California; Citronelle, Santa Barbara, California, Baltimore, Maryland, and Washington, D.C.; Michel's Bistro, Philadelphia, Pennsylvania; and Bistro M, San Francisco, California

Twice risen, Michel Richard's version of this favorite bread has a dense, satisfying texture.

2 cups bread flour or all-purpose flour	1 cup raisins
1/2 cup rye flour	1 cup walnut pieces, toasted in a 350°F oven until golden brown
1 1/2 teaspoons salt	1 teaspoon walnut oil (optional)
1/2 packet active dry yeast	
1 1/4 cups warm water	

1. In a food processor, process the flours, salt, and yeast until well blended. With the machine running, gradually pour the water through the feed tube and continue mixing until a very elastic dough forms, 3 to 5 minutes. Add the raisins, walnuts, and, if available, the walnut oil, and pulse them in. The dough will be very wet and sticky.

2. With a stiff rubber spatula, turn out the dough onto a floured work surface. Cover with a clean, damp kitchen towel and let the dough rise for 40 minutes.

3. Flour your hands and shape the dough into a ball, pulling its edges in toward the center and pinching them together to seal them. Line a 2-quart rounded bowl or basket with a kitchen towel and put the dough inside, pinched seam up. Cover with another kitchen towel and let rise at room temperature until almost doubled in volume, 1 1/2 to 2 hours.

4. Preheat the oven to 400°F.

5. Remove the top towel from the bread, place a baking sheet over the bowl, and invert them together to unmold the bread onto the baking sheet, seam side down. Remove the other towel. With the tip of a small, sharp knife, slash a large square on top of the loaf as a decoration.

6. Bake the bread until it is nicely browned and sounds hollow when its underside is tapped, about 1 hour. Transfer to a rack to cool before slicing.

Black and Green Olive Bread

1 loaf

Philippe Jeanty, Domaine Chandon, Yountville, California

"This is great served in the afternoon with a simple salad or spread with creamy goat cheese and topped with sun-dried tomatoes," says Philippe Jeanty of his recipe for a traditional loaf from the south of France.

1 package active dry yeast

2 teaspoons sugar

3/4 cup plus 2 tablespoons warm
  water

3 3/4 cups bread flour

1/4 cup olive oil

2/3 cup green olives, dried and pitted

2/3 cup Kalamata or other oil-cured
  black olives, dried and pitted

1 large egg, lightly beaten with
  1 tablespoon water

1. In a small mixing bowl, dissolve the yeast and sugar in the warm water, about 5 minutes.

2. Put the flour and olive oil in a mixer with the dough hook attachment, add the yeast mixture, and mix on low speed until well blended, about 3 minutes; or mix together in a large bowl with a wooden spoon. Add the olives and mix or knead 1 minute more.

3. Grease a 4-by-5-by-16-inch bread loaf mold and put the dough inside it; or form the dough by hand on a greased baking sheet into a similar-size loaf. Cover with a damp kitchen towel and let rise at warm room temperature until doubled in volume, about 1 hour.

4. Preheat the oven to 375°F.

5. Brush the top of the dough with the beaten egg mixture and bake until well risen and golden, 30 to 40 minutes. Unmold the loaf if necessary, and let cool before slicing and serving.

chapter

4

Desserts and Beverages

For many people, *dessert* and *comforting food* are synonymous terms. Sit down to a slice of freshly baked cake, a plate of cookies, a wedge of pie or spoonful of fruit crisp, a scoop of ice cream or sorbet, or even a simple dish of homemade applesauce and the world seems brighter, warmer, more kind. You'll find such sweet solace in abundance on the pages that follow, with a wide selection of familiar and eye-opening new recipes for cakes; cookies; pies, tarts, and crisps; ice creams and sorbets; and fruit desserts.

This extravaganza of desserts is followed by a selection of recipes for beverages that, whether hot or cold, provide comfort in their own particular way—chasing away winter's cold or summertime's heat and creating, in their place, a happy glow. Savor them at home, when you feel in need of a little extra comfort.

Polenta Pound Cake

Matthew Kenney, Matthew's, New York, New York

1 cake

Although Matthew Kenney makes this richly flavored golden pound cake as the foundation for his Apple Polenta Bread Pudding (page 204), you'll also find it incredibly comforting on its own, served with tea or coffee.

1 1/4 cups cake flour

1/2 cup yellow cornmeal

1/4 teaspoon salt

1 cup sugar

3/4 cup (1 1/2 sticks) unsalted butter, at room temperature

1 teaspoon pure vanilla extract

3 large eggs

1. Preheat the oven to 325°F. Butter and flour an 8 1/2-by-4 1/2-inch loaf pan.

2. In a medium-size mixing bowl, stir together the all-purpose flour, cornmeal, and salt. Set aside.

3. In another medium-size mixing bowl, use an electric mixer at medium to high speed to beat together the sugar and butter until light and fluffy, 5 to 6 minutes. Beat in the vanilla. One at a time, beat in the eggs until thoroughly combined.

4. With the mixer at low to medium speed, gradually beat in the dry ingredients, mixing just until blended.

5. Spoon the batter into the prepared pan. Bake until golden and a wooden toothpick inserted into the center comes out clean, about 1 hour. Cool on a wire rack.

Double Chocolate Brownies

Michael McCarty, Michael's, Santa Monica, California, and New York, New York

6 dozen

"I wanted to make an *adult* chocolate brownie," says Michael McCarty, "with a perfect, subtle balance of qualities—moist but not too gooey or fudgelike with a rich but not-too-sweet flavor and a great interplay of textures."

To that end, this recipe uses two different kinds of European chocolate—one to make the batter smooth, moist, and glossy, the other to form succulent nuggets of chocolate in the finished brownies. Michael recommends serving the brownies with a good-quality vanilla ice cream.

6 ounces semisweet chocolate, such as Valrhona Superior or Tobler Velma (see Note)

6 ounces bittersweet chocolate, such as Valrhona Caraque or Tobler Tobamera, broken by hand into small pieces (see Note)

3 tablespoons unsalted butter

3/4 cup granulated sugar

3 1/2 tablespoons water

2 large eggs

1 1/3 cups coarsely chopped walnuts

3/4 cup plus 1 tablespoon all-purpose flour

3/4 teaspoon salt

1 tablespoon confectioners' sugar

1. With a sharp, sturdy knife, carefully chop the semisweet chocolate into 1/4-inch pieces. Transfer them to a small bowl and refrigerate.

2. In a medium-size, heavy saucepan, combine the bittersweet chocolate, butter, granulated sugar, and water. Cook over the lowest possible heat, stirring occasionally with a wooden spoon until the chocolate has melted and the ingredients have blended, about 5 minutes.

3. Preheat the oven to 325°F. Butter two 9-inch-square cake pans.

4. Remove the chocolate mixture from the heat and beat in the eggs. Stir in the walnut, then gradually, the all-purpose flour and salt until a smooth batter forms.

5. Stir the chopped and chilled semisweet chocolate into the batter. Divide the batter evenly between the prepared pans. Bake until a toothpick inserted in their centers comes out clean, 20 to 25 minutes. Remove from the oven and let them cool in the pans for about 30 minutes.

6. Sprinkle the brownies with the confectioners' sugar and cut them into 1 1/2-inch squares. Transfer the brownies to individual paper candy cups. Store in an airtight container.

NOTE • *European chocolates are available in specialty food stores.*

Chocolate Slammer

Grant Showley, Showley's at Miramonte, St. Helena, California

"This intensely chocolate dessert," says Grant Showley, "will activate any endorphin known to man." He cautions you to serve it in small portions, "as it is super rich."

1 1/4 cups chocolate cookie crumbs	1 1/2 cups heavy cream
2 tablespoons unsalted butter, melted	3 large eggs (see Note page 208)
1 pound semisweet chocolate, broken into pieces (see Note)	2 tablespoons sugar

1. Preheat the oven to 350°F.

2. In a small mixing bowl, stir together the cookie crumbs and melted butter. Place the mixture in the bottom of a 9-inch springform pan and press down with your hands to pack it firmly and evenly until flat. Bake 10 minutes. Remove from the oven and cool to room temperature.

3. Put half the chocolate in the top half of a double boiler or in a heatproof bowl that fits inside the rim of a saucepan. Fill the bottom pan with enough water to come close to but not touch the top pan or bowl. Over low heat, bring the water to a bare simmer. Gently stir the chocolate until it has melted completely, about 10 minutes. Remove from the heat.

4. Put 1/2 cup of the cream in a medium-size mixing bowl and, with an electric mixer set on high, beat until the cream forms stiff peaks when the beaters are lifted out.

5. In a separate medium-size bowl, beat the eggs and sugar together at medium speed until they are fluffy and form a ribbon when the beaters are lifted out, 4 to 5 minutes. Add the whipped cream and half the melted chocolate, gently folding them together with a rubber spatula. Pour the mixture into the springform pan and refrigerate at least 3 hours or overnight.

6. About 1 1/2 hours before serving, melt the remaining chocolate. Remove from the heat and stir in the remaining cream until smoothly blended. Pour the mixture into the same springform pan and refrigerate until set, about 1 hour.

7. To serve, heat the blade of a sharp knife in a large glass or bowl of hot water and run it alongside the inner rim of the springform pan to loosen the cake. Remove the side of the pan. Dipping the knife repeatedly in the hot water before cutting, cut the cake into small individual wedges.

NOTE • *At Showley's, they use Valrhona chocolate, imported from Switzerland, which is available in specialty food stores.*

Mocha Truffle Torte with Caramel Sauce

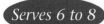

John Sedlar, Abiquiu, Santa Monica, California

Serves 6 to 8

Though sliced and served like a torte or cake, this dessert is nothing less than a giant truffle—"rich, gooey, and very comforting for chocolate lovers," says John Sedlar. He advises you to use a good-quality Belgian or French chocolate that is rich in cocoa butter.

Mocha Truffle:

3/4 cup heavy cream

10 ounces semisweet chocolate, broken into 1/2-inch pieces

1 tablespoon instant coffee powder

Caramel Sauce:

1 cup sugar

1 tablespoon water

3/4 cup heavy cream

For the mocha truffle:

1. Line an 8-inch round cake pan with a large circular coffee filter or a round of waxed paper large enough to come halfway up the side of the pan.

2. In a medium-size saucepan or the bottom of a double boiler, bring 2 inches of water to a boil over high heat. Reduce the heat to low to maintain a simmer.

3. Put the cream, chocolate, and instant coffee in a bowl large enough to rest inside the rim of the pan without touching the water or in the top half of the double boiler, and stir over the simmering water until the chocolate has melted completely and is fully blended with the cream and coffee, 7 to 10 minutes.

4. Pour the truffle cream into the lined pan. Refrigerate until solid, at least 2 hours.

5. To unmold the truffle, place a round of cardboard or a flat plate over the pan. Dunk the bottom of the pan in a sink filled with an inch or so of warm water to loosen the truffle. Then, holding the pan and cardboard or plate tightly together, invert them. Lift off the pan and peel off the coffee filter or waxed paper. Refrigerate, covered, until serving time.

For the caramel sauce:

1. Put the sugar and water in a heavy, medium-size skillet or saucepan. Over moderate heat, cook the sugar, stirring frequently, until it melts and turns a medium caramel brown, 10 to 15 minutes.

2. Immediately pour in the cream and stir until it is fully blended with the caramel. Remove the skillet from the heat. Let the sauce cool to room temperature.

3. To serve, spoon pools of caramel sauce onto individual serving plates. With a sharp knife, cut the truffle into wedges like a pie or cake and place a wedge on top of the sauce on each plate.

Warm Italian Cheesecake

Joyce Goldstein, Square One, San Francisco, California

Serves 6 to 8

Eating this cheesecake warm, "as if it were a soufflé," says Joyce Goldstein, emphasizes its delicate, creamy texture. For successful results, she stresses the importance of using fresh, creamy ricotta cheese and folding in the egg whites with a light hand. Start with all ingredients at room temperature. "If there is cake left," Joyce adds, "please do not refrigerate it; it really won't spoil overnight. For a second comforting experience, warm leftover cake before serving."

Crust:

1 1/2 cups all-purpose flour

1/2 cup (1 stick) unsalted butter, at room temperature

2 large egg yolks, whites reserved for cheesecake filling

2 tablespoons sugar

1 teaspoon grated lemon zest

1 tablespoon dry marsala

Filling:

1/2 cup golden raisins

1/4 cup dry marsala

1/4 cup pine nuts

1 pound ricotta cheese

1/2 cup sugar

1 tablespoon all-purpose flour

4 large eggs, separated, plus 2 extra whites reserved from crust preparation

1/2 cup sour cream or mixture of sour cream and heavy cream

1 teaspoon pure vanilla extract

2 teaspoons grated lemon zest

For the crust:

1. Put the all-purpose flour and butter in a food processor and pulse until they resemble crumbs. Add the egg yolks, sugar, lemon zest, and marsala and pulse until the mixture looks well combined, though it will not form a ball.

2. Press half the mixture onto the bottom of a 9-inch springform pan, forming a very thin layer. Snap on the side of the pan and press the remaining dough on the sides to form a very thin layer. Refrigerate the crust for up to several hours.

For the filling:

1. Put the raisins in a small saucepan and pour in the marsala. Warm over low heat for 4 to 5 minutes. Remove the pan from the heat and let the raisins sit in the marsala until plump, about 30 minutes.

2. Preheat the oven to 350°F.

3. Spread the pine nuts on a baking sheet and toast them, stirring once or twice, until golden brown, about 5 minutes. Set them aside, leaving the oven on.

4. Just before you are ready to complete the filling, remove the crust from the refrigerator.

5. Put the ricotta in the bowl of an electric mixer. Beat with the paddle on medium speed until the cheese looks light and fluffy, 2 to 3 minutes. Beat in the sugar and all-purpose flour just until blended. Then beat in the egg yolks, sour cream, and vanilla.

6. In another large bowl, beat the egg whites until soft peaks form when the beater is lifted out. Put one-third of the egg whites in the bowl with the ricotta mixture and beat just until combined. Then with a rubber spatula, gently fold the remaining egg whites, the pine nuts, and the raisins into the mixture, just until combined.

7. Pour the filling into the crust. Bake the cheesecake in the preheated oven until the filling appears set and no longer liquid but still wobbles noticeably when the cake is gently shaken, 50 to 60 minutes. Remove the pan from the oven and let the cheesecake cool in its pan for about 20 minutes. Then carefully remove the side of the pan and cut the cheesecake into wedges.

Classic Cheesecake

Marc Glassman, Cafe Majestic, San Francisco, California

Serves 8

"This dessert is the first one I ever learned to make when I started cooking," says Marc Glassman. With its graham cracker crust, cream cheese filling, and sour cream topping, this simple recipe yields a classic known to every cheesecake lover.

Graham Cracker Crust:

1 1/2 cups graham cracker crumbs

3 tablespoons sugar

1/2 cup (1 stick) unsalted butter, melted

Cream Cheese Filling:

2 pounds cream cheese at room temperature

1 1/2 cups sugar

1 tablespoon pure vanilla extract

1 tablespoon unflavored gelatin, softened in 2 tablespoons cold water

5 large eggs, separated

Sour Cream Topping:

2 cups sour cream

6 tablespoons sugar

2 tablespoons pure vanilla extract

For the crust:

1. Preheat the oven to 300°F.

2. In a medium-size mixing bowl, stir together the graham cracker crumbs, sugar, and the melted butter. Place the mixture in the bottom of a 9-inch springform pan and press down with your hands to pack it firmly and evenly until flat.

For the filling:

1. In a clean large bowl, stir together the cream cheese, sugar, vanilla, gelatin, and egg yolks until blended. In a separate large bowl, beat the egg whites until they form soft peaks when the beater is lifted out. With a rubber spatula, fold the egg whites into the cream cheese mixture.

2. Pour the cream cheese filling into the springform pan. Bake for 50 minutes. Remove from the oven and let cool for 30 minutes. Leave the oven on.

For the topping:

1. Stir together the sour cream, sugar, and vanilla. Pour it into the same springform pan and bake for 10 minutes more.

2. Remove the cheesecake from the oven and let it cool to room temperature. Then refrigerate overnight.

3. To serve, heat the blade of a sharp knife in a large glass or bowl of hot water and run it alongside the inner rim of the springform pan to loosen the cheesecake. Remove the side of the pan. Dipping the knife repeatedly in the hot water before cutting, cut the cheesecake into individual wedges.

Chocolate Chip Cookies

Emily Luchetti, Stars, San Francisco, California

2 1/2 dozen

"Big and full of chips, these cookies are loyal to the Toll House tradition," says Emily Luchetti of this recipe. "Yet they're not too cloyingly sweet."

1 cup (2 sticks) unsalted butter at room temperature

1 cup firmly packed light brown sugar

1 cup firmly packed dark brown sugar

2 large eggs

1 tablespoon pure vanilla extract

2 1/2 cups all-purpose flour

1 teaspoon baking soda

1 teaspoon salt

2 1/2 cups chocolate chips

1. Put the butter in the bowl of an electric mixer. Using the paddle attachment on medium speed, cream the butter until light and fluffy, about 2 minutes. Continuing to mix, slowly add both the brown sugars, again beating until light and fluffy, 4 to 5 minutes more. One at a time, add the eggs, then the vanilla, mixing until well incorporated. Fold in the dry ingredients and the chocolate chips.

2. With your hands, form the dough into 1 1/2-inch balls. Line baking sheets with parchment paper or grease them, and arrange cookies on them, spacing 3 to 4 inches apart. Chill at least 1 hour to discourage them from spreading while baking.

3. Preheat the oven to 350°F.

4. Bake the cookies one baking sheet at a time until golden brown, about 15 minutes. Let them cool for 10 minutes on the baking sheet and then remove them to a rack.

Oatmeal Cookies

JoAnn diLorenzo, JoAnn's Pantry, South San Francisco, California

3 dozen large cookies

"My very best friends and I all think this is the best oatmeal cookie ever," says JoAnn diLorenzo. "As a Virgo, earth sign, child of the sixties, I especially love grains and nuts. My friend and former baker, Nina Rannells, worked on this recipe for me."

1 3/4 cups (3 1/2 sticks) unsalted butter, softened

1 1/4 cups firmly packed light brown sugar

1 cup granulated sugar

2 extra-large eggs

1/2 cup water

2 teaspoons pure vanilla extract

2 cups all-purpose flour

1 teaspoon baking soda

3/4 teaspoon salt

1/2 teaspoon ground cinnamon

5 1/3 cups rolled oats

1 2/3 cups currants or raisins

1/2 cup lightly packed sweetened flaked coconut

1/4 cup toasted sesame seeds

1. Preheat the oven to 350°F.

2. In a large mixing bowl, use an electric mixer at high speed to cream together the butter and sugars until light and fluffy, 5 to 6 minutes. Add the eggs, water, and vanilla and beat briefly, just until combined.

3. In a medium-size bowl, sift together the all-purpose flour, baking soda, salt, and cinnamon. Add them to the egg mixture and, with the mixer set at low speed, beat until combined. Add the oats, currants, coconut, and sesame seeds and beat just until incorporated.

4. Line baking sheets with parchment paper or grease them. With an ice cream scoop, scoop up the dough, placing the scoops on the baking sheet several inches apart; prepare the dough in batches if necessary. Flatten each scoop slightly with the moistened palm of your hand and bake until nicely browned, 15 to 19 minutes. Transfer the cookies to a wire rack to cool, then store in airtight containers.

Biscotti

Gary Danko, The Dining Room, at The Ritz-Carlton Hotel, San Francisco, California

3 dozen

One of the most comforting experiences of Italian dining, Gary Danko points out, is dipping biscotti in a cup of coffee, espresso, or caffe latte. His recipe produces a classic version of Italy's "twice-baked" cookies. If you really want to indulge yourself, he suggests dipping the cooled biscotti in melted chocolate. The cookies store well for 2 or 3 weeks in an airtight container.

2 1/2 cups all-purpose flour

1 teaspoon baking powder

1 cup sugar

1/2 cup (1 stick) unsalted butter at room temperature

2 large eggs

1/2 cup whole shelled almonds, pistachios, or pine nuts

1 1/2 tablespoons whole anise seeds

2 teaspoons white or dark rum or pure vanilla extract

1. Preheat the oven to 350°F.

2. Line 2 baking sheets with parchment paper or grease them.

3. In a medium-size bowl, sift together the flour and baking powder. Set aside.

4. In a large mixing bowl, using an electric mixer set at high speed, cream together the sugar and butter until light and fluffy, 5 to 6 minutes. One at a time, beat in the eggs until thoroughly combined. At low speed, beat in the nuts, anise seeds, and rum or vanilla extract. Add the flour mixture and continue beating just until it is incorporated.

5. Divide the dough into 2 equal portions. On each prepared baking sheet, using lightly floured hands, pat a portion of dough into a flattened log 3 to 4 inches wide and 3/4 to 1 inch high.

6. Bake the logs until they are firm to the touch, about 20 minutes. Remove them from the oven, leaving the oven on, and let the logs cool on the baking sheets for about 5 minutes. Then use a large spatula to transfer them to a work surface. With a serrated bread knife, cut each log crosswise and at a slight angle into slices about 1/2 inch thick.

7. Lay the slices flat on the baking sheets and bake until they look lightly toasted, 5 to 10 minutes more. With the spatula, transfer them to wire racks to cool.

Applesauce Bars

Peter Harvey, Lake Merced Golf and Country Club, Daly City, California

About 32 bars

These old-fashioned bar cookies will remind you of something your mom used to make, right down to their corn flake topping, says Peter Harvey.

1 1/4 cups sugar

1 cup unsweetened applesauce

1/2 cup vegetable shortening at room temperature

2 cups all-purpose flour

1/2 tablespoon ground cinnamon

1 teaspoon ground nutmeg (or dash of ground cloves)

1 teaspoon baking soda

1/4 teaspoon salt

1 1/4 cups chopped walnuts

1 cup seedless raisins

1 teaspoon pure vanilla extract

2/3 cup crushed corn flakes

1 1/4 tablespoons unsalted butter, softened

1. Preheat the oven to 350°F.

2. Grease a 15 1/2-by-10 1/2-by-1-inch jelly roll pan.

3. In a large mixing bowl, stir together 1 cup of the sugar with the applesauce. Stir in the shortening.

4. In a medium-size bowl, sift together the all-purpose flour, cinnamon, nutmeg or cloves, baking soda, and salt. Add them to the applesauce mixture and stir until smooth. Stir in the walnuts, raisins, and vanilla. Spread the batter in the jelly roll pan.

5. In a small bowl, use your hands to rub together the corn flakes, butter, and remaining sugar. Sprinkle the mixture over the batter.

6. Bake until the bars are firm and a wooden toothpick inserted into the center comes out clean, about 30 minutes. Cool in the pan at room temperature. Then cut into 32 bars about 2-by-2 1/2 inches.

Ginger Pecan Shortbreads

Maria Helm, The Sherman House, San Francisco, California

12 pieces

A generous measure of ground ginger from the supermarket seasonings shelf gives these crunch cookies "spicy goodness," says Maria Helm. She bakes and forms them in the traditional Scottish way, cutting a large round into individual wedges right after they come out of the oven. They go especially well with her Maple Crème Brulée (page 195).

1/2 cup plus 1 tablespoon unsalted butter at room temperature

1/2 cup confectioners' sugar

2 tablespoons ground ginger

1/2 teaspoon pure vanilla extract

1/2 teaspoon salt

1/4 cup coarsely chopped pecans

1 cup less 2 tablespoons all-purpose flour

1 tablespoon cornstarch

1. Preheat the oven to 325°F.

2. With 1 tablespoon of the butter, grease a 9-inch pie pan.

3. In a large mixing bowl, use an electric beater set on high speed to beat the remaining butter until light and fluffy, 1 to 2 minutes. Add the sugar, ginger, vanilla, and salt and beat again until light and fluffy, 4 to 5 minutes more. Add the nuts and, on low speed, mix them in. Add the all-purpose flour and cornstarch and, still on low, mix just until combined.

4. Turn out the dough onto a lightly floured surface and knead lightly with your hands until smooth. Press the dough into the prepared pie pan and prick its surface evenly with a fork. Bake until golden, 35 to 40 minutes.

5. Carefully invert the pie pan onto a cutting board and, while the shortbread is still warm, use a long, sharp knife to cut it into 12 wedges. Cool to room temperature and store in an airtight container until serving.

Peach-Pecan Crisp

Lindsey Remolif Shere, Chez Panisse, Berkeley, California

"Peach crisp is summertime—picnics at the river, casual dinners with friends," says Lindsey Shere. She adds that this recipe is "a perfect carry-along dessert. It need not be kept cold. In fact, it benefits from sitting in the warm sun."

3 1/4 pounds ripe, flavorful peaches, peeled, pitted, and cut into 1/4-inch-thick slices (about 8 cups)

1 cup plus 1 1/2 tablespoons all-purpose flour

5 tablespoons granulated sugar

1/3 cup packed dark brown sugar

1/4 teaspoon salt

1/8 teaspoon ground cinnamon

6 tablespoons unsalted butter, at room temperature, cut into 1/2-inch slices

1/2 cup finely chopped pecans

Vanilla ice cream or heavy cream

1. Preheat the oven to 375°F.

2. In a large mixing bowl, toss the peaches with the 1 1/2 tablespoons of all-purpose flour and 3 tablespoons of the granulated sugar. Put them in a 2-quart shallow baking dish and smooth the top.

3. In a medium-size mixing bowl, thoroughly stir together the remaining all-purpose flour and granulated sugar with the brown sugar, salt, and cinnamon. Add the butter and, with a pastry blender, a pair of knives, or your fingertips, cut it in until the mixture begins to hold together and look crumbly. Add the pecans and stir just until the mixture resembles slightly moist-looking crumbs with no dry flour remaining.

4. Sprinkle the mixture evenly over the peaches. Bake until the topping is golden and the filling is bubbling, about 45 minutes. If the topping begins to brown too quickly, lay a piece of aluminum foil loosely over the top.

5. Serve warm, offering a scoop of vanilla ice cream or a drizzle of cream with each serving.

Pecan-Almond Tart with Nutmeg Crust

Serves 6 *Elizabeth Terry, Elizabeth on 37th, Savannah, Georgia*

"I love this tart," says Elizabeth Terry, "because it reminds me of old-fashioned south-ern pecan pie. But the nutmeg crust and the almonds add contemporary excitement." She cautions that, because the filling is thin, you should take care that there are no breaks in the crust that might allow the syrup mixture to leak through.

Nutmeg Crust:

1 tablespoon unsalted butter at room temperature

1/2 cup unbleached flour

1/4 cup whole-wheat pastry flour (see Note)

1/4 cup (1/2 stick) unsalted butter, chilled and cut into cubes

1 tablespoon sugar

1/2 teaspoon grated nutmeg

2 tablespoons very cold water

Pecan-Almond Filling:

3/4 cup light corn syrup (Karo)

1/2 cup sugar

3 tablespoons unsalted butter, chilled, cut into pieces

3 large eggs

1 teaspoon pure vanilla extract

1 cup chopped pecans, toasted

1/3 cup sliced almonds

For the nutmeg crust:

1. With the 1 tablespoon of room-temperature butter, grease a 9-inch tart or pie pan. Set it aside.

2. To make the nutmeg pastry, put the flours, chilled butter, sugar, and nutmeg in a food processor and process just until the mixture resembles coarse meal. With the machine running, pour in the water; continue processing just until the mixture comes together, in a few seconds. Remove the dough and, on a lightly floured surface, shape it into a flat disk. Wrap it in plastic wrap and refrigerate for 30 minutes.

3. On a floured surface, use a rolling pin to roll out the dough into a thin round. Roll up the round loosely around the rolling pin and unroll it onto the greased pan. Pat down the dough, taking care to seal any breaks. Trim the edge. Cover and refriger-ate at least 30 minutes or until ready to complete the tart.

For the filling:

1. Preheat the oven to 375°F.

2. To prepare the filling, stir together the syrup and sugar in a medium-size saucepan over medium heat. Bring to a boil and continue cooking until the sugar has dissolved, about two minutes. Remove the pan from the heat and stir in the cold butter until it melts. Leave the mixture to cool for 5 minutes more at room temperature.

3. In a medium-size mixing bowl, lightly whisk the eggs just until the yolks and whites are blended. Whisking continuously, pour in the syrup mixture and the vanilla. Pour the mixture through a fine seive into the chilled tart shell. Evenly sprinkle in the pecans, then the almonds.

4. Put the filled tart in the oven, placing a sheet pan on the shelf below to catch any drips. Bake for 30 minutes. Cool to room temperature before cutting into wedges and serving.

NOTE • *Whole-wheat pastry flour may be found in the baking section of well-stocked supermarkets or in health food stores.*

Basque Custard Torte with Cherries

Serves 8

Gerald Hirigoyen, Fringale, San Francisco, California

"Everyone thinks that their version of this traditional dessert from France's Basque country is the best," says Gerald Hirigoyen of his native land's version of a two-crust custard pie. "The truth of the matter is, they're all good. Any gâteau basque is comforting to me—especially when eaten first thing in the morning with my coffee. Never mind waiting for dessert!"

Pastry:

2 large egg yolks

1 cup sugar

1/2 cup (1 stick) unsalted butter, softened and cut into pieces

1 tablespoon dark rum

1/2 tablespoon almond extract

1/2 tablespoon Ricard or another anise-flavored liqueur

Pinch of salt

1/2 vanilla bean, split lengthwise, seeds scraped out and reserved, pod discarded

1 1/2 cups all-purpose flour

1/2 cup ground almonds

1 teaspoon baking powder

Filling:

2 large egg yolks

1/4 cup sugar

6 tablespoons plus 1 teaspoon all-purpose flour

1 cup milk

1/4 vanilla bean, split lengthwise

1/2 cup pitted fresh sweet cherries or drained canned cherries

For the pastry:

In a large mixing bowl, stir together the egg yolks and sugar until thoroughly combined. Add the butter, rum, almond extract, Ricard, salt, and vanilla seeds; stir until thoroughly combined. In a small bowl, stir together the all-purpose flour, ground almonds, and baking powder. Add them to the other ingredients and stir until they form a firm dough. Gather the dough into a ball, wrap in waxed paper or plastic wrap, and refrigerate 2 to 3 hours.

For the filling:

1. In a small mixing bowl, stir together the egg yolks and sugar until thoroughly combined. Thoroughly stir in the all-purpose flour and set aside.

2. Put the milk and vanilla bean in a medium-size saucepan and bring to a boil over medium heat. As soon as it comes to a boil, remove from the heat. Remove the vanilla bean, scrape the seeds into the milk, and discard the pod.

3. Whisking continuously with a wire whisk, pour half the hot milk into the egg-and-flour mixture.

4. Bring the remaining milk back to a boil and immediately pour the contents of the mixing bowl into the saucepan, stirring continuously. Continue stirring until the mixture is smooth and returns to a boil; cook, stirring, for 2 minutes more.

5. Remove the pan from the heat and set aside to cool at room temperature for 1 hour.

For the torte:

1. Preheat the oven to 350°F.

2. Butter and all-purpose flour a 10-inch cake pan.

3. Divide the chilled dough in half. Roll out one-half the dough into a 1/4-inch-thick round about 12 inches in diameter; press it into the bottom and side of the pan. Spread the pastry cream evenly over the dough. Scatter the cherries on top.

4. Roll out the remaining dough to a 10-inch diameter and place it on top of the cherries. With your fingers, gently pinch together the edges of the top and bottom layers of dough to seal in the filling

5. Bake until golden brown, 40 to 45 minutes. Remove from the oven and cool on a rack for 1 hour before cutting into wedges and serving.

Individual Hazelnut Tarts with Semisweet Fresh Cream

 Serves 6   *Sanford D'Amato, Sanford Restaurant, Milwaukee, Wisconsin*

"My father's uncle, who lived above our family's grocery store, used to roast hazelnuts in the shell in his oven and bring them downstairs to us as an afternoon snack," says Sanford D'Amato of the inspiration behind this rich-tasting, elegant-yet-homey dessert.

Tart Shells:

1/4 cup sugar

1/4 cup (1/2 stick) unsalted butter at room temperature, cut into pieces

1 large egg, beaten

1 1/2 cups all-purpose flour

1/4 teaspoon pure vanilla extract

1/2 cup sugar

1/2 cup dark corn syrup

1 1/2 tablespoons cider vinegar

1 tablespoon unsalted butter, melted and cooled

1/2 teaspoon pure vanilla extract

Pinch of salt

Hazelnut Filling:

2 cups (about 3/4 pound) shelled hazelnuts

3 large eggs, beaten

Semisweet Fresh Cream:

1 cup heavy cream

1/2 teaspoon confectioners' sugar

1/8 teaspoon pure vanilla extract

For the tart shells:

1. To make the tart shells, put the sugar and butter in a medium-size mixing bowl and beat with an electric beater on high speed until fluffy, 5 to 6 minutes. Add the egg and continue beating at low speed until well blended and smooth. Add the all-purpose flour and vanilla and mix well to form a soft, slightly sticky dough.

2. Divide the dough into 6 equal balls, wrap them in plastic wrap, and refrigerate for about 10 minutes.

3. Lightly flour a rolling pin and work surface and roll out each ball of dough into a 4 1/2-inch round. Lightly press each round into a 3 1/2-inch tartlet pan. Cover with plastic wrap and refrigerate until the pastry is firm, about 1 hour.

For the filling:

1. Preheat the oven to 350°.

2. While the dough is chilling, prepare the filling. Spread the hazelnuts on a baking sheet and toast them in the oven until golden brown, stirring once or twice, about 5 minutes. Leave the oven on. Put the nuts between the folds of a kitchen towel and rub vigorously to remove their skins. Then transfer them to a food processor and pulse the machine just until they are coarsely chopped.

3. In a medium-size mixing bowl, beat the eggs and sugar with the electric mixer on low speed just until well blended. Add the corn syrup, vinegar, melted butter, vanilla, and the salt; mix until smoothly blended. Stir in the hazelnuts.

4. Spoon the filling into the chilled tartlet shells; it should come to within 1/4 inch of their tops. Bake in the preheated oven until their centers are set and the crusts are golden brown, 15 to 20 minutes.

For the semisweet fresh cream:

1. While the tarts bake, prepare the cream. In a medium-size mixing bowl, beat the cream until it forms soft peaks. Fold in the confectioners' sugar and vanilla.

2. Serve the tarts warm, topping each one with a generous dollop of cream.

Lemon Sabayon in a Pine Nut Crust with Honey-Scented Mascarpone

Thomas Keller, The French Laundry, Yountville, California

Serves 8 to 10

Thomas Keller transforms his intensely lemony, creamy, and frothy version of sabayon—French cousin to Italy's zabaglione—into a filling for a tart shell intriguingly enriched with ground pine nuts. Served with lightly whipped cream sweetened with honey and given the added tang of the Italian fermented fresh cream known as mascarpone, the dessert, says Thomas, "sends the tongue to flight."

Pine Nut Crust:

1 1/2 cups all-purpose flour

2/3 cup pine nuts, pulsed in a food processor until finely ground

2 tablespoons sugar

1 egg

1/2 cup (1 stick) unsalted butter, at room temperature, cut into pieces

1/2 teaspoon pure vanilla extract

Lemon Sabayon:

3 large eggs, well chilled

3 egg yolks, well chilled

6 1/2 tablespoons sugar

3/4 cup plus 1/2 tablespoon lemon juice

1/2 cup (1 stick) unsalted butter cut into 1/2-inch pieces

Honey-Scented Mascarpone:

3/4 cup heavy cream

1/2 tablespoon mascarpone cheese

1 teaspoon honey, at room temperature

For the pine nut crust:

1. Preheat the oven to 350°F.

2. Generously butter and all-purpose flour a 9-inch tart pan with removable bottom and refrigerate it.

3. In a medium-size mixing bowl, using your hands or an electric beater, mix together the all-purpose flour, pinenuts, and sugar. Add the egg, butter, and vanilla and mix just until all the ingredients are combined to form a soft dough. Gather the dough together and refrigerate it for 10 minutes.

4. Remove the dough and the tart pan from the refrigerator. With your fingertips, press the dough into the side of the pan to form a thin rim, then press it into the bottom. Place on a baking sheet and bake until golden brown, 13 to 15 minutes, turn the baking sheet once halfway through so the crust bakes evenly. Don't worry if the crust cracks. Let it cool at room temperature.

For the lemon sabayon:

1. In a large metal mixing bowl, use a wire whisk to beat together the eggs, yolks, and sugar until smooth.

2. In a saucepan slightly smaller in diameter than the bowl, bring 1 1/2 inches of water to a boil over high heat. Reduce the heat to medium low to maintain a brisk simmer and place the bowl with the egg mixture on top of the pan. Whisking continuously and rotating the bowl slowly by its rim with your other hand, pour in about one-third of the lemon juice. Continue whisking and, as the mixture begins to thicken, pour in one-third more lemon juice. Continue whisking while you pour in the remaining juice. The mixture will look thick and frothy. Still whisking continuously and turning the bowl over the heat, add the butter a few pieces at a time until it is incorporated.

3. Pour the sabayon into the prebaked tart shell. Preheat the broiler while you let the tart sit for 15 minutes. Then place the tart under the broiler just until its top turns golden brown, 2 to 3 minutes. Refrigerate the tart until well chilled, about 1 1/2 hours.

For the honey-scented mascarpone:

1. Just before serving, prepare the honey-scented mascarpone. Put the cream, mascarpone, and honey in a medium-size mixing bowl and beat with a wire whisk just until it begins to thicken.

2. Carefully remove the side from the tart pan and cut the tart into wedges. Serve on individual plates, generously garnished with the honey-scented mascarpone.

Strawberry Rhubarb Pie

Gary Danko, The Dining Room at The Ritz-Carlton Hotel, San Francisco, California

Serves 8

One taste of this very traditional pie transports you to a farmhouse kitchen. Gary Danko serves it with his Iowa Buttermilk Ice Cream (page 213), which offers just the right creamy-yet-tangy complement to the pie's sweet-tart flavor.

Pie Shell:

1 1/2 cups sifted all-purpose flour

1 tablespoon sugar

1 teaspoon kosher salt

1/2 cup (1 stick) unsalted butter, well chilled and cut into 1/4-inch cubes

6 to 7 tablespoons ice water

Filling:

1 3/4 pounds fresh rhubarb, leaves trimmed and discarded, stalks cut into 3/4-inch dice (4 cups)

1 pint fresh strawberries, hulled and cut into 1/2-inch slices

2 tablespoons unsalted butter, well chilled and cut into 1/4-inch dice

1 tablespoon lemon juice

1 cup sugar

3 tablespoons tapioca flour, tapioca, or cornstarch

1 tablespoon finely grated orange zest

1/2 teaspoon ground cinnamon

1/2 teaspoon ground nutmeg

1/4 teaspoon salt

For the pie shell:

1. Put the all-purpose flour, sugar, and salt in a food processor and process for 5 seconds. Add the butter cubes and process until crumbs form, 10 to 15 seconds more. Add 6 tablespoons of the ice water and pulse the machine on and off until a moist, crumbly mass forms, about 15 seconds adding a little more water if necessary. Empty the dough onto a lightly floured work surface and, with your hands, gather it together into a ball. Cut the ball in half and pat each into two pieces, one slightly larger than the other, and into a round about 1 inch thick. Wrap with plastic wrap and refrigerate for at least 1 hour or up to several days.

2. With a rolling pin, roll out the larger round to a round about 1/8 inch thick and 12 inches in diameter. Loosely roll up the circle of dough around the pin and unroll it onto a 9-inch pie tin. Gently press the dough into the bottom and side.

For the filling:

1. Preheat the oven to 350°F.

2. In a large mixing bowl, toss together the rhubarb, strawberries, diced butter, and lemon juice. In a small bowl, stir together the remaining filling ingredients, then add them to the fruit and toss well.

3. Empty the filling into the lined pie tin. Dip your finger or a pastry brush into cold water and moisten the rim of the dough. With the rolling pin, roll out the remaining piece of dough into a circle large enough to cover the pie completely. Loosely roll it up around the rolling pin and unroll it over the filling. Using the tines of a fork, push down all around the rim to seal the top and bottom crusts together. With a small, sharp knife, trim off the excess dough and cut 3 small vents in the top.

4. Place the pie on a baking sheet and bake until golden brown and bubbly, about 1 hour. Remove from the oven and cool completely before serving.

Banana Cream Pie

Emily Luchetti, Stars, San Francisco, California

Serves 8 to 10

"A great banana cream pie should be full of bananas with just enough pastry cream to hold them together," says Emily Luchetti. Though the recipe looks long, each stage is quite easy, and the results are utter simplicity. Emily tops the pie with a thick layer of crème fraîche, providing a more tangy complement to the filling than the usual whipped cream. The final touch is a drizzle of a simple bittersweet chocolate sauce inspired by a James Beard recipe, which you'll also want to try over ice cream.

Brown Sugar Pastry Cream:

8 large egg yolks

1/2 cup firmly packed dark brown sugar

Pinch of salt

3 tablespoons cornstarch

2 1/2 cups milk

One 4-inch piece vanilla bean

1/4 cup heavy cream

2 tablespoons unsalted butter

Pie Shell:

1 1/2 cups all-purpose flour

1 tablespoon sugar

1/8 teaspoon salt

3/4 cup (1 1/2 sticks) unsalted butter, well chilled and cut into pieces

About 1 1/2 tablespoons ice water

Banana Filling:

5 medium-size bananas, peeled and cut into 1/8-inch-thick slices

1 teaspoon dark rum

1 teaspoon lime juice

3/4 cup crème fraîche

1 cup sour cream

Chocolate Sauce:

5 ounces heavy cream

1/4 pound bittersweet chocolate, coarsely chopped

For the pastry cream:

1. Put the egg yolks, brown sugar, and salt in a mixing bowl and whisk until well blended. Stir in the cornstarch.

2. In a medium-size, heavy-bottomed, nonreactive saucepan, put the milk and vanilla bean. Place the pan over medium heat and cook just until bubbles form around the edge.

3. Remove the milk from the heat and remove the vanilla bean. Whisking the egg-yolk mixture continuously by hand, slowly pour in the hot milk.

4. Return the egg-and-milk mixture to the saucepan and cook over medium-low heat, stirring constantly, until thick, 3 to 5 minutes. Remove the pan from the heat and stir in the cream and butter.

5. Pour the pastry cream through a fine strainer held over a bowl. Place plastic wrap directly on the surface of the pastry cream to prevent a skin from forming.

6. Refrigerate the pastry cream until cold, 1 to 2 hours. It will keep in the refrigerator for several days.

For the pie shell:

1. In the bowl of an electric mixer, combine the all-purpose flour, sugar, and salt. Using the paddle attachment on low speed, add the butter, beating until it is the size of small peas.

2. Still beating, slowly pour in only enough of the water so that the dough just comes together. It should look rough in the bowl but hold together if you squeeze it in your hand. Too much water will produce a tough dough.

3. Gather the dough together in a ball, cover in plastic wrap, and refrigerate for 30 minutes.

4. Preheat the oven to 350°F.

5. On a lightly floured surface, roll out the dough to a round 1/4 inch thick and about 13 inches in diameter. Loosely roll up the dough around the rolling pin and unroll it onto a 10-inch pie tin. Gently press the dough into the bottom and side and trim its edge.

6. Line the pie shell with a sheet of parchment paper or aluminum foil and fill it with pie weights, uncooked rice, or dried beans. Bake until the edge is golden brown, about 15 minutes. Remove the paper and weights, reduce the oven temperature to 325°F, and continue baking until the bottom of the shell is golden, about 15 minutes more. Let the shell cool to room temperature.

For the banana filling:

1. In a medium-size mixing bowl, toss the bananas with the rum and lime juice.

2. Spread about 3/4 cup of the prepared pastry cream in the bottom of the prebaked pie shell. Arrange the bananas evenly on top and cover with the remaining pastry cream.

3. Put the crème fraîche in the bowl of the electric mixer and, with the whisk attachment, whip it at medium-high speed until thick. Put the sour cream in a separate medium-size bowl and whisk it until smooth. Add the crème fraîche to the sour cream and fold them together. *Recipe continues • • •*

4. Top the pie with the cream mixture and refrigerate until ready to serve.

For the chocolate sauce:

1. About 10 minutes before serving time, pour the cream into a small, heavy-bottomed saucepan and heat over medium heat until bubbles form around the edge. Remove the pan from the heat and add the chocolate.

2. Cover the mixture and let it sit for 5 minutes. Uncover and stir until smooth.

3. Cut the pie into individual wedges and drizzle with the warm chocolate sauce. Pass any remaining sauce separately.

Vanilla Custard

Serves 6 *Lindsey Remolif Shere, Chez Panisse, Berkeley, California*

"A simple, perfectly flavored custard—creamy, not very sweet, and utterly soothing— is often exactly how I want to end a meal," says Lindsey Shere. "It makes me think of the custard pies my mother baked for my father, and the crème caramels I've eaten all over France and even Italy."

1 cup half-and-half	1/2 vanilla bean or 1/2 teaspoon
1 cup heavy cream	pure vanilla extract
3 tablespoons sugar	4 large egg yolks

1. Select a baking pan large enough to hold six 1/2-cup custard cups. Fill it half full of water, put it in the oven, and set the oven to 325°F while you make the custards.

2. Put the half-and-half, cream, and sugar in a heavy, medium-size saucepan; if using a vanilla bean, cut it in half lengthwise with a sharp knife and use the knife tip to scrape the seeds into the pan. Add the bean halves as well. Stir over low heat just until the sugar has dissolved and the cream is not hotter than your finger can stand.

3. Remove the vanilla bean from the hot cream; or stir the extract into the cream. In a medium-size mixing bowl, lightly whisk the egg yolks and then, whisking continuously, slowly pour in the warm cream mixture.

4. Pour the custard through a fine strainer into the 6 custard cups. Open the oven, carefully pull out the shelf with the water-filled baking pan, and place the cups in the pan. Cover the pan with aluminum foil. Bake until the custard in each cup is set about 3/4 inch in from the edge of each cup, but still wobbly in the center, about 30 minutes.

5. Remove the cups from the water bath and chill in the refrigerator before serving.

Maple Crème Brulée

Serves 6

Maria Helm, The Sherman House, San Francisco, California

The special appeal of this dessert, says Maria Helm, lies in the "sweet silkiness of the custard," a quality she likes to contrast by serving it with her Ginger Pecan Shortbreads (page 180). To give it crème brulée's signature crisp burnt-sugar topping, put the individual ramekins under a hot broiler; or take a tip from the chef and buy a small butane torch to neatly and efficiently caramelize each one!

6 large egg yolks

1 1/4 cups packed dark brown sugar

1/3 cup pure maple syrup

2 1/4 cups heavy cream

Pinch of salt

1. Preheat the oven to 350°F.

2. Bring a kettle of water to a boil and set aside.

3. In a medium-size mixing bowl, use a wire whisk to beat together the egg yolks, 1/2 cup brown sugar, and the maple syrup until blended.

4. In a small saucepan over medium heat, bring the cream to a boil. Whisking continuously, slowly pour the heated cream into the yolk mixture. Stir in the salt.

5. Pour the custard mixture through a fine strainer held over a bowl. Then ladle the strained custard into six 6-ounce heatproof ramekins. Place the ramekins in a baking or roasting pan and carefully pour hot water into the pan to come halfway up their sides.

6. Carefully place the baking pan in the preheated oven and bake the custards until they appear almost completely set, except in their very centers, 30 to 40 minutes. Remove from the oven and let cool to warm room temperature; then remove from the pan, cover, and refrigerate overnight.

7. Before serving, preheat the broiler. Place the ramekins on a sturdy baking sheet or broiler tray. Evenly sprinkle the top of each custard with the remaining brown sugar and place under the broiler until the sugar melts and caramelizes, 2 to 3 minutes.

Chocolate Pudding

Emily Luchetti, Stars, San Francisco, California

Serves 6

Emily Luchetti describes this recipe as "a chocolate pudding just as good as Mom used to make." In a spirit sure to evoke childhood memories, she adds that "it tastes even better if you make a hole in the middle just before serving and pour in some heavy cream."

6 large egg yolks

2 tablespoons plus 1 teaspoon sugar

Pinch of salt

2 teaspoons pure vanilla extract

2 1/2 cups heavy cream

3 1/2 ounces bittersweet chocolate, finely chopped

1. Preheat the oven to 300°F.

2. In a large mixing bowl, whisk together the egg yolks, sugar, salt, and vanilla. Set aside.

3. In a medium-size, heavy-bottomed saucepan, heat 1 cup of the cream over medium-high heat just until bubbles appear around the edge. Remove from the heat, add the chocolate, cover, and let stand for 5 minutes. Then stir until the mixture is smooth and the chocolate has completely melted.

4. In another heavy-bottomed saucepan, heat the remaining cream over medium-high heat just until bubbles appear around the edge. Whisk it into the chocolate-cream mixture. Then, whisking continuously, slowly pour the chocolate cream into the egg-yolk mixture, whisking until smooth.

5. Pour the pudding into six 6-ounce ovenproof ramekins. Place them in a baking pan and put it on the oven shelf. Pour hot water into the pan to come one-third to one-half the way up the sides of the ramekins. Cover the pan with aluminum foil. Bake the puddings about 40 minutes just until they are set around the edges, yet an area at their centers about the size of a half-dollar is not completely firm when the puddings are gently shaken. Be careful not to overcook them; they'll set more as they cool.

6. Refrigerate the puddings several hours to overnight. Before serving, let them sit at room temperature for 15 minutes.

Rice Pudding

Kevin Taylor, Zenith American Grill, Denver, Colorado

Serves 4 to 6

At first glance, Kevin Taylor's take on rice pudding looks impeccably traditional, with its creamy grains of rice, its golden raisins, and its hints of cinnamon and orange. Taste it, though, and you'll find he's added some intriguing innovations, cooking it entirely on the stovetop and enriching the texture and flavor with ground roasted almonds.

1/3 cup blanched almonds	2 large egg yolks
2 1/2 cups milk	1 large egg
5 tablespoons round-grain or short-grain rice	1/4 cup heavy cream
	1/4 cup sugar
1/4 cup golden raisins	1/2 teaspoon pure vanilla extract
1/4 teaspoon grated orange zest	1/4 teaspoon ground cinnamon

1. Preheat the oven to 325°F.

2. Spread the blanched almonds on a baking sheet and toast them in the oven, stirring once or twice, until they just begin to turn golden, 5 to 7 minutes. Remove from the oven and let cool to room temperature. Then put the nuts in a food processor and pulse just until the almonds are finely ground. Set them aside.

3. In a medium-size saucepan, bring the milk to a boil over medium heat. Stir in the rice, raisins, ground almonds, and orange zest and continue stirring until the mixture returns to a boil. Reduce the heat to low and simmer gently, stirring occasionally, until the rice is tender, about 30 minutes.

4. In a medium-size mixing bowl, stir together the egg yolks, egg, cream, sugar, vanilla, and cinnamon. Pour in the rice mixture and stir until blended. Return the mixture to the saucepan and, over medium heat, stir until the mixture comes to a boil. Spoon into individual soufflé or custard cups and serve.

Taro and Tapioca Pudding

Alice Wong, Hong Kong Flower Lounge, Millbrae, California

Serves 6 to 8

If you've never eaten taro before, Alice Wong suggests you think of this sweetened mixture of two tropical roots—the tuberous taro and tapioca, extracted from the manioc root—as Hong Kong's answer to the rice pudding of Western nurseries. Like rice pudding, the dessert is smooth, rich, and soothingly bland.

3 ounces (about 1/2 cup) tapioca (not instant)

One 1-pound taro root, peeled and cut into 3/4-inch-thick slices (see Note)

1 cup milk

3/4 cup unsweetened coconut milk (see Note)

2 cups water

1 1/2 cups sugar, plus extra if necessary

1. Put the tapioca in a bowl, add cold water to cover, and leave to soak for 30 minutes.

2. While the tapioca is soaking, put the taro root in a steamer over simmering water and cook until very soft, 20 to 30 minutes. In a medium-size mixing bowl, mash the taro slices with the milk and coconut milk to form a smooth paste.

3. Drain the soaked tapioca well in a fine strainer and transfer it to a medium-size saucepan. Add more cold water to cover, bring to a boil over medium-high heat, reduce the heat to low, and simmer gently until the tapioca looks transparent, about 5 minutes. Remove from the heat, let the tapioca stand for about 5 minutes more, and drain in a fine strainer.

4. In a medium-size nonstick saucepan, bring the 2 cups of water and the sugar to a boil over medium-high heat, stirring to dissolve the sugar. Add the tapioca and the taro paste and, stirring constantly, bring the mixture back to a boil. Taste and adjust the sweetness with more sugar. Serve immediately.

NOTE • *You'll find taro as well as canned coconut milk in well-stocked food stores or in Asian or Caribbean markets.*

Tiramisu

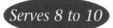 *Jeff Forman, Palio D'Asti, San Francisco, California*

Serves 8 to 10

"Unabashedly rich and completely satisfying" is how pastry chef Jeff Forman describes this version of the popular Italian dessert, a perfect treat for entertaining friends or for a special family dinner. Jeff points out that tiramisu is at its best made a day or two in advance, "to give it time for the flavors to blend and the textures to harmonize."

9 large egg yolks	40 ladyfingers
3/4 cup plus 3 tablespoons sugar	2 cups brewed espresso or double-strength black coffee, chilled
3/4 cup dark rum	
21 ounces mascarpone	2 ounces bittersweet chocolate, very finely chopped
1 1/4 cups heavy cream	

1. In a medium-size saucepan, bring 2 inches or so of water to a boil, then reduce the heat to maintain a gentle simmer.

2. In a stainless-steel bowl large enough to fit inside the rim of the saucepan without touching the water, stir together the egg yolks, 3/4 cup of the sugar, and the rum and immediately nest the bowl on top of the saucepan. Whisk continuously with a wire whisk while the mixture cooks and thickens enough so that when a spoonful is poured back into the bowl, it forms a smooth ribbon, 3 to 5 minutes. (If you have a candy thermometer, the mixture should register 140°F.) This mixture is a classic Italian zabaglione.

3. Immediately set the bowl into a larger bowl filled with ice and water and let the mixture chill, whisking occasionally.

4. Meanwhile, in a large bowl, use a wire whisk or an electric mixer on medium-low speed to beat together the mascarpone, cream, and remaining sugar until the mixture forms soft peaks when the whisk or beaters are lifted out.

5. Assemble the tiramisu in a 2- or 2 1/2-quart soufflé dish or similar straight-sided dish. Dip ladyfingers a few at a time in the espresso and arrange a single layer of them—about a third of the total amount—in the bottom of the dish. Spread one-third of the zabaglione over the ladyfingers. Top with one-third of the mascarpone mixture. Continue layering in this way until all the ladyfingers, zabaglione, and mascarpone have been used up, ending with a smooth layer of the mascarpone mixture.

6. Refrigerate, covered, until serving time, for up to 3 days. Spoon into large bowls or dishes, topping each serving with chopped chocolate.

Polenta Pudding Soaked in Blackberry Compote with Mascarpone Cream

Serves 12 — *Philippe Jeanty, Domaine Chandon, Yountville, California*

This dessert from Philippe Jeanty recalls a classic summer pudding of cake soaked in sweet berry juices. But there's one notable exception: The cake here is freshly baked and distinguished by the golden color, rich flavor, and rustic texture of polenta.

Polenta Cake:

1 1/2 cups (3 sticks) unsalted butter at room temperature, cut into pieces

4 cups confectioners' sugar

1/4 vanilla bean (preferably Tahitian), split in half lengthwise, seeds scraped out and reserved, bean reserved for another use (see Note)

4 large eggs

2 large egg yolks

2 cups bread flour

1 cup uncooked polenta

Blackberry Compote:

3 pints blackberries, fresh or frozen (no need to thaw), about 6 cups

1/2 cup granulated sugar

Mascarpone Cream:

1 cup heavy cream

1/2 cup mascarpone

3 tablespoons granulated sugar

12 small mint sprigs

For the polenta cake:

1. Preheat the oven to 325°F.

2. Grease and flour a 12-inch round or a 13-by-9-inch rectangular round cake pan.

3. Put the butter, confectioners' sugar, and vanilla seeds in a large mixing bowl and beat with an electric mixer at medium speed until creamy, 2 to 3 minutes. One at a time, beat in the eggs and then the egg yolks until blended. Add the flour and polenta and beat until a smooth batter forms. Pour the batter into the prepared cake pan and bake until a wooden toothpick inserted into the center comes out clean, about 1 hour and 15 minutes. Unmold the cake onto a wire rack and leave to cool.

For the blackberry compote:

While the cake cools, prepare the berry compote. Put 5 cups of the berries in a large saucepan, reserving 1 cup for a garnish. Add the sugar and cook over medium heat, stirring occasionally, until the sugar has dissolved and formed a syrup with the berries' juices, about 10 minutes.

To assemble the pudding:

Cut the cooled cake into 12 equal wedges or rectangular pieces. Place them in a shallow baking dish large enough to hold them in a single layer with some space between the pieces. Pour the cooked berries and their juices over and around the cake pieces. Cover the dish with plastic wrap and refrigerate overnight, occasionally uncovering it and basting the cake pieces with the juices.

For the mascarpone cream:

1. Before serving the pudding, put the heavy cream, mascarpone, and sugar in a medium-size mixing bowl. Beat with a wire whisk or an electric mixer at medium speed until the mixture forms soft peaks when the whisk or beaters are lifted out.

2. Place each piece of cake on a serving plate with some of the blackberry compote. Spoon a dollop of mascarpone cream on top and garnish with some of the uncooked berries, a drizzle of the berry juices, and a sprig of mint.

NOTE • *You can use the scraped-out vanilla bean to make vanilla-scented sugar. Simply bury the bean in a jar of sugar. Covered tightly, it lasts indefinitely.*

Blueberry Bread Pudding with Maple Whiskey Sauce

Margaret Fox, Cafe Beaujolais, Mendocino, California

Serves 12

"Although I was a custard and rice pudding fan from the get-go," says Margaret Fox, "bread pudding is something I never had until I was older. Such soft, nursery foods just mean family and security to me. Frankly, I don't see why we bother with anything else!" Though you can make the pudding with a fresh loaf of bread, Margaret says that a slightly stale loaf will do fine.

Bread Pudding:

4 1/3 cups milk

1/2 vanilla bean or 1/2 tablespoon pure vanilla extract

1 pound blueberries, fresh or frozen (no need to thaw)

1 pound loaf brioche or egg bread, crusts trimmed off, bread cut into 1-inch cubes

6 large eggs

4 large egg yolks

1 1/4 cups sugar

Maple Whiskey Sauce:

1 cup half-and-half

3 large egg yolks

1/3 cup pure maple syrup

1/4 cup whiskey

2 tablespoons sugar

1 teaspoon cornstarch

For the bread pudding:

1. Preheat the oven to 325°F.

2. Put the milk in a medium-size saucepan. If using the vanilla bean, cut it in half lengthwise with a sharp knife; use the knife tip to scrape the tiny seeds out of the bean into the milk. Add the scraped pod to the milk. Over medium heat, bring the milk to a boil. Cover, remove from the heat, and leave to infuse for 10 minutes.

3. Spread half the blueberries on the bottom of a 9-by-13-inch loaf pan. Cover them with the bread cubes and top with the remaining berries.

4. In a medium-size mixing bowl, lightly whisk the eggs, yolks, and sugar together, just until combined. Remove the vanilla bean from the milk. Whisking the egg mixture continuously, pour in the warm milk; if using vanilla extract, add it now.

5. Pour the liquid mixture evenly over the berries and bread cubes. Place a baking pan in the oven and place the pudding pan in the baking pan. Carefully pour enough hot water into the baking pan to come halfway up the side of the pudding. Bake until the center of the pudding is set and the top is lightly browned, about 45 minutes.

For the maple whiskey sauce:

1. While the pudding is baking, make the maple whiskey sauce. In a small saucepan over medium heat, bring the half-and-half to a boil. Meanwhile, in a small mixing bowl, whisk together the egg yolks, maple syrup, whiskey, sugar, and cornstarch.

2. Whisking continuously, slowly pour the hot half-and-half into the yolk mixture. Return the mixture to the saucepan over medium heat and cook, stirring constantly with a wooden spatula or spoon, until it thickens to a light, pourable custard consistency, about 175°F on a cooking thermometer. Immediately pour the sauce through a sieve into a small bowl set over a medium-size bowl of ice water; or plunge the bottom of the saucepan into an ice bath to stop cooking. Cover and keep warm.

3. When the pudding is done, cut it into generous pieces and serve the warm sauce over it.

Apple Polenta Bread Pudding
with Hard Sauce

Matthew Kenney, Matthew's, New York, New York

"Children all over the globe love bread pudding," says Matthew Kenney. "This updated version combines apples and cinnamon with Polenta Pound Cake instead of bread. Yet it still has that very satisfying consistency and flavor we all remember from childhood."

Hard Sauce:

1 cup confectioners' sugar

5 tablespoons unsalted butter at room temperature

2 to 3 tablespoons brandy

1/2 teaspoon pure vanilla extract

Pudding:

4 large egg yolks

3 large eggs

1/2 cup granulated sugar

1 3/4 cups milk

1 1/4 cups heavy cream

1/2 tablespoon ground cinnamon

3 medium-size apples, peeled, cored, and cut into 1/2-inch dice

1/2 cup seedless golden raisins

Polenta Pound Cake (page 168) cut into 16 pieces, each about 4-by-4 inches and 1/2 inch thick

For the hard sauce:

In a medium-size mixing bowl, cream together the confectioners' sugar and butter. Add the brandy to taste and the vanilla and beat until smooth and creamy. Cover and refrigerate.

For the pudding:

1. In a medium-size mixing bowl, whisk together the egg yolks, eggs, and granulated sugar. Set aside.

2. Combine the milk, cream, and cinnamon in a medium-size, heavy saucepan over medium-high heat and heat only until bubbles appear around the edge.

3. Whisking the egg mixture continuously, slowly pour in the hot milk and cream. Pour the mixture through a strainer held over another medium-size mixing bowl.

4. Toss together the apples and raisins. In each of eight 1-cup ramekins or soufflé dishes, put enough of the apple-raisin mixture to cover the bottom.

5. Dip a slice of pound cake into the custard mixture and place it into a ramekin. Add enough of the apple-raisin mixture to cover it well. Dip another piece of cake into the custard and place it on top. Repeat with the remaining ramekins. Then distribute the remaining custard mixture among the ramekins.

6. Place the ramekins in a baking pan large enough to hold them all without touching. Cover them with plastic wrap and let them sit at room temperature for 30 minutes.

7. Meanwhile, preheat the oven to 325°F.

8. Uncover the ramekins and pour hot water into the pan to come about one-quarter of the way up their sides. Bake until a small, thin-bladed knife inserted into the center of one of the ramekins comes out almost completely clean, about 30 minutes.

9. Place the ramekins on top of individual serving plates and serve, topping each with a spoonful of hard sauce.

Chocolate Bread Pudding with Sun-Dried Cherries and Crème Fraîche

Serves 6 *Hiro Sone and Lissa Doumani, Terra, St. Helena, California*

"Especially on a cold winter day, this combination of warm chocolate and cognac-soaked sun-dried cherries will keep you cozy and happy," say Hiro Sone and Lissa Doumani.

1/2 cup sun-dried cherries (see Note)

1/3 cup cognac

1/2 loaf French baguette, crusts trimmed off, bread cut into 1/2-inch cubes

1/2 pound bittersweet chocolate, broken into pieces

3 large eggs

1 cup heavy cream

1/2 cup sour cream

1/2 cup granulated sugar

1 teaspoon pure vanilla extract

1/4 teaspoon ground cinnamon

1 cup crème fraîche

1 tablespoon confectioners' sugar

1. Preheat the oven to 350°F.

2. Put the sun-dried cherries in a small mixing bowl and add the cognac. Leave the cherries to soak for 1 hour.

3. Meanwhile, spread the bread cubes on a baking sheet and bake them in the oven until lightly toasted, 10 to 15 minutes. Set aside.

4. When the cherries have finished soaking, put the chocolate in a medium-size mixing bowl and bring 2 inches of water to a boil over high heat in a saucepan large enough to support the bowl in its rim without the bottom of the bowl touching the water. Reduce the heat to maintain a bare simmer, put the bowl on top of the pan, and melt the chocolate, stirring occasionally. Remove the bowl from the heat.

5. While the chocolate melts, put the eggs, cream, sour cream, sugar, vanilla, and cinnamon in another medium-size mixing bowl and stir with a whisk just until blended. Stirring the melted chocolate continuously, pour in the egg mixture and continue stirring until thoroughly blended.

6. Add the cherries, cognac, and toasted bread cubes to the bowl and stir well. Set aside at room temperature until the bread completely soaks up the mixture, about 2 hours.

7. Preheat the oven to 325°F.

8. Bring a kettle of water to a boil.

9. Divide the pudding mixture among six 8- to 10-ounce ovenproof ramekins or soufflé dishes. Put them in a baking pan large enough to hold them all without touching. Slide out the oven shelf, put the pan on the shelf, and pour in boiling water to come halfway up the sides of the ramekins. Bake until the puddings are fully set but still moist, about 35 minutes.

10. Just before the puddings are done, whisk together the crème fraîche and confectioners' sugar. Place the ramekins on individual serving plates and spoon the crème fraîche on top of each pudding. Serve immediately.

NOTE • *You can find sun-dried cherries in specialty food shops.*

Simple Chocolate Mousse

Michel Richard, Citrus, Los Angeles, California; Citronelle, Santa Barbara, California, Baltimore, Maryland, and Washington, D.C.; Michel's Bistro, Philadelphia, Pennsylvania; and Bistro M, San Francisco, California

Serves 4 to 6

If you want to make the easiest chocolate mousse ever, try this bistro-style recipe from Michel Richard.

5 ounces semisweet chocolate, coarsely chopped

1/2 cup (1 stick) unsalted butter, cut into small pieces

5 large eggs, separated (see Note)

1/4 cup sugar

1. In a small, heavy saucepan over very low heat, melt the chocolate. Remove from the heat and add the butter, stirring with a wooden spoon until well mixed. One at a time, stir in the egg yolks.

2. In a medium-size mixing bowl, with a wire whisk or an electric mixer at medium speed, beat the egg whites until soft peaks form when the whisk or beaters are lifted out. Sprinkle in the sugar and continue beating until the whites form stiff peaks but are not yet dry.

3. With a rubber spatula, gently fold the chocolate mixture into the egg whites until completely blended.

4. Spoon the mousse into 4 to 6 serving dishes and chill in the refrigerator until completely set, at least 3 hours.

NOTE • *You needn't give up dishes with raw or lightly cooked eggs such as Chocolate Mousse, made at home, unless you are very young or old or ill.*

Rich Chocolate Mousse

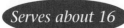

Marc Glassman, Cafe Majestic, San Francisco, California

"Fast, easy, and a surefire crowd pleaser," is how Marc Glassman describes this basic, virtually foolproof recipe for great chocolate mousse. The ingredients can easily be halved or quartered to serve fewer people. "It can also be made into ice cream," Marc adds. All you have to do is process it in an ice cream maker, following manufacturer's directions, instead of chilling in the refrigerator.

3/4 cup water

3/4 cup sugar

1/4 cup hazelnut liqueur (optional)

1 pound semisweet chocolate, coarsely chopped

8 large egg yolks, lightly beaten (see Note page 208)

1/2 gallon heavy cream

1. In a large, heavy saucepan over low heat, stir together the water and sugar until the sugar has completely dissolved. Raise the heat to medium high and bring to a boil; boil for 1 minute, then remove from the heat. Stir in the liqueur if using.

2. Add the chocolate and stir until it has completely melted. Add the egg yolks and stir until smooth.

3. In a large mixing bowl, beat the cream with an electric beater on medium speed until soft peaks form. A little at a time, add the chocolate mixture to the whipped cream, folding them together with a rubber spatula. Cover the bowl and refrigerate until thoroughly chilled, at least 3 hours.

Meyer Lemon Fallen Soufflés

Bruce Hill, Oritalia, San Francisco, California

Serves 4

Deliberately allowing these individual soufflés to fall eliminates the anxiety that often accompanies soufflé making and produces a creamy, almost puddinglike consistency that contrasts wonderfully with the distinctively aromatic juice and zest of Meyer lemons. If you can't find Meyer lemons, substitute regular lemons or a mixture of orange and lemon.

Soufflés:

2 large eggs, separated

1/4 cup plus 1 tablespoon sugar

1 tablespoon all-purpose flour

1 tablespoon unsalted butter, melted

1/2 cup milk

1/3 cup freshly squeezed Meyer lemon juice (see Note)

1 tablespoon finely grated Meyer lemon zest

Fresh mint sprigs

Soufflé Dishes:

2 teaspoons unsalted butter, softened

1/4 cup sugar

1. Preheat the oven to 350°F.

2. Prepare four 1/2-cup soufflé dishes by lightly coating them with the butter and sprinkling them with the sugar. Set aside.

For the soufflés:

1. In a medium-size mixing bowl, use an electric mixer on medium speed to beat together the egg yolks and the 1/4 cup of sugar until just combined. Add the all-purpose flour and melted butter and continue beating until the sugar has completely dissolved, about 3 minutes. Add the milk and the Meyer lemon juice and zest and beat just until smoothly combined.

2. In a separate medium-size mixing bowl, beat the egg whites until frothy. Sprinkle in the remaining 1 tablespoon of sugar and continue beating until the whites form stiff peaks when the beaters are lifted out. With a rubber spatula, gently fold the egg whites into the yolk mixture just until combined.

3. Spoon or ladle the soufflé mixture into the prepared soufflé cups. Place the cups in a shallow baking pan and add about 1/4 inch of cold water to the pan. Put the pan in the oven and bake the soufflés until puffed and golden, about 40 minutes.

4. Remove the soufflés from the oven and transfer them to the refrigerator to chill for at least 30 minutes.

5. To serve, invert each soufflé onto a dessert plate, using a small knife if necessary to loosen it from the sides of the soufflé dish. Garnish with mint.

NOTE • *Meyer lemons are a large variety of thin-skinned lemon with a sweet, intensely aromatic flavor. They may be found in well-stocked supermarkets or specialty produce shops.*

Vanilla Bean Ice Cream

Hiro Sone and Lissa Doumani, Terra, St. Helena, California

This simple, ultrarich recipe for vanilla ice cream is sure to please everyone. Hiro Sone and Lissa Doumani like to top it with a peppered sauté of fresh strawberries in sweetened cabernet sauvignon (page 218).

2 cups heavy cream

2 cups milk

1 vanilla bean, split in half lengthwise

8 large egg yolks (see Note page 208)

1/2 cup sugar

1. Put the cream, milk, and vanilla bean in a medium-size saucepan and bring to a boil over medium-high heat. Turn off the heat, cover the pan, and let the mixture steep for 10 minutes.

2. In a large mixing bowl, beat the egg yolks with a wire whisk until smooth. Whisking continuously, gradually pour in the sugar until thoroughly combined. Still whisking, slowly pour in the hot cream mixture, removing the vanilla bean.

3. Return the mixture to the saucepan over low heat and cook, stirring constantly with a wooden spoon, until the mixture is thick enough to heavily coat the back of the spoon, 10 to 15 minutes.

4. Return the mixture to the mixing bowl and place it inside a larger bowl half filled with ice cubes and cold water. Leave it, stirring frequently, until cool, about 30 minutes.

5. Pour the mixture through a fine strainer. Then transfer it to an ice cream machine and freeze, following manufacturer's instructions.

Iowa Buttermilk Ice Cream

Gary Danko, The Dining Room, The Ritz-Carlton Hotel, San Francisco, California

The companion of choice to Gary Danko's Strawberry Rhubarb Pie (page 181), this farmhouse-style ice cream can bring you simple pleasure on its own—or served with a topping of your choosing—on a hot summer afternoon.

10 large egg yolks (see Note, page 208)

1 cup sugar

3/8 teaspoon kosher salt

1 1/2 cups heavy cream

1 1/2 cups milk

1/4 vanilla bean, split

1 1/2 cups buttermilk

1. In a medium-size stainless-steel saucepan, whisk together the egg yolks, sugar, and vanilla beans, salt just until smoothly combined. Whisking constantly, slowly pour in the cream and milk. Put the pan over medium heat and cook, stirring constantly with a wooden spoon, until the mixture thickens enough to lightly coat the back of the spoon, 10 to 15 minutes.

2. Stir the buttermilk into the saucepan. Then pour the mixture through a fine-meshed strainer set over a medium-size mixing bowl. Return the mixture to the pan and set the bottom of the pan in a baking pan filled with ice and water. Stir occasionally until the mixture is cool.

3. Transfer the mixture to an ice cream machine and freeze, following the manufacturer's directions.

Afternoon in July Strawberry Ice Cream

Derek Burns, Elka, San Francisco, California

About 2 1/2 quarts

"When I was growing up, no summer dinner party was complete without the kids fighting over who got to turn the crank on the old ice cream freezer," recalls Derek Burns. "Living in southern California, we had seemingly endless supplies of strawberries in the summer months, and this ice cream was a favorite way to consume them." Derek adds that the recipe works just as well in newfangled electric ice cream freezers as in the old-fashioned hand-cranked variety.

4 pint baskets ripe strawberries

3 tablespoons sugar

1 quart heavy cream

1 vanilla bean, split lengthwise, seeds scraped out and reserved, or 1 teaspoon pure vanilla extract

6 large egg yolks (see Note page 208)

1. Hull the strawberries and cut them in 1/4-inch-thick slices into a medium-size mixing bowl. Sprinkle them with the sugar and let them stand, loosely covered, at room temperature for at least 3 hours, stirring occasionally, to let the sugar draw out their juices.

2. In a heavy-bottomed, medium-size saucepan, stir together the cream and the vanilla seeds (do not add vanilla extract at this point). Over low heat, warm the cream until bubbles just begin to form at the edge. Remove from the heat, and if using vanilla extract, pour it in at this stage.

3. Put the egg yolks in a large mixing bowl and beat them lightly with a wire whisk. Stirring continuously, slowly pour in the hot cream. Stir in the strawberries and their juices.

4. Freeze the mixture in an ice cream freezer, following manufacturer's instructions.

Blackberry-Mint Sorbet

Ercolino Crugnale, Stouffer Stanford Court Hotel, San Francisco, California

Serves 6 to 8

"The silken texture of this sorbet, combined with the zing of the mint, is revitalizing, especially on a hot day," says Ercolino Crugnale.

1 3/4 cups sugar	1/4 cup packed fresh mint leaves
1 1/2 cups water	1 teaspoon lemon juice
4 cups fresh blackberries	Pinch of salt

1. In a small saucepan, stir together the sugar and water. Bring to a boil over medium heat, stirring until the sugar dissolves. Reduce the heat to low and simmer 1 minute more. Cool to room temperature. This simple syrup may be stored, covered, in the refrigerator indefinitely.

2. Put the blackberries and mint, in batches if necessary, in a blender or a food processor and process until smoothly pureed.

3. To remove the blackberry seeds, pour and press the puree through a strainer held over a medium-size mixing bowl. Stir in 1 1/4 cups of the syrup along with the lemon juice and salt.

4. Freeze the mixture in an ice cream machine, following the manufacturer's instructions. Store in the freezer in a covered container. If the sorbet freezes rock-solid, let the sorbet soften slightly at room temperature.

Pineapple Sage Sorbet

About 1 quart *Robert Calderone, Anago Bistro, Cambridge, Massachusetts*

"This sorbet, the creation of our pastry chef Kathryn Walsh, is delicious any time of year," says Robert Calderone. "But it's particularly refreshing when the weather is hot and steamy." Robert says she likes to accompany it with biscotti.

Sugar Syrup:
5 cups water

1 1/4 cups sugar

Sorbet:
Juice and grated zest of 1 orange

Juice and grated zest of 1 lemon

1/2 cup packed fresh pineapple sage leaves or mint, washed and patted thoroughly dry (see Note)

For the sugar syrup:

Put the water and sugar in a 2-quart saucepan over medium heat. Bring to a boil, stirring occasionally, to dissolve the sugar. Boil for 2 to 3 minutes. Remove from the heat and pour half the syrup into another saucepan. Set aside.

For the sorbet:

1. Add the zests of the orange and lemon to one of the saucepans of syrup. Put the pan over low heat and simmer for 10 minutes. Measure equal parts of orange and lemon juice to equal 1/3 cup and pour them into the simmering syrup. Remove the pan from the heat; and leave at room temperature.

2. Meanwhile, stir the pineapple sage leaves into the other pan of syrup. Bring to a boil over medium heat; then reduce the heat to very low and let the leaves infuse in the barely simmering syrup for 10 to 15 minutes.

3. Hold a strainer over the pan containing the citrus-flavored syrup and pour the pineapple sage syrup into it. Discard the leaves. Stir the syrups together and let them cool to room temperature. Then cover and refrigerate several hours until thoroughly chilled.

4. Put the syrup mixture in an ice cream machine and freeze, following manufacturer's directions. Or make it into a granita by pouring the chilled syrup into a 9-by-13-inch metal pan and putting it into the coldest part of your freezer, stirring with a fork ever 30 minutes or so until it forms a mass of coarse crystals; then freeze at least 8 hours until completely solid.

NOTE • *Look for pineapple sage, its flavor reminiscent of pineapple; in produce shops, at specialty farmers' markets, or in nurseries specializing in herbs.*

Chocolate Sorbet

 Philippe Jeanty, Domaine Chandon, Yountville, California

"This sorbet," says Philippe Jeanty, "has a wonderfully deep, rich chocolate flavor and a sensual texture." Added to those appealing characteristics is the fact that it comes together so quickly with no fuss at all.

4 1/2 cups water

7 ounces (about 2 1/3 cups)
  unsweetened cocoa powder
  (see Note)

2 cups plus 2 tablespoons sugar

1. Put the water, cocoa, and sugar in a heavy saucepan. Over medium heat, bring to a boil, stirring continuously.

2. Fill a baking pan with ice and water and place the bottom of the saucepan in the ice bath. Stir frequently until the mixture is cool.

3. Transfer the mixture to an ice cream machine and freeze, following the manufacturer's directions.

NOTE • *Philippe Jeanty uses Valrhona cocoa powder, but any good-quality unsweetened cocoa may be substituted.*

Sautéed Strawberries in Cabernet Sauvignon and Black Pepper Sauce

Serves 6 | *Hiro Sone and Lissa Doumani, Terra, St. Helena, California*

"Strawberries and ice cream comfort everyone," say Hiro Sone and Lissa Doumani. "With the addition of cabernet and black pepper, it becomes adult comfort food." The dessert is especially sensuous, as vanilla ice cream—their recipe or your own favorite brand—melts into the hot strawberries and sauce.

1 1/4 cups cabernet sauvignon wine

6 tablespoons sugar

1/4 vanilla bean, split in half lengthwise

3/4 teaspoon cornstarch

2 tablespoons unsalted butter

2 pints fresh strawberries, hulled and cut lengthwise into quarters

Pinch of black pepper

6 generous scoops Vanilla Bean Ice Cream (page 212)

1. In a medium-size saucepan, stir together 1 cup of the wine with the sugar and vanilla bean. Bring to a boil over medium-high heat.

2. Meanwhile, in a small mixing bowl, stir together the remaining wine and the cornstarch until the cornstarch dissolves. Whisking continuously, slowly pour the cornstarch mixture into the boiling cabernet. Remove from the heat and set aside.

3. In a medium-size sauté pan or skillet, melt the butter over high heat. Add the strawberries and cook, stirring, just until heated, about 1 minute. Pour in the sauce and sprinkle in the pepper. Bring the liquid back to a boil and simmer briefly, about 10 seconds. Remove vanilla bean before serving.

4. Spoon or ladle the strawberries and sauce into individual serving bowls and top each with a scoop of vanilla ice cream. Serve immediately.

Warm Strawberries with Balsamic Vinegar

Faz Poursohi, Circolo, Faz Cafe, and Cafe Latte, San Francisco, California

Serves 6

"The sweet scent of these warmed fresh berries captures the essence of summer," says Faz Poursohi of this quickly prepared, light, and elegant dessert. He suggests topping them, if you like, with dollops of whipped cream.

3 tablespoons unsalted butter

1 1/2 cups packed brown sugar

1 cup balsamic vinegar

3 pints ripe strawberries, washed and hulled

1/4 cup lemon juice

Fresh mint sprigs

1. In a large skillet, melt the butter over medium heat, taking care not to let it brown. Add the brown sugar and vinegar and cook, stirring, until the sugar has dissolved completely and the mixture has reduced to a light, syrupy consistency, 7 to 10 minutes.

2. Add the strawberries and, still over medium heat, gently toss them in the syrup until they are warmed through and evenly coated, about 1 1/2 minutes more. Stir in the lemon juice and remove from the heat.

3. Serve immediately on plates or bowls, garnished with the mint.

Golden Delicious Applesauce

Alice Waters, Chez Panisse, Berkeley, California

Serves 4

If you start with good apples, you need virtually nothing else to make good applesauce, as this recipe proves. "This is simple and warming," says Alice Walters. "And, because tasty apples will make sweet applesauce without any sugar at all, it's especially nourishing." Sometimes, she suggests, if the apples are too sweet, you might even have to add a little lemon juice.

1 pound apples, quartered, peeled, and cored

1/4 cup water

Crème fraîche

Put the apples and water in a medium-size saucepan over medium heat. Bring to a gentle simmer; then cover and cook, stirring occasionally, until soft, 20 to 30 minutes. With a wooden spoon, mash to the desired texture. Serve warm, drizzled with crème fraîche.

Sweet Crepes with Apples and Chocolate

12 Crepes *Sylvie Le Mer, Ti-Couz, San Francisco, California*

"What I love about crepes is their versatility," says Sylvie Le Mer, who also contributes a savory version on page 120. "They lend themselves to traditional and seasonal fillings, like these apples, and they're delicious any time of the day or night." Don't even attempt to serve them all at once; each requires individual preparation and should be enjoyed at its best, right out of the skillet. You could also eat them plain, with coffee, or filled with other sweet fillings of your choice: butter with orange or lemon juice, brown sugar or honey, jam, toasted nuts, ice cream, and so on.

To get the right consistency with easy measurements, the batter quantities given below yield enough for twice as many crepes as you'll need. But the batter keeps well, covered in the refrigerator, for 2 days or so. And unfilled cooked crepes may be refrigerated, covered, for 2 to 3 days, or frozen for several months.

Crepes:

4 1/2 cups milk

4 1/2 cups water

1 tablespoon pure vanilla extract

1 large egg, lightly beaten

2 1/2 cups all-purpose flour

1/2 cup whole-wheat flour

1 cup sugar

1 tablespoon salt

1/2 cup (1 stick) salted butter, at room temperature

Filling:

1 tablespoon salted butter

6 Granny Smith apples, halved, cored, peeled, and thinly sliced

1 cup heavy cream

1/2 pound bittersweet or semisweet chocolate, broken into small pieces

1 1/2 cups crème fraîche or lightly whipped cream

For the crepes:

1. In a large mixing bowl, use a wire whisk to stir together the milk, water, vanilla, and egg until well blended. Whisk in the all-purpose and whole-wheat flours, sugar, and salt until a smooth batter forms. Cover with plastic wrap and let the batter rest in the refrigerator for at least 1 hour.

2. While the batter rests, prepare the filling.

For the filling:

1. Melt the 1 tablespoon of salted butter in a large skillet over medium heat. Add the apples and cook, stirring frequently, until they are soft, 20 to 25 minutes, adding a little water if they appear to get too dry.

2. Put the cream in the top half of a double boiler or a heat-resistant bowl, set above—not touching—a few inches of simmering water. When the cream is warm, add the chocolate and stir until it melts and blends completely with the cream. Turn off the heat and cover the chocolate cream to keep warm.

3. To prepare the crepes, swirl about 1 teaspoon of salted butter in a 12-inch nonstick skillet over medium heat to coat its bottom. Briefly stir the batter, ladle about 3 ounces (measuring with a measuring cup) of it into the skillet, and swirl it around to coat the bottom and side; then place it on the heat. When the crepe's edge starts turning light brown, after 1 to 2 minutes, use a spatula to peel it from the skillet and flip it over. Cook 1 minute more, then flip it over again.

4. With a rubber spatula, spread the crepe with about 1 teaspoon of the butter. Still over the heat, spread a generous 1/4 cup of the apple filling in the center of the crepe and drizzle with 2 tablespoons of the chocolate cream. Fold the bottom edge, sides, and then the top edge of the crepe over the filling to enclose it in a square package. Continue cooking until the bottom is crisp and brown, about 1 minute more. With a spatula, flip the crepe over onto a heated serving plate and garnish with a dollop of crème fraîche or whipped cream.

5. Repeat the procedure with the remaining batter and filling.

Roasted Pear with Champagne Gastrique, Cracked Black Pepper, and Roquefort

Serves 4 *Alain Rondelli, Alain Rondelli, San Francisco, California*

"A dish of surprises and contrasts" is how Alain Rondelli describes this "takeoff on the very classical pairing of fresh pear and Roquefort cheese, in which the crispness of the pear plays off the creaminess of the cheese, and the pear's sweetness contrasts with the tanginess of the gastrique (a sweetened vinegar-butter sauce) and the spiciness of the cracked black pepper." Popular on the menu of Chef Rondelli's eponymous restaurant, this out-of-the-ordinary dessert may be served with equal success as an appetizer.

4 ripe, firm Comice or Bosc pears

3/4 cup sugar

5 ounces Roquefort cheese cut into 4 equal wedges

3/4 cup champagne vinegar

1 tablespoon coarsely cracked black pepper

2 tablespoons unsalted butter at room temperature

Pinch of kosher salt

1. Cut each pear in half lengthwise and cut out the seeds, tough cores, and stems. Cut each half lengthwise into 3 wedges; do not peel.

2. Preheat a large, nonstick skillet over medium-high heat. Spread the sugar on a plate and dip one skinless side of each pear wedge in the sugar, immediately transferring the wedge, sugared side down, to the hot skillet. Cook the pear wedges until the sugared sides are golden brown, 2 to 3 minutes.

3. On each of 4 serving plates, arrange 6 pear wedges in a star pattern, sugared sides up. Stand a wedge of Roquefort in the center of each plate. Set the plates aside.

4. Put the remaining sugar in a medium-size saucepan over medium-low heat and cook, stirring occasionally, until it dissolves and turns a light caramel brown, 5 to 7 minutes. Quickly add all the vinegar and the black pepper and cook, stirring constantly to prevent the sugar from crystallizing, until the liquid reduces by half, 7 to 10 minutes. Add the butter and stir just until it melts and blends with the other ingredients. Season to taste with a pinch of kosher salt.

5. Spoon the champagne gastrique sauce over the pear slices and serve immediately.

Swedish Pancakes with Lingonberries and Ice Cream

Christer Larsson, Christer's, New York, New York

Serves 6

"Children, however old they are, love this typical Swedish dessert," says Christer Larsson. "It was the greatest culinary experience of my childhood."

1 quart good-quality vanilla ice cream

2 large eggs, lightly beaten

1 1/4 cups all-purpose flour

3 cups milk

2 tablespoons unsalted butter, melted

1/2 teaspoon salt

2 cups lingonberry jam (see Note)

1. Preheat the oven to its lowest setting and warm an ovenproof dish or platter. Remove the ice cream from the freezer and let it soften slightly at room temperature while you prepare the pancakes.

2. In a medium-size mixing bowl, whisk together the eggs, all-purpose flour, and just enough of the milk to form a smooth, lump-free paste. Whisk in the remaining milk, butter, and salt.

3. Heat a small cast-iron or nonstick skillet over medium heat and ladle in enough batter to form a thin film, swirling the skillet to coat the bottom. Cook the pancakes until golden, 1 to 2 minutes per side. As each pancake is finished, transfer it to the platter or dish to keep warm in the oven.

4. When all the pancakes are done, spoon some ice cream along the center of each, top with lingonberry jam, and loosely roll it. Depending on the pancakes' size, place 2 or 3 on each serving plate and serve immediately.

NOTE • *You'll find lingonberry jam in specialty food shops and well-stocked supermarkets.*

Mulled Apple Cider

Serves 6 to 8   *Anne Rosenzweig, Arcadia, New York, New York*

Mugs of this hot spiced cider from chef Anne Rosenzweig are the perfect warmers for a chilly autumn or winter evening. For grownups, use hard cider if you like.

2 quarts apple cider

1/2 cup brandy

5 whole cloves

3 cinnamon sticks

Pinch of ground allspice

Combine all the ingredients in a large saucepan. Bring almost to a boil over medium heat. Reduce the heat to low and simmer gently for 5 minutes. Ladle into mugs.

Hot Buttered Rum with Apple Cider

Serves 1   *Joyce Goldstein, Square One, San Francisco, California*

"If I think I'm about to get a cold and fell achy and chilled, I know it's time for hot cider with rum," says Joyce Goldstein. "It warms me from within and keeps the cold at bay. Drink it slowly and feel better."

1 cup apple cider

1/4 cup Myers dark rum

2 whole cloves

1 cinnamon stick

1 tablespoon unsalted butter

1. Put the cider in a small saucepan and bring to a simmer over medium heat.

2. Pour the rum into a large mug. Add the cloves, cinnamon stick, and butter. Pour in the hot rum.

Eggnog

George Mahaffey, The Little Nell, Aspen, Colorado

About 3 quarts

"This recipe yields a rich, slightly thick-textured eggnog entirely unlike commercial products," says George Mahaffey of his version of the traditional holiday cup of cheer. Speaking of the cheering element, he says the choice and proportion of liquors you use are entirely a matter of preference; but he advises that "an all-whiskey formula yields a more aggressive flavor, whereas no whiskey at all is contrary to my southern heritage."

You can even make an alcohol-free nog, substituting milk for the liquor to maintain the consistency. And if you're concerned about using raw eggs, leave the beaten whites out—though the consistency will be diminished and the yield reduced, requiring you to use about 25 percent less alcohol.

8 large eggs, separated (see Note, page 208)

1 cup sugar

1/2 cup 80-proof bourbon whiskey

1/4 cup rum

1/4 cup brandy

1 quart half-and-half

1 teaspoon nutmeg

3/4 cup heavy cream

1. In the top half of a double boiler over simmering water, use a wire whisk or an electric mixer on low speed to whisk together the egg yolks and sugar until they form a thick, pale yellow foam.

2. Transfer the egg-yolk mixture to a medium-size mixing bowl and whisk in the bourbon, rum, brandy, half-and-half, and nutmeg until smoothly blended.

3. In another bowl, whisk or beat the egg whites until they form soft peaks when the whisk or beaters are lifted out. Gently fold the whites into the eggnog mixture.

4. Clean out the egg-white bowl and whisk or beat the heavy cream until it is slightly thickened but still fluid. Add it to the eggnog and whisk until smoothly blended.

5. Transfer the eggnog to a chilled punch bowl, or refrigerate, covered, until serving. The nog will separate as it rests, so use the serving ladle to stir it gently before pouring.

The Last Resort

Chris Schlesinger, East Coast Grill, Cambridge, Massachusetts

"Something like a frozen Planter's Punch or Mai Tai, this drink is as refreshing as a trade wind," says Chris Schlesinger of an exclusive drink created at the East Coast Grill "one long, arduous night after work during an R&D session at the bar."

Two 12-ounce cans guava juice
One 12-ounce can papaya juice
1 1/4 cups pineapple juice
1 1/3 cups orange juice
One 8-ounce can Coco Lopez

1/2 cup grenadine
2 cups light rum (see Note)
8 slices fresh mango or papaya
Dark rum

1. In a 2 1/2- to 3-quart container with a tight-fitting lid, combine the guava, papaya, pineapple, and orange juices, the Coco Lopez, and the grenadine. Mix well.

2. To make one drink, fill a 16-ounce glass with ice. Add one shot (2 ounces) of light rum. Fill the glass to the top of the ice level with the fruit-juice mixture. Pour the contents of the glass into a blender and blend until completely combined and smooth, about 1 minute.

3. Pour the finished drink into a fancy glass and garnish with a slice of papaya or mango. Float a splash of dark rum on top.

NOTE • *Colorless light rum, also known as silver rum, may be found in any well-stocked liquor store.*

Contributors

The following chefs generously contributed the recipes that appear in this book.

Nestor Arrañaga
Project Open Hand, San Francisco, California

Nestor Arrañaga came to San Francisco from Guadalajara, Mexico, in 1975, and began working in the restaurant Casa de Cristal. Seven restaurants and eleven years later, he was founding chef of Los Arcos, working there until 1988. Nestor lived with a man from Colombia who became very sick with an undiagnosed illness; Nestor helped him to eat well, and the man lived for 8 more years. Then, Nestor's best friend from Mexico became ill with HIV, and before dying he made Nestor promise to help people with AIDS by providing them with good food. Nestor came to the kitchens of Project Open Hand in 1989, where he serves as sous-chef.

Derek Burns
Elka, San Francisco, California

Derek Burns hails from Portland, Oregon, and was introduced to the food business by his father, an executive with Saga Food Corporation. In 1985, he became sous-chef at Pava's in Sacramento, eventually becoming head chef before moving on in 1987 to Acappelia's in San Francisco. He further refined his cooking skills from 1988 to 1992, first under Joyce Goldstein at Square One, and then with Julian Serrano at Masa's. In 1992, he became chef of 231 Ellsworth, leaving in September 1994 to explore the bold union of French and Asian cuisine as chef de cuisine of Elka Gilmore's Elka restaurant.

Robert Calderone
Anago Bistro, Cambridge, Massachusetts

Born and raised in Somerville, Massachusetts, Robert Calderone trained extensively in restaurant kitchens, serving as chef for the Hilton in Dedham, Massachusetts, the Lafayette Hotel in Boston, and Panache in Cambridge. In July 1992, he and partner Susan Finegold purchased 798 Main Street in Cambridge, transforming it into Anago Bistro, which features Robert's New England–accented American and European regional cuisine.

Fernando Castillo
Project Open Hand, San Francisco, California

Fernando Castillo came to San Francisco from Mexico in 1972 and attended the Berlitz Institute of Language, graduating in 1975. In 1976, he began two years of training at the prestigious California Culinary Academy, and from 1979 to 1984 he served as executive chef for two very successful local restaurants, one Mexican, the other French. He then opened his own very successful restaurant, but he sold it after his business partner died of AIDS. Wishing to better his knowledge of how to help people with HIV and AIDS, Fernando enrolled in nutrition classes at City College of San Francisco in 1991. Soon after, he began to work at Project Open Hand, where he is now sous-chef and specials chef.

Jesse Cool
Flea Street Café, Menlo Park, California

Jesse Cool is widely recognized in the Bay Area for her dedication to and advocacy of locally grown, farm-to-table, clean, organic foods. She has appeared on television regularly to discuss seasonal produce on Oakland's Fox Network News, and has served as a demonstrator and chef each year since 1988 at the Chef's Holidays program at The Ahwanee Hotel in Yosemite.

Ercolino Crugnale

Stouffer Stanford Court Hotel, San Francisco, California

Ercolino Crugnale was born and raised in Denver in a family of avid food enthusiasts. After graduation from the Culinary Institute of America, he polished his skills at such renowned establishments as the Hotel Bel-Air in Los Angeles, The Cloister Hotel in Sea Island, Georgia, and the Salishan Lodge in Glenedon Beach, Oregon, before his appointment as executive chef of the Stanford Court Hotel. He prides himself in using marinades, vinaigrettes, vegetable juices, fresh herbs, and organic produce to bring out intense natural flavors and create healthful recipes.

Sanford D'Amato

Sanford Restaurant, Milwaukee, Wisconsin

Born and raised in Milwaukee, Sanford D'Amato graduated from the Culinary Institute of America in 1974, staying on for a one-year fellowship in the Escoffier Room. After working in various New York City restaurants, he returned home in 1980, receiving national attention at John Byron's Restaurant. In December 1989, he and his wife, Angela, opened Sanford in the former site of his father's and grandfather's grocery store. The restaurant has since received widespread local and national accolades.

Gary Danko

Dining Room at The Ritz Carlton, San Francisco, California

Gary Danko began his training at the age of 6, baking cookies and cakes from Betty Crocker cookbooks in his mother's kitchen in Massena, New York. Upon graduating from the Culinary Institute of America in 1977, he worked briefly in San Francisco, Vermont, and New York before refining his skills and knowledge with the legendary Madeleine Kamman from 1984 to 1986. He then spent five acclaimed years at the restaurant of Chateau Souverain Winery in Geyserville, California, before joining the new Ritz Carlton San Francisco in 1991, where his outstanding regional cooking has won accolades nationwide.

JoAnn diLorenzo

JoAnn's Cafe & Pantry, South San Francisco; JoAnn's B Street Cafe, San Mateo, California

Born into an Italian immigrant family, JoAnn diLorenzo prides herself in serving homespun seasonal foods at JoAnn's Cafe, opened in 1982, and her subsequently opened JoAnn's B Street Cafe and JoAnn's Pantry. Her restaurants have consistently been praised in local and national publications, especially for serving some of the best breakfasts in the Bay Area.

Lissa Doumani

Terra, St. Helena, California

Lissa Doumani's family owned restaurants in Los Angeles as well as the acclaimed Stag's Leap Winery in the Napa Valley. She learned pastry-making under the tutelage of Nancy Silverton at Wolfgang Puck's Spago, where she met her future fiancé and business partner, Hiro Sone. After working as pastry chef for Roy Yamaguchi at 385 North in Los Angeles, she left in 1988 to open, with Hiro, their award-winning restaurant Terra.

Dean Fearing

Mansion on Turtle Creek, Dallas, Texas

The son of a Louisville, Kentucky, innkeeper, Dean Fearing trained at the Culinary Institute of America. He began his career at Cincinnati's Maisonette, followed by The Pyramid Room at The Fairmont Hotel in Dallas. When The Mansion on Turtle Creek opened in 1980, he served as executive sous-chef, later leaving to be chef and part owner of the very successful Agnew's. Soon, however, he returned to The Mansion as executive chef, where he has since been a pioneer of the new southwest cuisine, cooking his innovative dishes for such luminaries as George Bush, Bill Clinton, and Queen Elizabeth II. Dean is the author of *The Mansion on Turtle Creek Cookbook* and *Dean Fearing's Southwest Cuisine*.

Barbara Figueroa
B Figueroa, Seattle, Washington

Trained at James Beard's cooking school in 1977 and 1978, and a 1980 graduate of New York City Technical College, Barbara Figueroa went on to work at Le Cirque and Jams in New York, with Wolfgang Puck at Spago in Los Angeles, and with Elka Gilmore at Camelions in Santa Monica. As executive chef of Seattle's Sorrento Hotel from 1987 to 1992, she garnered several prestigious local and national awards—among them the James Beard/Seagram Restaurant Award as Best Chef in the Northwest—before taking over the kitchen at Victor's in San Francisco's Westin St. Francis Hotel. In 1995 she returned to Seattle to open her own restaurant, B. Figueroa.

Bobby Flay
BOLO, New York, New York

Born and raised on the East Side of Manhattan, Bobby Flay fell into cooking at the age of 17 when he took a job at Joe Allen's, so impressing the management that Joe Allen paid his tuition to the prestigious French Culinary Institute, where he graduated in 1984. Bobby compiled an impressive list of honors as executive chef at Mesa Grill and his latest restaurant, BOLO, a colorful and energetic Spanish restaurant that melds his name (BO) with that of partner Laurence (LO) Kretschmer. Recognized in 1993 as a Rising Star Chef by the James Beard Foundation, and recipient of the first-ever French Culinary Institute Outstanding Graduate Award, he is also the author of *Bobby Flay's Bold American Food*.

Jeff Forman

Palio d'Asti, San Francisco, California

A New York native, Jeff Forman trained under Jacques Pepin at the French Culinary Institute in Manhattan. After completing a classical French course of study, he worked with Jacques on the public television series "Today's Gourmet," produced by KQED in San Francisco. In addition to serving as pastry chef at Palio d'Asti, Jeff travels annually to Trattoria da Mario in Padua, Italy, where he teaches his dessert techniques to consumers and professionals alike.

Margaret Fox

Cafe Beaujolais, Mendocino, California

Margaret Fox grew up baking alongside her mother, and by her midteens was teaching bread-making and selling baked goods to stores in Berkeley. After graduating from U.C. Santa Cruz, she moved to Mendocino, working there as baker at the Mendecino Hotel and then as manager of a local cheese shop. In 1977, she and two partners bought Cafe Beaujolais, of which she became sole proprietor in 1979. The breakfasts and desserts she created there won widespread acclaim, and she chronicled the restaurants in her books *Cafe Beaujolais* and *Morning Food*. In 1984, she hired classically trained Christopher Kump as her dinner chef. They married in 1988.

Marc Glassman

Cafe Majestic, San Francisco, California

Second-generation San Franciscan Marc Glassman has eight years of kitchen experience in the Napa Valley which led to his first job as chef of the Cafe at Saks Fifth Avenue. After working as executive chef at the Princeton Inn and owner/chef of Ma'Shaun's in San Rafael, he was invited in 1993 by Tom Marshall and Rolf Lewis, owners of the Majestic Hotel, to become chef of Cafe Majestic. There he serves a

California cuisine combining classic French techniques and Asian flavors, in harmony with the establishment's reputation as "the most romantic restaurant in San Francisco."

Joyce Goldstein
Square One, San Francisco, California

Award-winning owner-chef of Square One, Joyce Goldstein founded San Francisco's California Street Cooking School. A frequent commentator on local television, she also writes for the *San Francisco Chronicle*, as well as *San Francisco Focus* and *Food & Wine* magazines. She is the author of several acclaimed cookbooks, including *Back to Square One*, *The Mediterranean Kitchen*, *Mediterranean the Beautiful Cookbook*, and, with Williams-Sonoma founder Chuck Williams, *Festive Occasions* and *Casual Occasions*. Her restaurant and books have won numerous awards, including several James Beard Awards.

Christopher Gross
Christopher's and Christopher's Bistro, Phoenix, Arizona

Born in Missouri and raised from the age of 12 in Phoenix, Christopher Gross began working in kitchens when he was 14. He went on to cook at the Century Plaza in Los Angeles and a small restaurant in London before snaring a position at the famed Chez Albert in Paris. He returned to the U.S. to work at L'Orangerie in Los Angeles and La Champagne at Scottsdale's Registry Resort before becoming chef/partner at Le Relais in Scottsdale. *Food & Wine* named him one of America's Ten Best New Chefs in 1989. In 1990, he opened Christopher's and Christopher's Bistro, which highlight his dedication to serving the freshest ingredients, simply prepared and exquisitely presented.

Peter Harvey
Lake Merced Golf and Country Club, Daly City, California

Raised in Massachusetts, Peter Harvey graduated from the Culinary Institute of America and apprenticed at the Hotel Pierre in New York. He subsequently broadening his skills and experience at the Stanford Court and the Four Seasons Clift Hotel in San Francisco, the Hyatt Regency Maui, and the Highlands Inn. Named chef de cuisine of the Pan Pacific Hotel in 1993, he delights in offering California comfort cuisine, featuring fresh local ingredients simply prepared with the help of classic techniques—an approach to cooking he continues to explore at the Lake Merced Golf and Country Club.

The Haussner Family
Haussner's Restaurant, Baltimore, Maryland

Haussner's was founded in Baltimore in 1926 by young Bavarian master chef William Henry Haussner, and its continued success owed much to his partnership with his wife, Frances, who emigrated from Germany in 1924 and married William in 1935. Today, Haussner's is a Baltimore institution for its superior continental cuisine, for its outstanding art collection amassed by Mr. and Mrs. Haussner, and for the attentive service provided by second and third generations of the family and more than 200 employees.

Maria Helm
The Sherman House, San Francisco, California

A native of New York, Maria Helm began cooking professionally after school at the age of 16. After graduating from Union College, she ran a part-time catering business in Boston while working full time in advertising—finally leaving after three years to attend San Francisco's California Culinary Academy, followed by the Conditerei Tivoli Pastry School in Denmark. She worked at several Bay Area restaurants before joining the Sherman House as a pastry chef and baker in 1988, eventually becoming its executive chef. Her food, which blends the styles of California and France, also imaginatively incorporates Asian ingredients.

Lisa Hemenway
Lisa Hemenway's, Santa Rosa, California

A self-taught chef, Lisa Hemenway hails from the small California town of Oroville. At the age of 20, she opened a natural-food bakery, then first gained celebrity as pastry chef at Santa Rosa's John Ash & Co. In 1983, she and partner Robert Muszynski opened Lisa Hemenway's Restaurant, with a down-to-earth, eclectic menu that offers "a walk in all cultures" and emphasizes heart-healthy food. At her delicatessen, Tote Cuisine, she provides a wide range of take-out fare to local residents and businesses, as well as to many holiday picnickers in the Wine Country.

Bruce Hill
Oritalia, San Francisco, California

In 1981, Bruce Hill moved from his hometown of Washington, D.C., to Albuquerque, where—an aspiring drummer—he earned money as dishwasher in a hospital kitchen. Soon he had moved up to the position of food operations manager. After stints back home at the Georgetown Bar & Grill and The Intrigue, he moved to San Francisco, where he worked at Stars from 1985 to 1988. He went on to found Ace Cafe and to work at the Four Seasons Clift Hotel and Aqua. In May 1993, he became executive chef of Nori Yoshida's Oritalia, continually refining that restaurant's signature merger of the cuisines of East and West.

Gerald Hirigoyen
Fringale, San Francisco, California

Born and raised in France's Basque country, Gerald Hirigoyen began his culinary apprenticeship at the age of 13. In 1980, he moved to San Francisco and his cooking won admiration at a number of restaurants before he opened his own acclaimed 50-seat bistro, Fringale, in 1991. His eclectic fare has been widely recognized on both local and national levels, and *Food & Wine* named him one of the Top New Chefs in America. His first cookbook, *Bistro*, is part of the "Casual Cuisines" series.

Barr Hogen
Project Open Hand, San Francisco, California

Katharin Barr Hogen began her culinary training with several different, talented Bay Area caterers, eventually starting her own small catering company, Barr None Catering, which she still operates. In 1989, she was asked to become executive chef of a new whole-foods restaurant in San Francisco, Val 21, where she spent two and a half years. Following a four-month trip to Turkey and Eastern Europe, Barr came to Project Open Hand as a specials chef, and one and a half years later she became special diets supervisor.

Todd Humphries
Campton Place Hotel, San Francisco, California

Todd Humphries grew up in Regina, Saskatchewan, Canada, where he gained an appreciation of the simple foods that came from his family's kitchen garden. After high school, be began cooking professionally at a restaurant in his home town, eventually becoming its chef. He then attended the Culinary Institute of America, graduating in 1988 and going on to cook in several leading hotels and restaurants in New York City before assuming the position of executive chef at the Campton Place Kempinski Hotel, where he creates traditional American fare with touches of Asia, India, and the Middle East.

Philippe Jeanty
Domaine Chandon, Yountville, California

Born into a family of growers and winemakers in Champagne, Philippe Jeanty trained in the kitchens of some of France's greatest chefs, including Joseph Thuet, Gaston Lenotre, Gerard Boyer, Jean Pierre Lallement and Pierre and Michel Troisgros. As executive chef of Domaine Chandon in the Napa Valley, he bases his cuisine on local products, the traditions he was raised with, his classical training, and the new traditions he has acquired since living in and learning the culinary heritage of America.

Thomas Keller
The French Laundry, Yountville, California

Born in Southern California, Thomas Keller self-trained in southern Florida and New England before gaining recognition in New York at Raoul's and the Polo Restaurant of the Westbury Hotel. To build his career, he then apprenticed in the kitchens of some of France's greatest restaurants, before returning to New York to open Rakel in 1986. There, and subsequently at Checkers Hotel in Los Angeles, he refined his style of interpretive, spontaneous cooking with architectural drama— an art he now practices at the French Laundry. His cooking has been recognized by the American Institute of Wine and Food, Chefs in America, and the James Beard Foundation, among many others.

Matthew Kenney
Matthew's, New York, New York

Born in Connecticut, Matthew Kenney grew up along the coast of Maine. As a student at the French Culinary Institute in New York City, he worked in the kitchens of La Caravelle and Malvasia. From there, he went on to cook at Alo Alo, and then became executive chef of Banana Cafe. In 1993, with partner Ricardo Amaral, he opened Matthew's, where the menu reflects his love of seafood and of Mediterranean cooking with Moroccan influences. *Food & Wine* magazine named him one of America's Ten Best New Chefs.

Robert Kinkead
Kinkead's, Washington, D.C.

A three-time James Beard Award nominee for "Best Mid-Atlantic Chef," Bob Kinkead gained restaurant experience at such establishments as Joseph's in Boston, the Sheraton Commander Hotel in Cambridge, and Chillingsworth in Brewster, Massachusetts, before becoming head chef, and later a partner, at Twenty-One Federal in Nantucket. He first won national prominence at Twenty-One Federal in Washington. In September 1993, he opened the widely acclaimed Kinkead's on Pennsylvania Avenue's historic Red Lion Row, which he describes as "an American brasserie with a heavy emphasis on seafood."

Christer Larsson
Christer's, New York, New York

Christer Larsson apprenticed as a cook in his home town of Vetlanda, Sweden, and went on to work at hotels in Sweden and Denmark owned by Scandinavian Airlines. He moved to the United States in 1980, serving as chef for Westin hotels, the Century Plaza in Los Angeles, and the Hyatt Regency in Hilton Head. Following a position as executive chef at Aquavit in New York, he opened his own restaurant, Christer's, in November 1993, where he celebrates his love of seafood and offers freshly realized interpretations of Scandinavian classics.

Sylvie Le Mer
Ti-Couz, San Francisco, California

Born and raised in Quimper in the French province of Brittany, Sylvie Le Mer moved to the United States in 1983, eventually settling in San Francisco in late 1985. There, in 1992, she and her husband, restaurateur Joey Altman, opened Ti-Couz (Gaelic for "old house"), specializing in the sweet and savory crepes of her native Brittany.

Emily Luchetti
Stars, San Francisco, California

After working in restaurant kitchens in New York, Paris, and San Francisco, Emily Luchetti joined the staff of Jeremiah Tower's Stars restaurant when it opened in the summer of 1984, where she swiftly secured her reputation as one of America's leading pastry chefs. She is the author of *Stars Desserts*, and her recipes for glorious, classic desserts have also appeared in *Food & Wine*, *Bon Appétit*, and *Chocolatier* magazines.

George Mahaffey
The Little Nell, Aspen, Colorado

After receiving a B.A. in philosophy from Virginia Commonwealth University, Virginia-bred George Mahaffey obtained his formal training with a three-year chef's apprenticeship under the auspices of the American Culinary Federation. He gained valuable experience at The Cloister Hotel on Sea Island, Georgia, and Hotel Hershey in Hershey, Pennsylvania, before becoming executive chef of Hotel Bel-Air in Los Angeles, where he coauthored *The Bel-Air Book of Southern California Food and Entertaining* with Norman Kolpas. In October 1992, he took over the kitchen of The Little Nell, where his American Alpine Cooking has been recognized by numerous national publications and with a 1994 James Beard Award nomination for Mahaffey as "Top Chef in the Southwest."

Michael McCarty
Michael's, Los Angeles, California, and New York, New York

Born and raised in Briarcliff Manor, New York, Michael McCarty moved to Paris following his secondary studies, receiving his Certificate d'Aptitude Professionelle from the Ecole Hotelier de Paris; the Grande Diplome from the Cordon Bleu; and a diploma from the Academie du Vin. In 1974, he returned to the U.S., earning a B.A. in the Business and Art of Gastronomy from the University of Colorado. He opened Michael's in Santa Monica in 1979, at the age of 25, becoming a driving force in the California Cuisine movement. His cookbook, *Michael's Cookbook*, coauthored with Norman Kolpas, demonstrates his continuing commitment to the worlds of good food, fine wines, and contemporary art.

Carlo Middione
Vivande, San Francisco, California

Carlo Middione, owner/chef of Vivande, celebrates his Sicilian heritage in his Fillmore Street trattoria, which has won widespread praise for its authentic, imaginative Italian cooking. He is the author of *The Food of Southern Italy* and *Italian: Pure and Simple*, and is seen nationwide as a cooking-show host on The Learning Channel.

Law Ming
Harbor Village, San Francisco, California

Law Ming began his culinary career in 1970 as an apprentice in a Hong Kong restaurant, and went on to work as a stir-fry and dim-sum chef in several famous establishments there before joining Harbor Village's parent restaurant in 1981. In 1985, he emigrated to the United States to help open the Harbor Village in San Francisco, and as master dim-sum chef heads a staff of 12 who prepare about 5,000 fresh dumplings each weekday, and 12,000 per day on weekends.

Jean-Louis Palladin
Jean-Louis at the Watergate Hotel, Washington, D.C.

Born in Gascony, Jean-Louis Palladin began his cooking apprenticeship at age 12, eventually returning to his home town to open La Table des Cordeliers and becoming, at 28, the youngest chef in France ever to win two Michelin stars. In December 1979, he was enticed to Washington, D.C., to open the intimate 42-seat restaurant Jean-Louis at the Watergate Hotel, where he combines classical techniques with his highly personal contemporary approach to combining ingredients. He is also the author of *Jean-Louis: Cooking with the Seasons.*

Georges Perrier
Le Bec-Fin, Philadelphia, Pennsylvania

Born in Lyon, Georges Perrier began his apprenticeship at 14, training for more than nine years with some of France's greatest chefs. He came to Philadelphia in 1967 as head chef of La Panetiere. Three years later, he opened Le Bec-Fin, "the good taste," which quickly became a Philadelphia institution and won attention as one of the finest restaurants in the nation—winning Five-Star status from the Mobil Travel Guide since

1985 and Five-Diamond status from AAA since 1989. In 1989, 200 French chefs worldwide selected him as Perrier's "Chef of the Year" and awarded him the coveted Silver Toque.

Faz Poursohi

Circolo, Faz Cafe, and Cafe Latte, San Francisco, California

Faz Poursohi's success as a restaurateur can be attributed to his childhood in Tehran, where the family table always featured freshly baked breads and produce from the family farm. In 1974, he moved to the United States to attend the University of Illinois, eventually going to work with renowned restaurant creator Rich Melman. He then moved to the Bay Area, joining Spectrum Foods, before launching his own first restaurant, Circolo, in 1986. Faz went on to reopen the Santa Fe Bar & Grill in Berkeley and to open Cafe Latte and Faz Cafe in San Francisco and Faz Restaurant in Danville. His latest venture is the new Faz Restaurant, on the site of Circolo, featuring Mediterranean cuisine with Middle Eastern roots.

Michel Richard

Citrus, Los Angeles, California; Citronelle, Santa Barbara, California, Baltimore, Maryland, and Washington, D.C.; Michel's Bistro, Philadelphia, Pennsylvania; and Bistro M, San Francisco, California

Apprenticed in a restaurant at the age of 13, Michel Richard moved to Paris six years later, quickly rising to become the topmost pastry chef for the legendary Gaston Lenotre. He came to the United States in 1974 to open Lenotre's first shop in New York, moving to Los Angeles three years later to open his own pastry shop. Michel opened his celebrated Citrus in 1987 and has since gone on to open numerous restaurants serving his innovative bistro cuisine in Santa Barbara, Santa Monica, San Francisco, Washington, D.C., Baltimore, and Philadelphia. Recipient of numerous top awards and accolades, Michel is also the author of *Michel Richard's Home Cooking with a French Accent.*

Judy Rodgers
Zuni Cafe & Grill, San Francisco, California

As a high school exchange student in 1973, Judy Rodgers wound up at the Troisgros family's hotel in Roanne, France. After graduation from Stanford, she worked as lunch chef at Chez Panisse. Working with Marion Cunningham, she opened the Union Hotel in Benecia, California, serving simple American fare and gaining election in 1983 to the first Who's Who in Cooking in America. In 1987, she became chef at Zuni Cafe, winning acclaim for her honest yet sophisticated food from the heart.

Alain Rondelli
Alain Rondelli, San Francisco, California

Born in Paris, Alain Rondelli began his culinary apprenticeship at the age of 19, going on to serve for a time—during his military service—in the kitchen of France's presidential mansion, the Elysee Palace. For a while, he ran his own acclaimed restaurant in Provence, before a visit to San Francisco induced him to accept a job in the kitchen of the legendary Ernie's restaurant. After three years there, Alain went on to open the bistro that bears his name, where he has won widespread admiration for his contemporary interpretations of French cuisine.

Anne Rosenzweig
Arcadia, New York, New York

Anne Rosenzweig came to the culinary world through her work as an anthropologist, traveling extensively in India, Nepal, and East and West Africa. In her hosts' kitchens, she fell in love with food, developing the techniques and palate that influence her cooking today. In 1984, she opened Arcadia, serving hearty food with rural roots and urban polish. In 1987, while still maintaining her role at Arcadia, she became part of the team brought together to rejuvenate New York's legendary "21" Club. Her recipes appear in *The Arcadia Seasonal Mural and Cookbook.*

Chris Schlesinger

East Coast Grill, Cambridge, Massachusetts

Raised in Virginia, Chris Schlesinger trained at the Culinary Institute of America and immersed himself in the vibrant foods of the Caribbean before working at the Harvest in Cambridge, Massachusetts. In 1985, he opened the first of his own successful area restaurants, the East Coast Grill in Cambridge, winning widespread acclaim for a fresh and lively cuisine that combines the influences of his childhood, his training, and his travels. He is the author, with John Willoughby, of *The Thrill of the Grill*; *Salsas, Sambals, Chutneys and Chow-Chows*; and *Big Flavors of the Hot Sun*.

Jimmy Schmidt

The Rattlesnake Club, Detroit, Michigan

Extensively educated in food and wine in France and the United States, Jimmy Schmidt became executive chef of Detroit's London Chop House in 1977. In 1985, with former partner Michael McCarty, he opened the first Rattlesnake Club in Denver, followed by another in Detroit in 1988 and Adirondacks in Washington, D.C., in 1989. That year, Jimmy took over sole proprietorship of The Rattlesnake Club in Detroit, and has since opened numerous area restaurants. Recipient of many awards, including the 1993 James Beard Award as Best Chef of the Midwest, Jimmy has also been named to the Honor Roll of American Chefs and Who's Who in American Cooking. The author of *Cooking for All Seasons*, he writes for the *Detroit Free Press* and *Bon Appetit*.

Cory Schreiber

Wildwood, Portland, Oregon

For more than a century, the Schreiber family has been involved in the shellfish business in the Pacific Northwest, and Cory began his own career at the age of 11, working in their Portland restaurant, Dan & Louis Oyster Bar. He went on to work with Lydia Shire at the Seasons Restaurant in the Bostonian Hotel; Gordon Sinclair at Gordon's in Chicago; and Bradley Ogden at the Lark Creek Inn in Marin County.

He was executive chef of John Cunin's Cypress Club in San Francisco before opening his own Wildwood in May 1994, serving fresh regional ingredients in season, many of them cooked in a wood-fired brick oven.

John Sedlar
Abiquiu, Santa Monica, California

John Sedlar grew up in Santa Fe, New Mexico, but his heritage has deep roots in the pueblo of Abiquiu, where his great-grandparents Eloisa and Pablita maintained the family ranch. He had already gained local acclaim as a chef in L.A.'s South Bay when he apprenticed himself to legendary French chef Jean Bertranou at L'Ermitage. After opening his own first restaurant, Saint Estephe in Manhattan Beach, California, John evolved Modern Southwest Cuisine, combining classic French techniques with the ingredients and vernacular of New Mexican food. In 1991, he went on to win further raves with Bikini, in Santa Monica, and opened Abiquiu in 1994. The recipient of numerous professional accolades, he is the author of *Modern Southwest Cuisine*.

Piero Selvaggio
Valentino, Los Angeles, California

A native of Sicily, Piero Selvaggio emigrated to the United States at the age of 17, and soon settled in Los Angeles. In 1972, he opened Valentino there, setting an exceptional standard for elegant Italian dining that remains unequalled: The 1991 *Zagat Southern California* guide described Valentino as "one of the great restaurants of the world." In 1985, Piero opened Primi, also in Los Angeles, and followed that with Posto, in the nearby community of Sherman Oaks.

Lindsey Remolif Shere
Chez Panisse, Berkeley, California

Raised on a family farm in Sonoma County and educated at UC Berkeley, Lindsey Shere taught herself desserts and pastry by carefully studying the books and methods of such greats as Julia Child, Elizabeth David, and Richard Olney. In 1971, she joined Alice Waters in opening Chez Panisse, and her devotion to fresh ingredients and highly developed flavors—and to combining the pastry work of haute cuisine, the ice creams of Italian cooking, and the simplicity of homespun American desserts—was recognized with the 1993 James Beard Award as "Pastry Chef of the Year." She is the author of *Chez Panisse Desserts*.

Grant Showley
Showley's at Miramonte, St. Helena, California

As proprietors of a popular cafe and charcuterie in Newport Beach, California, Grant Showley and his wife, Sharon, often visited the Napa Valley, falling in love with its relaxed style and innovative cuisine. In 1990, they opened Showley's there in a historic building dating from 1860. Grant's cooking celebrates the best of California cuisine, creatively accented with French and Italian influences that express the heritage of the Wine Country.

Chaiwatt Siriyarn
Marnee Thai, San Francisco, California

Natives of Thailand, Chaiwatt Siriyarn and his wife, May, opened Marnee Thai in 1986. The restaurant has consistently won rave reviews, as well as awards from *Sunset* magazine and the Chefs in America Awards Foundation. In 1993 and 1994, Marnee Thai was selected one of the Bay Area's top five Thai restaurants by the San Francisco *Zagat* guide.

Hiro Sone
Terra, St. Helena, California

Hiro Sone trained at the Ecole Technique Hoteliere Tsuji in Osaka. In 1983, he became sous-chef at the Tokyo branch of Wolfgang Puck's Spago, later moving to Los Angeles to become Spago's pasta chef and then head chef. In November 1988, he and Lissa Doumani, his fiancée and Spago's former pastry cook, opened Terra, serving foods combining the tastes and traditions of southern France, northern Italy, and Asia.

Sarah Stegner
The Dining Room, The Ritz Carlton, Chicago, Illinois

Sarah Stegner joined the Ritz Carlton, Chicago, upon graduation from Cooking School Dumas Pere. Following six years working there in various culinary capacities, she was promoted to chef of the Dining Room, and has since won many local and national awards and gained distinction as one of America's most creative young women chefs. A three-month tour of France, where she trained in the kitchens of leading chefs, has led her to create a menu expressing a refreshing approach to contemporary French cuisine. In 1994, the James Beard Foundation named her the year's Rising Star Chef.

Craig Stoll
Palio d'Asti, San Francisco, California

Craig Stoll trained at the Culinary Institute of America, Florida International University's School of Hospitality Management, and the International Culinary Institute in Torino, Italy. He went on to work as sous-chef at San Francisco's Campton Place Hotel, Postrio, and Splendido, followed by a year in 1992 at Ristorante da Delfina in Florence. Returning to San Francisco, he won a 3 1/2-star rating at Tutto Bene before taking over the kitchen of restaurateur Gianni Fassio's acclaimed Palio d'Asti.

Allen Susser
Chef Allen's, North Miami Beach, Florida

Drawn to the warmth of Miami, Brooklyn-born Allen Susser—trained at the New York City Technical College, Florida International University, Le Bristol Hotel in Paris, and Le Cirque in New York—opened Chef Allen's restaurant in 1986. There he continues to develop a "New World Cuisine" combining Caribbean, Latin American, and Modern American influences. In 1994, he was honored by the James Beard Awards as Best Chef in the Southeast Region.

Kevin Taylor
Zenith American Grill, Denver, Colorado

A native Coloradan, Kevin Taylor began working in the kitchen of a local country club at the age of 14. His enthusiasm there led the chef and sous-chef to offer him an exhaustive classical apprenticeship, and he went on, at 18, to become sous-chef of the exclusive Cherry Hills Country Club. He further honed his skills at a variety of Denver restaurants before opening Zenith in December 1987, a restaurant where his inventive dishes avoid such rich ingredients as butter and cream, which can mask flavors, in pursuit of clean, fresh, eye-opening tastes.

Elizabeth Terry
Elizabeth on 37th, Savannah, Georgia

Elizabeth Terry worked in the wine and cheese business in Atlanta before opening, in 1979, a small soup and sandwich shop called Thyme for You. In 1981, she opened Elizabeth on 37th with her husband, Michael, who also serves as wine steward. Her updated versions of Savannah's coastal company cooking of the 18th and 19th centuries has won her recognition locally and nationwide, including selection in 1991 by the James Beard Foundation as best regional chef.

Irene Trias
Appam—Cuisine of Old India, San Francisco, California

Irene Trias learned the skills and secrets of the Indian kitchen from her grandmother, as well as through her extensive travels throughout India since her teen years. With Lia Kath, her business partner and now her husband, in 1982 she opened the Community Blend coffee house in San Francisco's Haight District. There she began to steam herbed eggs, Indian style, for her customers, and eventually expanded into the next-door space to open Indian Oven. In 1992, she opened Appam, featuring regal clay-pot recipes that date back more than three centuries. She now also owns and operates Oddball Cafe, specializing in healthful lunches inspired by India and the Southwest.

Andy Wai

Harbor Village Restaurants, San Francisco,
Monterey Park, California

Andy Wai began cooking in 1973 at the age of 15 at Boss Restaurant in his native Hong Kong. Completing his apprenticeship in 1979, he joined the city's famed Tung Fung as fourth wok chef. He went on to work as wok chef at some of Hong Kong's most celebrated restaurants before moving to San Francisco as Harbor Village's second wok chef in 1989. In 1992, he became executive chef, overseeing a kitchen staff of 40.

Alice Waters

Chez Panisse, Berkeley, California

Alice Waters, widely regarded as the mother of California cuisine and the new American cooking, opened Chez Panisse in August 1971. The restaurant's dedication to serving the highest quality products according to the season has led her to develop a network of farmers and ranchers who steadily supply it with pure, fresh ingredients. Widely honored with virtually every leading restaurant award, she is the author of several books, including *Chez Panisse Menu Cookbook, Fanny at Chez Panisse,* and *Chez Panisse Vegetables.*

Hans Wiegand

The Pavilion Restaurant at The Claremont Resort,
Oakland, California

Born, raised, and trained in the culinary arts in Germany, Hans Wiegand served as executive chef of the St. Francis Hotel and the Pan Pacific Hotel in San Francisco before becoming executive chef of the Claremont Resort and Spa. A member of the American Culinary Federation and the National Executive Chef Association, he was named San Francisco Bay Area "Chef of the Year" in 1994 by the Executive Chef Association. Subsequently, he took over the kitchen of the Ritz Carlton in Boston.

Alice Wong
Hong Kong Flower Lounge, Millbrae, California

After opening four successful Flower Lounge restaurants in Hong Kong in the mid-1980s, Alice Wong brought to the San Francisco Bay Area her successful concept of serving fine classic and contemporary Chinese cuisine in an atmosphere of elegant appointments and attentive service.

Roy Yamaguchi
Roy's Restaurant, Honolulu, Hawaii

Born and raised in Japan, Roy Yamaguchi graduated from the Culinary Institute of America in 1976. Moving to Los Angeles, he worked in the kitchens of several restaurants, including the legendary L'Ermitage on La Cienega and Michael's in Santa Monica. In 1981, he excited local diners by combining Asian and French cooking styles at the Sheraton Plaza La Reina, moving on in 1984 to become executive chef and partner of 385 North. In late 1988, he moved to Hawaii, opening Roy's Restaurant. His many honors include recognition as one of the nation's best regional chefs by the James Beard Foundation. He is the author of *Feasts of Hawaii*.

Regional Listing of Chefs

Northeast

Robert Calderone	Anago Bistro	Cambridge, Massachusettes
Chris Schlesinger	East Coast Grill	Cambridge, Massachusettes

Middle Atlantic

Bobby Flay	BOLO	New York, New York
The Haussner Family	Haussner's Restaurant	Baltimore, Maryland
Matthew Kenney	Matthew's	New York, New York
Robert Kinkead	Kinkead's	Washington, D.C.
Christer Larsson	Christer's	New York, New York
Michael McCarty	Michael's	New York, New York
Jean-Louis Palladin	Jean-Louis at the Watergate Hotel	Washington, D.C.
Georges Perrier	Le Bec-Fin	Philadelphia, Pennsylvania
Michel Richard	Citronelle	Baltimore, Maryland
	Citronelle	Washington, D.C.
	Michel's Bistro	Philadelphia, Pennsylvania
Anne Rosenzweig	Arcadia	New York, New York

South and Southeast

Allen Susser	Chef Allen's	Miami Beach, Florida
Elizabeth Terry	Elizabeth on 37th	Savannah, Georgia

Midwest

Sanford D'Amato	Sanford Restaurant	Milwaukee, Wi.
Jimmy Schmidt	The Rattlesnake Club	Detroit, Michigan
Sarah Stegner	The Dining Room at The Ritz Carlton	Chicago, Illinois

West

| George Mahaffey | The Little Nell | Aspen, Colorado |
| Kevin Taylor | Zenith American Grill | Denver, Colorado |

Southwest

| Dean Fearing | Mansion on Turtle Creek | Dallas, Texas |
| Christopher Gross | Christopher's Bistro | Phoenix, Arizona |

California

Nestor Arrañaga	Project Open Hand	San Francisco
Derek Burns	Elka	San Francisco
Fernando Castillo	Project Open Hand	San Francisco
Jesse Cool	Flea Street Cafe	Menlo Park
Ercolino Crugnale	Stouffer Stanford Court Hotel	San Francisco
Gary Danko	The Ritz Carlton	San Francisco
JoAnn diLorenzo	JoAnn's B Street Cafe	San Mateo
	JoAnn's Cafe & Pantry	San Francisco
Lissa Doumani	Terra	St. Helena
Margaret Fox	Cafe Beaujolais	Mendocino
Marc Glassman	Cafe Majestic	San Francisco
Joyce Goldstein	Square One	San Francisco
Peter Harvey	Lake Merced Golf and Country Club	Daly City

Maria Helm	The Sherman House	San Francisco
Lisa Hemenway	Lisa Hemenway's	Santa Rosa
Bruce Hill	Oritalia	San Francisco
Gerald Hirigoyen	Fringale	San Francisco
Barr Hogen	Project Open Hand	San Francisco
Todd Humphries	Campton Place Hotel	San Francisco
Philippe Jeanty	Domaine Chandon	Yountville
Thomas Keller	The French Laundry	Yountville
Sylvie Le Mer	Ti-Couz	San Francisco
Emily Luchetti	Stars	San Francisco
Michael McCarty	Michael's	Santa Monica
Carlo Middione	Vivande	San Francisco
Law Ming	Harbor Village	San Francisco
Faz Poursohi	Circolo	San Francisco
	Faz Cafe	San Francisco
	Cafe Latte	San Francisco
Michel Richard	Citrus	Los Angeles
	Citronelle	Santa Barbara
	Bistro M	San Francisco
Judy Rodgers	Zuni Cafe & Grill	San Francisco
Alain Rondelli	Alain Rondelli	San Francisco
John Sedlar	Abiquiu	Santa Monica
	Abiquiu	San Francisco
Piero Selvaggio	Valentino	Los Angeles
Lindsey Remolif Shere	Chez Panisse	Berkeley
Grant Showley	Showley's at Miramonte	St. Helena

Chaiwatt Siriyarn	Marnee Thai	San Francisco
Hiro Sone	Terra	St. Helena
Craig Stoll	Palio D'Asti	San Francisco
Irene Trias	Appam	San Francisco
Andy Wai	Harbor Village	Monterey Park
		San Francisco
Alice Waters	Chez Panisse	Berkeley
Hans Wiegand	The Pavilion Restaurant at The Claremont Resort	Oakland
Alice Wong	Hong Kong Flower Lounge	Millbrae

Northwest and Pacific

Barbara Figueroa	B Figueroa	Seattle, Washington
Cory Schreiber	Wildwood	Portland, Oregon
Roy Yamaguchi	Roy's Restaurant	Honolulu, Hawaii

Index